CLAIMING
ABRAHAM

Given in Memory of

Doug Maxwell

by

Judy & Gene Sharp

&

Rusty & Jerry Sharp

CLAIMING ABRAHAM

Reading the
Bible and the Qur'an
Side by Side

MICHAEL LODAHL

Brazos Press

a division of Baker Publishing Group
Grand Rapids, Michigan

© 2010 by Michael Lodahl

Published by Brazos Press
a division of Baker Publishing Group
P.O. Box 6287, Grand Rapids, MI 49516-6287
www.brazospress.com

Printed in the United States of America

Library of Congress Cataloging-in-Publication Data
Lodahl, Michael E., 1955–
    Claiming Abraham : reading the Bible and the Qur'an side by side / Michael Lodahl.
        p.   cm.
    Includes bibliographical references and index.
    ISBN 978-1-58743-239-2 (pbk.)
    1. Abraham (Biblical patriarch) 2. Abraham (Biblical patriarch)—In the Koran. 3. Bible. O.T. Genesis—Criticism, interpretation, etc. 4. Bible. O.T. Genesis—Islamic interpretations. 5. Koran—Relation to the Bible. I. Title.
    BS580.A3L63 2010
    220.6—dc22   2009045339

In loving memory of my teacher, Paul van Buren (1924–1998)—

"May he be remembered for a blessing"—

and in gratitude to David Hartman and the Shalom Hartman Institute

CONTENTS

Acknowledgments

I am grateful to God for the many colleagues, friends, and students who have read and commented upon various chapters of *Claiming Abraham*. Their perceptive insights and suggestions have been rich sources of wisdom and encouragement; more importantly, their friendships continue to uphold my life with love and joy.

In addition to my loving and longsuffering wife Janice, these friends served as constructive critics as this book gradually took shape: Michael Christensen, Denny Clark, Patty Dikes, Rachel Herman, Brad Kelle, Michael Leffel, Bradford McCall, Bettina Pedersen, Tom Phillips, Sam Powell, Brent Strawn, Karen Winslow, and John Wright. A number of graduate students in theology at Point Loma Nazarene University, where I am privileged to teach theology, have provided sage and witty responses to the manuscript in various stages of its development. Most memorable in this regard are Kala Carruthers, Timothy Gaines, Gary Reynolds, Renee Robertson, and Will Tuchrello. Thank you, too, to my graduate students at Africa Nazarene University, Nairobi, Kenya, who journeyed through contemporary theology with me in August 2004 and especially engaged with the Bible's and Qur'an's stories of Adam's naming of the animals: Girmawi Bush, Righton Kyomba, Joseph Lilema, Emmanuel Mwase, Julius Njuki, Emmanuel Wafula, and that great and joyous giant known to me only as Samuel the Nigerian.

I am grateful to Point Loma for a sabbatical leave dedicated to the rewarding labors of research and writing, and particularly to the university's Wesleyan Center for 21st Century Studies, for its generous bestowal of several grants in the past few years toward the end of completing this volume. Similarly, I remember the month of January 2005 with fondness, spending long hours holed up in the research library of ACOR (American Center for

Oriental Research) in Amman, Jordan. I was there with a group of professors from schools in the Council of Independent Colleges who were happy beneficiaries of a generous grant from the Council of American Overseas Research Centers to participate in the Teaching about Islam and Middle Eastern Culture program. Gary Scudder, Faith Childress, Jonathan and Darla Schuum—your friendship and scholarship were, and are, a wellspring of great inspiration.

Closer to home, a huge thank you goes out to San Diego's Sisterhood of the Sermon on the Couch—Barbara Burnette, Paula Carbone, Ana Christopher, Frankie Contestable, Dulce Dehaven, Carolyn Johnson, June Melin, and Ginna Olsen—for their unremitting questions, unbeatable hospitality, unfeigned laughter, and uncontainable enthusiasm for theological conversation. I must also express warm appreciation to Norma, owner of Newbreak Coffee Co., purveyors of the finest French Roast I've ever tasted—and right there on San Diego's Ocean Beach, no less. Probably half of *Claiming Abraham* was written in this most excellent of surfer hangouts.

Deep gratitude also goes to the good folks at Brazos Press with whom I worked most closely—Rodney Clapp, Lisa Ann Cockrel, Lisa Beth Anderson, BJ Heyboer, and Jeremy Wells—for their kindness, encouragement, professionalism, and expertise. I am beholden to you all.

Of all these friends who have shared in the journey that is this book, my deepest gratitude goes to Denny Clark, whose close and critical reading of the manuscript often felt like iron sharpening iron. Denny's hard work made this a much better book, and I am in his debt even as I anticipate the publication of his own work in this blossoming area of Christian-Muslim comparative theology.

Opening

Arguing over Abraham

Hear, O Israel:
The LORD is our God, the LORD is one.

        —The Shema

For us there is one God, the Father,
from whom are all things, and for whom we exist,
and one Lord, Jesus Christ,
through whom are all things and through whom we exist.

        —Paul the Apostle

There is no God but God,
and Muhammad is His prophet.

        —The Shahada

As an outsider, may I be allowed to say this:
you People of the Book had better get along
and get to know each other sometime soon.

        —John Yokota, Shin Buddhist

How shall we Christians and Muslims speak with one another? How do we get to know one another, let alone get along? What ideas, experiences, or practices can provide a basis for conversation? Can we really speak with one another, or are we destined only to speak past one another? With our

1

common history all too often marked by violence and venom—Crusaders and colonialism on one side, jihad and terrorism on the other, not to mention media that tend to play up the differences for all their sensationalistic worth—will our words toward each other ever be more than accusations, caricatures, and curses?

I do not pretend to be able to offer a definitive answer to these questions. But I and many others desire to affirm a far deeper sense of hope regarding the Muslim-Christian conversation than all of the tired clichés and typical caricatures would allow. Arguably it is required of us all to nurture such hopes, for it appears that the future of our world, at least humanly speaking, may well hang in the balance. There is undeniably a kind of contesting under way between Islamic culture, particularly in the Middle East, and so-called Western culture—a culture perceived by the great majority of Muslims, more or less correctly, as having been profoundly shaped by the Jewish and Christian traditions. This contesting poses a seemingly constant danger of bursting and flaming out of control not only in the West Bank but also on the West Coast, not only at Israel's borders but also in Indonesia, not only in the Philippines but also in Philadelphia. The pressure is on: it is incumbent upon people of faith, but also people simply of goodwill, to begin the hard task of listening to, appreciating, and hopefully even loving one another across the often harshly drawn lines of varying religious traditions.

In this book I propose one avenue that such difficult conversations might take. I do not think it is the only avenue, and possibly it is not even the best, but I believe it is an interesting and potentially fruitful one. It is the avenue of attempting to read, carefully and sympathetically yet also critically, the sacred texts of religious traditions not our own. This possibility suggested itself to me the first time I read through the entirety of the Qur'an—in English translations, admittedly—several years ago.

I am a Christian minister and theologian, pursuing my vocation primarily as a university professor. One of my interests through the years has involved the challenging task of attempting to understand, and then to communicate to my students, something of the riches of religious traditions other than my (and usually their) own. It is a difficult undertaking, this attempt to engage, appreciate, and even learn from the religious "other"—or, to employ the biblical term, the "stranger." But I, along with many others, have found it to be an undertaking that is inherently rewarding. Most of us have heard the injunction of the book of Leviticus to "love your neighbor as yourself" (19:18), but far fewer of us know that later in the same chapter the Israelites were commanded also to "love the alien as yourself" (19:34). It seems important, too, to add that this commandment to love the stranger is followed by a hauntingly compelling rationale: "for you were aliens in the land of Egypt."

It is as though God called to the fledgling community of Israel—and calls to us even today—to remember what it is like to be the outsider, the excluded, the forgotten one. Remember what it feels like—and know that the "alien" or "stranger" is also a fellow human being, and thus one who can feel the pain of exclusion, of marginalization, of dehumanization. In my best moments, I have tried to nurture in my own heart, as well as the hearts of my students, a glimmer of what it might mean for us to love the *religious strangers*—that is, people of religious convictions and practices that might appear alien to us—as ourselves. I am hopeful that a sense of this love for "the stranger" will permeate the lines and spaces of this book.

In the light of this biblical calling to love the stranger as oneself, it occurred to me a few years ago that since part of my job is to teach something of Islam to my predominantly Christian students, it might behoove me actually to read through the entire Qur'an! Certainly I had read much of it, mostly in anthologies that offer snippets of the scriptures of the world's great religions. But especially given what had occurred the previous September (the now infamous and immediately recognizable 9/11), it seemed to me that I owed it to myself and to my students to read the entire Qur'an with them. And so, in the spring of 2002, we did.

What I found in that reading was a bit of a shock. I was (and still am) struck by the undeniable power of many passages in the Qur'an, even though I experience them only in English translations. (I have begun the process of learning Arabic during the writing of this book.) But I also was struck by the considerable number of biblical characters whose exploits are renarrated and whose stories are retold—often in noticeably different ways—in the Qur'an. While I am not trained as a biblical scholar per se (by which I mean that my doctoral work was not in biblical studies), my vocation as a theologian demands that I try to be a careful reader of texts, biblical and otherwise. In this book I attempt to read the texts of the Bible and the Qur'an precisely as a theologian, which means constantly asking about the theological assumptions, whether explicit or implicit, animating and arising from the text. Similarly, in asking such questions of the text, we are confronted by the inescapable fact that we readers approach the text already with our own, often unexamined, theological assumptions. To the extent that we acknowledge this, perhaps we may at least occasionally allow our assumptions and prior commitments themselves to be challenged, chastened, or even changed. Our primary goal will be to interpret and reflect upon what the text either implies or directly claims about God and God's relation to the world. To engage in such interpretation is also to wonder about the practical implications these theological claims have for the way we live. What I believe I have found in reading relevant and comparable texts from the Bible and the Qur'an are, at least in some cases we shall explore, distinct theological trajectories. In other words, if I am correct in my reading, then the Bible and the Qur'an often construe God, humans, and the world as a whole in noticeably different ways—and in ways that make for significant differences both in theology and in practice. These significant differences are largely what this book is about.

The idea for this book, in fact, occurred to me first during that spring of 2002 as I read the Qur'an's retelling of one of the Bible's stories of Abraham, found in Genesis 18. I was repeatedly struck by the differences in detail found in these two narratives; I was also aware of the traditional Muslim assumption that when there are differences between the Bible and the Qur'an, it is to be understood that the latter provides God's correction of the former.[1] While I confess that as a non-Muslim this is not my assumption, the question still can be raised: Are these differences between the Bible and the Qur'an of any significance? Do the differences make a difference, particularly as the stories in question have been recited, heard, read, studied, and memorized by their respective communities of faith over these many centuries? I suspect that at least sometimes the differences do matter, including those that arise in the telling of the story of Abraham.

But we should appreciate the irony here. It is not uncommon to hear appeals to the fundamental consonance of Judaism, Christianity, and Islam as "Abrahamic" faiths. It is certainly true that the basic plot of the Abraham story provides a lot of common ground for Jews, Christians, and Muslims. But like all clichés, the one that flaunts the notion that these three great monotheistic traditions are "Abrahamic faiths" has just enough truth—and more than enough falsity—to make it dangerous. On the one hand, it is true that believers within all three of these traditions lay claim to Abraham as their father. On the other hand, the ways in which they construe Abraham's patronage and story are so divergent as to yield some very different Abrahams. When my children were much younger, a song they sang regularly in Sunday school began, "Father Abraham had many sons, many sons had Father Abraham." The intertextual exercise we shall undertake in chapter 1, soon to follow, should make it evident that those many sons (and daughters) in turn have, over the centuries, given birth to many different Abrahams!

To be sure, only the most superficial reading of these traditions would come to a less complicated conclusion, such as "Well, we all have Abraham as our father—now isn't that nice? Shouldn't we all just try to get along?" To begin with, many of us recognize that there are real differences simply between Jews and Christians regarding the nature of Abraham's offspring. Indeed, it was probably some of those differences, adamantly and vocally disputed, that brought the issue most sharply to Muhammad's mind. These questions are typical of the Qur'an: "O People of the Book, why do you dispute concerning Abraham, when the Torah and the Gospel were only revealed after him? Do you have no sense?" (Q 3:65).[2] Traditionally, Jews trace their physical lineage to Abraham, through his son Isaac, down to Jacob, who through his God-wrestling became Israel.[3] Christians, following the argument of the apostle Paul, trace their lineage spiritually through Jesus back to Abraham, the ancestor "not only [of] the adherents of the law but also [of] those who share the faith of Abraham (for he is the father of all of us . . .)" (Rom. 4:16). There are hints aplenty in the Qur'an that the disputations between Jews and Christians regarding Abraham's true progeny, some of which occurred within earshot of Muhammad, cried out for a solution—a solution the Arabic prophet attempted to offer particularly during his years in Medina (622–32 CE).

In chapter 1 we will attempt a careful look at how the Qur'an retells the story of the divine visitation of Abraham as told in Genesis 18. I believe it will provide a fitting and powerful opening exercise in intertextual study. Before doing so, however, I want to acknowledge some of the challenges involved in undertaking a study such as this. First of all, I am not a Muslim. I am not, nor do I seriously entertain the possibility that I might become, a believer within the *umma*, the worldwide Islamic community. I do not share in their practices, convictions, or culture(s). I am an outsider; thus, from the vantage point(s) of the Muslim community and its rich traditions, it is I who am "the stranger." Given this reality, is it possible for me to pick up the Muslims' holy text and read it truly? Do I not need the help of their history of living with, and within, and out of, the Qur'an? Is it in fact at least a little voyeuristic to read this text as an outsider, bereft of the history of interpretations that shapes Muslim readers and practitioners of the Qur'an? I have tried to mitigate this problem by reading extensively and carefully from a variety of Islamic commentators and writers. Nonetheless, I still stand outside the Islamic circle of conviction and practice. This is a thorny, difficult issue. But it is not the only one.

Next, as I briefly mentioned earlier, I presently do not know the Arabic language well. I cannot read the Qur'an with any facility in its original tongue, and while I am moved by hearing it recited by Muslims trained in the art of its recitation, I am lucky just to pick out an occasional word or phrase. Meanwhile, Muslims traditionally have insisted that to hear the Qur'an truly as *God's vocalized, recited Word*, one must hear it in its Arabic purity and clarity. In this book, on the other hand, we will be encountering the Qur'an in English translation; this is already a serious dilution, Muslims insist, of the text's inherent and divine power. According to the Qur'an itself, the only miracle that the prophet Muhammad was given to perform was, well, the Qur'an itself—and according to Islamic tradition, in its native Arabic the

Qur'an's miraculous nature is indisputable. "This Qur'an could never have been produced except by Allah . . . There is no doubt about it. It is from the Lord of the Worlds" (Q 10:37). So I am not only an outsider to this rich tradition of practice and interpretation of the Qur'an; I am a stranger also to its cadences, rhythms, poetic beauty, and—by Muslim standards—its miraculous power.

This poetic or aesthetic, ostensibly even miraculous, element of encountering the Qur'an is not, by the way, a minor consideration. Indeed, like many other religious traditions, Islam celebrates the *performative* dimension of its scripture reading. By this term scholars mean that the power of religious tradition's scriptures is not exhausted simply by understanding the basic meaning of a passage. Beyond the cognitive meaning, the oral *performance* involved in reading or reciting the text is experienced as possessing a profoundly formative influence upon all who hear it.[4] Simply stated, to *per*form the text is not simply to *in*form hearers but in fact to *trans*form them—or at least to provide the setting in which such transformation may be possible.

It is helpful to acknowledge that this is far from unique to Islam. Many Buddhists experience recited texts such as the Lotus Sutra in a comparable way, and Hindus' recitation of their ancient scriptures, the Vedas, is also performative. When traditional Catholics who do not actually know the Latin language nonetheless desire to hear the Mass performed in Latin, we are dealing with a comparable phenomenon. Fundamentalist Protestants who insist on using the King James Version of the Bible are probably themselves motivated by a similar fascination with the perceived power of its now-distinctive English prose—a style of language that, by lifelong association and habituation, has become widely identified with the sounds of holiness. I know that in my own churchly upbringing, sometimes the very feelings evoked by the King James idiom were far more powerful in their effects than any perception of cognitive meaning arising from the text.

The point is that, while it is not difficult to understand the idea of a religious text's exercising a performative role in the lives of its devoted readers, this performative function of the Qur'an—utterly crucial for countless Muslims—cannot play a significant role in this book. Instead, we will be reading primarily for theological purposes, attempting to discern how the Qur'an renders biblical narratives and describes characters, including God. Again, I will be reading not as a practicing Muslim from within the Islamic history of tradition but as a Christian theologian who attempts to read these texts critically yet respectfully. This means I will assume that the historical, social, and religious milieu in which the Qur'an came to be is of vital importance for understanding its nature as well as its message. While I will assume that the Qur'an is a historical document, I will also attempt to heed respectfully its claims for itself as well as its claims for God, whom Muslims take to be the very Author of the Qur'an. I presume, however, that listening respectfully to those claims does not require the reader to accept them.

While I do not share the traditional Muslim assumption regarding the purely divine origin of the Qur'an, I hope to proceed with openness to the question of its status as revelation. For now, we can at least admit that, even in translation, there are times when the Qur'an's poetic and literary power is palpable. Particularly in some of Muhammad's earlier revelations, it is difficult to miss the apocalyptic urgency, the world-shattering power, erupting right through the very lines of the text. For example: "When the heaven is rent asunder; and hearkens to its Lord and is judged—and when the earth is spread out; and casts out what is within it and is voided; and hearkens to its Lord and is judged—O man, you strive unto your Lord and you shall meet Him" (Q 84:1–6).[5]

Even as we grant this rhetorical power of the Qur'an, in this book we will largely restrict ourselves to the task of encountering the Qur'an for its theological themes rather than for its transformational power—that is, for *what* we read on its pages rather than for *how* we might feel when we hear it recited. Similarly, while I do not read it "religiously," I do intend to read it theologically, with respect and care, even as I read it, inescapably, as a person of Christian faith. My primary consolation in this approach is that along with whatever performative and transformative capacities Muslims experience in the recitation or hearing of the Qur'an, they also hear it for what it claims for God and the human relation to God—including the nature of our responsibility before God. Hence it is that Muslim scholars can write learned and detailed commentaries on the Qur'an, engaging in the task of interpretation and application of the text for the sake of faithful Muslim believing and living. It is at this point of attempting to come to terms with the theological message of the Qur'an, then, that we will approach this text. So we will build on the simple observation that, to varying degrees at various times in his ministry, Muhammad understood himself to be offering a message from God that had the potential to heal the rift between Jews and Christians, to say nothing of his message to the growing Muslim community of his own day. To put it simply, Muhammad claimed to be the bearer of *a message*—something to be heard and understood not only by Muslims but also by Jews and Christians and others. In a sense, then, despite a sense of historical and theological alienation from the Qur'an on the part of most non-Muslims, its claims do invite our careful and critical attention.

With these important provisos in mind, hopefully we are in a position to explore the Qur'an's dramatically divergent retellings of biblical stories, of alternative interpretations of biblical figures and ideas. These differences between the Bible and the Qur'an become evident by laying respective passages, all in English translation, side by side. This procedure itself, however, raises yet another important issue to acknowledge in the early going. My assumption is not at all that Muhammad had written copies of the Jewish and Christian scriptures, or of subsequent Jewish and Christian commentaries on those scriptures, from which he worked. I do not assume that he could have laid written versions of the biblical and qur'anic stories side by side, as I am about to do in most of the chapters to follow. I have no suspicion that Muhammad was intentionally changing details or theological ideas as found in biblical narratives. The Qur'an—a term which, after all, means "recitation"—was produced in an oral culture, where most people's encounter with their sacred scriptures would have been through oral performance. The "Bible" Muhammad would have known, presumably, was a dynamic, fluid stream of oral transmission.[6] Even though the Qur'an is filled with references to "the Book," this notion of "book" would be far less captive to the columns on a page than our own books are.

Further, I have come to appreciate, even if slowly, that there is a certain ethics of reading that is at risk in this venture. What once seemed to me to be a relatively innocent idea—to lay columns of text from the Qur'an and from the Bible side by side, like parallel passages telling the same story—has grown increasingly complicated.

How and why did I choose the texts that I did? Can they simply be laid side by side like that, as though in each case the passages in question were serving comparable purposes for their faith communities?[7] One can even raise the question whether when the biblical passage is placed in the left-hand column and the qur'anic passage is on the right, the author or editor who so arranges these texts is already prejudicing readers in at least some subtle ways. I can only confess to an awareness of the weightiness of these issues and assure my readers that I have attempted to pursue this work with these important ethical questions always near at hand. I hope my efforts to be attentive to such issues will be judged to have been at least relatively successful. This does not mean that I expect or even hope that Muslims will find my characterizations of the Qur'an's message to be the same as their own; I am certain that they will not. But I do hope that my engagement will be perceived as respectful, honest, sensitive, and conducive to further conversations.

1

ARGUING OVER ABRAHAM
ARGUING WITH GOD

> Say: "Allah has spoken the truth. Follow then the religion of Abraham, the upright; he was not one of the polytheists . . . O People of the Book, why do you disbelieve in the Revelations of Allah, when Allah witnesses whatever you do?"
>
> —Qur'an 3:95, 98

It is not unusual to hear appeals to the possibility of concord among Jews, Muslims, and Christians around the figure of Abraham. Often such an appeal is framed by the notion of all three traditions sharing in what is called "Abrahamic faith." The question I raise in this chapter, very simply put, is: How helpful is this appeal? While certainly it is true that the figure and story of Abraham appear in all three religious traditions (and in many of their offshoots), we will see that Abraham provides at least as much contested ground as common ground.

In this chapter I hope to unearth some of that contested ground for our surveying. We will of necessity restrict ourselves to a single episode in the Abraham story shared by the biblical book of Genesis and the Qur'an; many other episodes could be explored, but I offer this one for its particular interest and importance. It is the story of the mysterious divine visitation of Abraham in Genesis 18, which ends with an intriguing conversation between God and Abraham regarding the ethical merit of God's plan to destroy the cities of Sodom and Gomorrah. This strange and compelling narrative is mentioned in the Qur'an several times, most extensively and with greatest detail in Surah 11.[1] My intention is to explore these parallel passages from Genesis 18 and Surah 11, interspersing theological commentary along the way. In my recitation of both passages in the following pages, nothing is deleted from either passage; each will be explored in its entirety.

The Bible	The Qur'an
Genesis 18:1–5	*Surah 11:69*
The LORD appeared to Abraham	Our messengers indeed came to Abraham
by the oaks of Mamre, as he sat at the	bearing good news.
entrance of his tent in the heat of the day. He looked up and saw three men standing near him. When he saw them, he ran from the tent entrance to meet them, and bowed	
down to the ground. He said, "My lord, if	They said, "Peace,"
I find favor with you, do not pass by your servant. Let a little water be brought, and	
wash your feet, and rest yourselves under	he said, "Peace."
the tree. Let me bring a little bread, that you may refresh yourselves, and after that you may pass on— since you have come to your servant."	

What may attract our attention immediately is that in the Genesis version God actually "makes an appearance" of sorts as "the LORD"—the traditional translation for the four-letter designation for God (*YHWH*) that English-speaking Christians have sometimes rendered as "Jehovah" or "Yahweh." This name, often referred to by scholars as the Tetragrammaton (literally, "four letters"), is deemed in the Jewish tradition to be too holy for human lips; hence, "the LORD" (or in Hebrew, *Adonai*) is a typical Jewish circumlocution for the divine name, though in recent years some Jews prefer *HaShem* ("the Name") and others *G-d*. In deference to the most common Jewish usage, however, throughout this book I will utilize the term *Adonai* to designate the holy, unutterable divine name of YHWH.

The fundamental point is that this divine name, in the long development of Jewish tradition, eventually came to designate God's considerable—if not infinite—holiness and transcendence. It may be surprising, then, that in the early chapters of Genesis it is particularly in those narratives when God is designated by this holy name that we encounter the most obvious and dramatic examples of anthropomorphism—of God's being portrayed in very human ways. Surely the story before us bears out this tendency.

Never mind that later in the Torah Adonai will reply to Moses's request to see God's glory, "You cannot see my face; for no one shall see me and live" (Exod. 33:20)—or, for that matter, that the Johannine writings in the New Testament insist that "no one has ever seen God" (John 1:18; 1 John 4:12). Here in Genesis we read that Adonai "appeared to Abraham." Some Jewish commentators, most notably the great Maimonides (1135–1204), have tried to sidestep the difficulty by suggesting that Abraham's experience was a vision, much as an earlier episode in Abraham's life appears to have been (Genesis 15). However, Genesis 18 has far less of the mysterious, visionary hues that are evident in Genesis 15. For example, the story in Genesis 15 occurs as the sun is setting; in fact, in language that suggests something of a twilight-zone atmosphere, we read that "a deep sleep fell upon Abram, and a deep and terrifying darkness descended upon him" (15:12). Genesis 18, by contrast, describes its theophany as occurring "in the heat of the day" (18:1). In the earlier story, Abraham has a vision or dream in which God, oddly enough, appears as "a smoking fire pot and a flaming torch" (15:17). In our story, Genesis 18, Adonai's appearance is not only in broad daylight but in an accessible, human form. Further, this experience involves an extensive meal, and Abraham's wife Sarah also gets involved later in the conversation. None of this means that Genesis 18 cannot be interpreted as the description of a visionary experience; it just means that the text is less obvious in suggesting just exactly how we should interpret it. Against Maimonides's understandable sensibilities, the quaint yet mysterious story of Genesis 18 seems to offer a tangible, nearly human deity.

The Qur'an appears to be grappling with this problem by changing the subject of this appearance from God to angels. (Subsequent Muslim tradition would identify them as Gabriel, Michael, and Israfil.) Immediately by stating that these visitors are not the appearing of God per se but rather messengers of God, the Qur'an succeeds in quieting the disquieting problem of blatant anthropomorphism, of conceiving of God as though God were essentially a human being writ large. For in making this observation regarding the Qur'an's retelling of the story, we must appreciate the fact that the biblical depictions of God such as encountered in Genesis 18 created interpretive problems for Jewish (and later, Christian) readers. What kind of God is it who, earlier in Genesis, like a potter molds the *adam* (earthling) out of *adamah* (dirt of the ground); or who takes a stroll through the Garden of Eden, hunting down Adam and Eve and engaging them, along with a talking serpent, in a long and complicated interrogation; or who places a rainbow in the clouds to remind himself about his promise not to flood the earth again? Is this God not "all too human"? It seems quite clear that the stories cannot be interpreted literally—so how should they be read?

In addressing the problems created by anthropomorphism, well before the time of Muhammad, Jewish teachers had developed an interpretive scheme that was to prove useful for their own and, later, Christian reflection upon the biblical text. The rabbis argued that the scriptures offered imagery for God that was accessible to the human mind. Our limitations require of God a downward movement of accommodation, so that when scripture describes God in human terms—such as having a face, hands, feet, or a heart, or as walking and talking and so on—this is divine revelation "stooping down," we might say, to our level. Thus, such figures of speech regarding God were to be interpreted not literally but figuratively; rabbis frequently employed the phrase *k'b'yakol*, translated "as it were" or "so to speak," to remind themselves and their students that anthropomorphisms are unavoidable though not literally true. Given the notion of divine accommodation—an idea that John Calvin honed expertly in his writings—modern and contemporary Christian theologians generally tend to read these ancient stories of Adonai for what the stories may teach us *theologically*. This means we attempt to read them seriously and carefully, but usually not literally. In other words, such a story as Genesis 18 should be read with the question in mind, "Without needing to assume that this passage gives us a simple, literal description of God, what does it suggest to us theologically regarding God and God's ways with the world?" If this approach is fruitful, it implies that we ought to treat these stories far more like parables than like newspaper accounts, with the assumption that one of the very important ways human beings have attempted to put into words their most noble and subtle notions regarding divine matters is through the use of story, parable, myth. The words of the Genesis text, then, that "the LORD appeared to Abraham by the oaks of Mamre," might be interpreted as portraying through narrative the theological claim that God truly can, and truly does, draw near in communication and communion with human beings—and does so in particular times and places.

Genesis 18:5–8	Surah 11:69–70
So they said, "Do as you have said." And Abraham hastened into the tent to Sarah, and said, "Make ready quickly three measures of choice flour, knead it,	
and make cakes." Abraham ran to the	Then he brought a roasted calf at once.

12

Genesis 18:5–8	Surah 11:69–70
herd, and took a calf, tender and good, and gave it to the servant, who hastened to prepare it. Then he took curds and milk and the calf that he had prepared, and set	
it before them; and he stood by them	But when he saw that their hands did not
under the tree while they ate.	reach out to it, he became suspicious of them and conceived a fear of them. They said: "Fear not, we have been sent to the people of Lot."

Now the stakes are raised! In the Genesis version of the story, not only has Adonai made an appearance to Abraham in the heat of the day, but Abraham has set about busily to provide rich hospitality for his mysterious guest(s?). Genesis goes into far greater detail than the qur'anic parallel, but in both stories it is obvious that Abraham is fulfilling the praiseworthy role of host to strangers, an act highly prized among Middle Eastern peoples. But of course the big difference then emerges: in Genesis the three strangers (one of whom, it seems, is Adonai) actually partake of the feast, while in the Qur'an the angelic beings do not. In this Genesis passage there is the possibility of material sharing between the divine and the human; there is fellowship, conversation. In the Qur'an God is absent from the narrative, except as represented by "messengers" who are themselves too heavenly, too transcendent, to avail themselves of Abraham's hospitality. Abraham's understandable reaction to this turn of events is to feel afraid of these mysterious strangers. Though they are then able to calm his trepidation, an important qur'anic point has been made: the heavenly realm of Allah does not traffic in earthly things. Eighth-century Muslim exegete Ibn Kathir commented, "According to the People of the Book, the fatted calf was roasted and served with three rolls, fat, and milk. And, according to them, the angels ate, but this is not right."[2]

Meanwhile, in Genesis: please pass the curds and milk.

Genesis 18:9–21	Surah 11:71–73
They said to him, "Where is your wife Sarah?" And he said, "There, in the tent." Then one said, "I will surely return to you in due season, and your wife Sarah shall	
have a son." And Sarah was listening at	His wife was standing by,
the tent entrance behind him. Now Abraham and Sarah were old, advanced in age; it had ceased to be with Sarah after	

13

Genesis 18:9–21	Surah 11:71–73
the manner of women. So Sarah laughed	so she laughed.
to herself, saying,	Thereupon We announced to her the good news of Isaac, and after Isaac, of Jacob.
	She said: "Woe is me, shall I bear a child
"After I have grown old,	while I am an old woman,
and my husband is old, shall I have	and this, my husband, is an old man too?
pleasure?"	
	That is truly a very strange thing."
The LORD said to Abraham, "Why did	They said:
Sarah laugh, and say, 'Shall I indeed bear	
a child, now that I am old?' Is	"Do you wonder at Allah's Command?
anything too wonderful for the LORD? At the	May the Mercy and Blessings of Allah be
set time I will return to you, in due season,	upon you, O people of the House [of Abraham].
and Sarah shall have a son." But Sarah denied, saying, "I did not laugh"; for she was afraid. He said, "Oh yes, you did laugh."	
	Surely He is Praiseworthy and Glorious."
Then the men set out from there, and they looked toward Sodom; and Abraham went with them to set them on their way. The LORD said, "Shall I hide from Abraham what I am about to do, seeing that Abraham shall become a great and mighty nation, and all the nations of the earth shall be blessed in him? No, for I have chosen him, that he may charge his children and his household after him to keep the ways of the LORD by doing righteousness and justice; so that the LORD may bring about for Abraham what he has promised him." Then the LORD said, "How great is the outcry against Sodom and Gomorrah and how very grave their sin! I must go down and see whether they have done altogether according to the outcry that has come to me; and if not, I will know."	

We now encounter a truly remarkable development in our intertextual reading. On the one hand, we find a striking similarity between the two narratives regarding the announcement of Sarah's impending miraculous pregnancy, along with her understandable reaction. On the other hand, the next part of the Genesis narrative, immediately above, has no qur'anic parallel whatsoever. In Genesis, the narrator pulls back the curtain on Adonai's own reflective process—we read of God, *as it were* (to borrow the rabbinic phrase), mulling something over: "So should I hide this from Abraham, or not? I suppose I really should tell him, since out of him I intend to create a mighty nation that will bless all the nations." Some rabbis suggested that God's line of reasoning was that if indeed God was about to make Abraham the "father of many nations" or peoples (*goyim*), it would hardly make sense to conceal from Abraham a plan to destroy the *goyim* of Sodom and Gomorrah: no time like the present to start putting Abraham to work as a father-figure who has "charge [over] his children" (18:19). But does God really need to think things through? Our traditional theological notion of divine omniscience—of God's immediate and absolutely thorough knowledge of all of the details of creation, past, present, and future—would seemingly preclude the proposition that God would need to sift through some possible courses of action.

Further, Adonai describes the impending action against Sodom and Gomorrah in distinctively anthropomorphic imagery. "I must go down," says Adonai, and "see" what the situation is like in these twin cities of sin. It is as though God is saying, "I need to go down and check it out to see if it's as bad as what I've heard—and if it isn't, well, I'll find that out too." Again, language like this plays havoc with traditional notions of God's omniscience and omnipresence. What would it mean for a God who is present, presumably, throughout all of creation to "go down and see"? No wonder the Jewish and Christian traditions have labored hard to understand these anthropomorphisms as God's humble method of communicating with finite and frail human beings; no wonder, too, that the Qur'an also attempts in its own ways to avoid at least the more obvious anthropomorphisms of the Bible.

Genesis 18:22–25	Surah 11:74–75
So the men turned from there, and went toward Sodom, while Abraham remained standing before the Lord. Then Abraham came near and said, "Will you indeed sweep away the righteous with the wicked?	Then when fear left Abraham and the good news came to him, he started pleading with Us concerning the people of Lot.
Suppose there are fifty righteous within the city; will you then sweep away the place and not forgive it for the fifty righteous who are in it? Far be it from you	Abraham is truly clement, contrite, penitent.
to do such a thing, to slay the righteous with the wicked, so that the righteous fare as the wicked! Far be that from you! *Shall not the Judge of all the earth do what is just?'*	

15

"Shall not the Judge of all the earth do what is just?" is one of the great questions in the Bible—raised by a human being, challenging the Creator and Sustainer of all things to do right. *Amazing!*—and for the Qur'an, inconceivable. The Qur'an's relative silence on this part of the Abraham story certainly is understandable; after all, it is not only a wonderful question but a troubling one too. Does God really need Abraham to issue this challenge? Does God need to have God's ethical horizons broadened by the likes of this puny human, hospitable though he was? And what is the standard of justice or fairness to which Abraham appeals? Why is this a standard that the holy Creator of all things would necessarily recognize or embrace? Do human beings and God share some common ideals about justice? What would it mean for God to be answerable to some standard of justice? Whose standard is it, anyway?

But for all of that, it is a compelling question. It is a marvelous narrative scene. Abraham the human, made of "dust and ashes" (18:27), gets in God's face, so to speak, and holds God accountable. It is a compelling portrait of biblical humanism we encounter here, where the human insists that its deity hew to just and equitable practices.

Genesis 18:26–33	Surah 11:76
And the LORD said, "If I find at Sodom fifty righteous in the city, I will forgive the whole place for their sake." Abraham answered, "Let me take it upon myself	"O Abraham, desist from this; the Command of your Lord has come and an irreversible punishment shall surely smite them."
to speak to the Lord, I who am but dust and ashes. Suppose five of the fifty righteous are lacking? Will you destroy the whole city for lack of five?" And he said, "I will not destroy it if I find forty-five there." Again he spoke to him, "Suppose forty are found there." He answered, "For the sake of forty I will not do it." Then he said, "Oh do not let the Lord be angry if I speak. Suppose thirty are found there." He answered, "I will not do it, if I find thirty there." He said, "Let me take it upon myself to speak to the Lord. Suppose twenty are found there." He answered, "For the sake of twenty I will not destroy it." Then he said, "Oh do not let the Lord be angry if I speak just once more. Suppose ten are found there." He answered, "For the sake of ten I will not destroy it." And the LORD went his way, when he had finished speaking to Abraham; and Abraham returned to his place.	

And so, not surprisingly, where Genesis offers one of the great bartering-for-justice stories in the history of human narration, the Qur'an is silent. Or nearly so. More precisely, in the Qur'an it is Abraham who is told to be silent, to hold his tongue, to submit to Allah's judgment. While the Qur'an does offer a brief hint of Abraham's pleading and bartering—immediately qualified, if not effectively denied, by insisting that Abraham was "clement, contrite, penitent"—any pleading for Sodom is quickly cut off. "Don't waste your breath, Abraham. The decree has been issued, and nothing can change that."

Anthropomorphisms abound in the Genesis story before us: God, in cahoots with a couple of mysterious fellow-travelers, wanders into Abraham's campsite and sits down to a big Middle Eastern spread; God holds an internal conversation about how much to let Abraham in on the divine plan; God engages in a social ethics debate with Abraham; God could perhaps even have been "talked down" out of nuking the sinners—who knows? But again we must ask: Is this any way for a deity to behave?

No wonder the Qur'an cleans up God's image. The qur'anic version of the story is much cleaner, crisper, and godlike. God the transcendent Creator does not play a narrative role, but the messengers know exactly how to deliver God's unchangeable decree and get God's things done.

Clearly, this process of side-by-side reading yields some fascinating differences. It is not difficult to trace the significant shifts these differences might make in a community of interpretation, over time, regarding God and God's relationship to the world and to oneself. However, further reflection suggests that we cannot lay these two narratives "side by side" quite so simply and readily. After all, there was several centuries' worth of reading the biblical texts, by both Jews and Christians (if not others as well), that had already accumulated by the time of Muhammad. In other words, there were already many layers of Jewish and Christian interpretation, oral and written, that interpose themselves between the Genesis and Qur'an columns on a page. To draw on James Kugel's title and terminology, we must take into account the "Bible as it was" that lies between Genesis 18 and Surah 11.[3] Stated simply, "the Bible as it was" means *the Bible as it was interpreted*—as it was read, recited, heard, grappled with, commented upon, and applied by Jewish (and then later, also Christian) scribes within, and in behalf of, their particular communities of faith and practice. The Bible never stands apart from the communities of faith and practice that embrace it; such communities are the reason, historically speaking, that the Bible even exists. But of course the opposite is also true: these communities take shape and thrive as they draw strength and vision from their holy texts. The Bible is far from simply words on thin

17

pages; it is a history of readings, of discussion and debate, of questions and replies, of lives seriously lived in historical communities of interpretation and application. All of this lies in the space separating the biblical and qur'anic texts we have been comparing.

Here is an example pertinent to our present purposes: several centuries' worth of rabbinic commentary on the book of Genesis was collected and collated near the end of the fourth and into the early fifth centuries CE (which means roughly two centuries before Muhammad's time). This material, called *Genesis Rabbah*, provides an authoritative Jewish sourcebook of readings of the Genesis text by and for the Jewish community not only of two millennia ago but even of today. Interestingly, what it demonstrates is that the differences between Genesis and the Qur'an are to some extent accounted for (or at least softened a bit) by the history of Jewish interpretation itself. In other words, our undertaking is far from simply a matter of showing "how far the Qur'an departed" from the Bible; instead, it is a matter of seeing that the qur'anic versions of biblical narratives often already imbibed the ambience of Jewish readings of the biblical text—readings intended, often, to deanthropomorphize God in a discernible tendency toward greater theological sophistication. Let us take another intertextual look, this time at the rabbinic exposition of Genesis 18 found in *Genesis Rabbah*, laid alongside the Qur'an's narrative:

Genesis Rabbah[4]	*Surah 11:69*
"*And Thy condescension hath made me great*" (Ps. 18:35): with what condescension did the Lord make Abraham great? In that he sat while the *Shechinah* stood; thus it is written,	
"And the Lord appeared unto him . . . as he sat."	Our messengers indeed came to Abraham bearing good news.
. . . Thus it is written, "And he lifted up his eyes and looked" (18:2)—he saw the *Shechinah* and saw the angels . . .	

While the rabbis did not deny that it was God who appeared to Abraham, they found it useful to make a linguistic shift. When wanting to denote God's presence and activity within the creaturely realm, they tended to employ a subtle circumlocution, the term *Shechinah*. This designation, derived from the Hebrew word for "dwelling" (*shakhan*), provided the rabbis a way to speak of God as being near to, present with, and active in the world without actually saying it was *God*—even though it is.[5] Let us simply say that the Shechinah is the divine presence, and thus that the rabbis' theological strategy does not undercut Genesis's insistence upon God's desire and capacity for true communion with human beings or with the creaturely realm generally. Indeed, the rabbis playfully observe in this story of divine visitation that God, like an observant Jew, undertakes a *mitzvah*—a good deed that makes the world a better place—of visiting the sick. A cursory glance at the end of Genesis 17, the previous chapter, reminds the reader that Abraham has only recently been circumcised. So he is one sore old man! Thus, the God of all creation bends low to visit the ailing Abraham, allowing him to remain seated while the Shechinah stands.

Genesis Rabbah	Surah 11:70
"And they said, 'Do as you have said'"	
(18:5). "As for us," said they,	But when he saw that their hands did not
"we neither eat nor drink; but you	reach out to [the meal], . . .
who do eat and drink, do as you have said . . ."	
Above [in the heavenly sphere] there is no eating and drinking; hence when Moses ascended on high he appeared like them [the angels], as it says, *Then I abode in the mount forty days and forty nights; I did neither eat bread nor drink water* (Deut. 9:9). But below, where there is eating and drinking, we find, "And he stood by them under the tree, and they did eat" (18:8). Did they then eat? They pretended to eat, removing each course in turn.	

In the light of the rabbinic commentary on Genesis 18, it seems likely that the Qur'an's denial that the heavenly messengers even lifted a hand toward Abraham's nice spread shares with the Jewish interpretive tradition a hesitation to portray God in such anthropomorphic ways. In the rabbinic readings preserved in *Genesis Rabbah*, the divine party only "pretended to eat"—an explicit undercutting of the surface meaning of the Genesis text, surely. But, again, it is not a surprising reading the rabbis offered, for it certainly seems much more in keeping with the idea of divine transcendence: "above there is no eating and drinking."

It is noteworthy, too, that even as the rabbis could speak of the Shechinah, the presence of God, as paying a visit to Abraham, they also identified all three visitors as angels. Thus, in anticipation of what we read also in the Qur'an, God is not identified with any one of the angels. Rabbinic tradition identified the three as Michael, Gabriel, and Raphael; according to *Genesis Rabbah*, Rabbi Hiyya taught that Abraham conversed with "the most important of them, Michael"[6]—who is thus being identified functionally as God's stand-in.

Genesis Rabbah	*Surah 11:75–76*
"Abraham remained standing before the LORD" (18:22). Rabbi Simon said: This is an emendation of the Soferim [lit., "bookmen" or scholars; scribes from the time of Ezra to the Maccabean period, roughly 450—100 BC], for the *Shechinah* was actually waiting for Abraham. *(The issue is that another, early and reliable, manuscript tradition reads "while the* LORD *remained standing before Abraham"—i.e., as though standing as a servant before a superior.)*	
"'Far be it from you to do such a thing, to slay the righteous with the wicked, . . . Far be that from you!" R. Judan interpreted: It is a profa- nation for Thee; it is alien to Thy nature . . . R. Abba said: Not [simply] "to do such a thing" is written here, but "to do anything after this manner": nei- ther this nor anything like it nor anything even of a lesser nature.	Abraham is truly clement, contrite, penitent.
"Suppose five of the fifty righteous are lacking? Will you destroy the whole city for lack of five?" (18:28). R. Hiyya b. Abba said: Abraham wished to descend from fifty to five, but the Holy One, blessed be He, said to him: "Turn back" (i.e., "This is too big a jump").	"O Abraham, desist from this; the Command of your Lord has come and an irreversible punishment shall surely smite them."

The rabbinic interpreters could even be explicitly self-aware of their theological wrestlings with, and renderings of, the biblical text. Here in *Genesis
Rabbah* the observation is attributed to Rabbi Simon that earlier Jewish
scribes actually had made a change in the language of the Genesis text they
had inherited: even if Abraham boldly engaged the Almighty in a little
discussion of theological ethics, surely it is not acceptable to say that God
stood "before Abraham"—as many of the oldest manuscripts actually had
it—as a servant stands before the master. Rather, surely it was the case that
the Jewish scribes of Ezra's time had been correct to insist that in fact Abraham had stood "before God." Yet it is not at all clear that Rabbi Simon was
sympathetic with this revision of the text; he appears to be saying something
like "As a matter of fact, it was God's Presence, the Shechinah, that was
waiting upon Abraham."[7]

In his commentary on Genesis, the contemporary Christian biblical scholar Walter Brueggemann has written regarding this interchange between Abraham and God:

> It is as though Abraham is Yahweh's theological teacher and raises a question that is quite new for him. The question concerns Yahweh's willingness to set aside the closed system and approach the world in another way. Abraham is the bearer of a new theological possibility. He dares to raise risky questions with Yahweh. The relation of Abraham and Yahweh in this passage is worth noting in detail ... [A] very early text note (not to be doubted in its authority and authenticity) shows that the text before any translation actually read, "Yahweh stood before Abraham." The picture is one which agrees with our comment about Abraham as Yahweh's theological instructor ... But that bold image of Yahweh being accountable to Abraham for this theological idea was judged by the early scribes as irreverent and unacceptable ... But the earlier version suggests with remarkable candor what a bold posture Abraham assumes and how presumptuous is the issue he raises.[8]

Even if the narrative image of God "standing before" Abraham was judged to be "irreverent and unacceptable," the rabbis were nonetheless quite willing to elaborate on Abraham's moral challenge to God. "It would be utterly alien to your nature to destroy the innocent along with the wicked," the rabbinical Abraham theologizes. "Far be it from you to do such a thing, or even anything remotely like it!" The most beautifully compelling argument, however, is attributed to Rabbi Levi, who interpreted Abraham's challenge to be "If you want to have a world, there can be no justice, and if justice is what you want, there can be no world. You are holding the rope at both ends; you want a world and you want justice. If you don't give in a bit, the world can never stand."[9] It is an appeal to the Creator to recognize and even embrace the inherent limitations in creaturely existence, to temper heavenly ideals with earthly realities.

Indeed, Rabbi Hiyya ben Abba is said to have remarked that God had to apply the brakes to Abraham's impulses toward mercy. According to this imaginative rabbinic strand of interpretation, Abraham had dropped the hypothetical number of righteous Sodomites from fifty down to five in a single leap! "Turn back," the rabbinically rendered Shechinah replies; that is too big a jump all at once; let's slow down, back up, and work the number down a little more gradually! But even this is a far cry from the Qur'an's rendering of the angels who, speaking on God's behalf, order Abraham to "desist from this" hopeless plea-bargaining entirely.

We detect, then, a set of subtle but fascinating shifts in this Abrahamic story as it is molded by rabbinic reading. The rabbis did not deny that it was truly God who visited Abraham and Sarah; they did, however, soften the rhetoric of the biblical text from the use of God's Holy Name (YHWH), a name of great mystery and holy transcendence, by employing instead the term Shechinah. Granted, the Shechinah is God—but God specifically imagined, narrated, and experienced as present within creation. As the rabbinic tradition has come to say it, the Shechinah is God walking, "as it were," among us and conversing with us. True, said the rabbis, God has no legs upon which to stand, literally, and no actual mouth whereby to speak. But God can nonetheless come and sit down, "so to speak," by Abraham's and Sarah's encampment because the Shechinah is God dwelling among us, in communiqué with us. Yet there was clearly a further move made by at least some rabbis, in which even the Shechinah's presence is embodied in a trio of angels. But whether God or angels, the rabbis insisted, no otherworldly being could actually eat earthly, material food. And while the God of the rabbis is willing to engage in discussion with Abraham regarding the fate of the Sodomites, God finds it necessary as well to place a check upon Abraham's apparently overly generous proclivity for mercy.

Interestingly enough, during roughly the same years that these playful rabbinic musings on Genesis were being collected and collated into *Genesis Rabbah*, one of the greatest ever of Christian theologians, St. Augustine (354–430), bishop of Hippo in North Africa, was writing his *Confessions* and many other materials for the benefit of fellow Christians. Augustine was one of the earliest theologians to see glimmers of the Trinity in Genesis 18. This should not be surprising, given the facts that the doctrine of the Trinity received its most serious attention and development precisely during the late fourth century and that Augustine was one of its most important contributors. In fact, in his book *On the Trinity* Augustine, sounding every bit like a Christian rabbi, comments on our story:

> Now under the oak tree at Mamre, Abraham saw three men, whom he invited in and received with hospitality, serving them as they dined. Yet Scripture does not say . . . "three men appeared to him," but "the Lord appeared to him." Then, however, recounting how it was that the Lord did in fact appear to him, it adds the matter of the three men, whom Abraham invites to his hospitality in the plural number—though afterward he speaks to them in the singular, as if One . . .[10]

Over the subsequent centuries, the story of Genesis 18 would for Christians not only provide an apt model of hospitality but also increasingly come to be understood to provide a foreshadowing of the triune God. In medieval Christian exegesis and art, Genesis's mysterious portrait of Abraham's three visitors as somehow also being or representing "the LORD" became a defining image. Even today, one of the most enduring images in Christian iconography is the fifteenth-century Russian Andrei Rublev's *Icon of the Old Testament Trinity*, a rendering of three angelic beings seated at a table, gathered around an elevated plate (the Orthodox tradition's *diskos*) upon which a piece of bread rests.[11] Kugel, in his massive and helpful tome *Traditions of the Bible*, includes a facsimile of this same icon, adding this presumably lighthearted comment beneath it: "The angels visited Abraham. They didn't have much to eat."[12] But whether in jest or not, Kugel misleads his readers on an extremely critical point: this meal is not simply a single chunk of bread to be shared three ways. Closer examination yields that the bread has a face! This only makes all the more obvious what the viewer might have suspected already: the humble meal at the center of this heavenly trio is none other than the church's sacramental meal, the Eucharist, the body and blood of Jesus. This is a meal that, for Christians, is of infinite supply and boundless spiritual nutrition; contrary to Kugel, there is plenty to eat! But if Rublev's icon represents the triune God, what sense does it make for the divine figures to be seated at the Eucharistic table?

Contemporary Roman Catholic theologian Elizabeth Johnson has written a sparkling little commentary on this icon that helps to answer this question. Johnson muses,

> What catches the meditating eye most is the position of the three figures. They are arranged in a circle inclining toward one another but the circle is not closed. What the image suggests is that the mystery of God is not a self-contained or closed divine society but a communion in relationship. Moreover, its portrayal of the figures evokes the idea that this divine communion is lovingly open to the world, seeking to nourish it. As you contemplate, you begin intuitively to grasp that you are invited into this circle. Indeed, by gazing, you are already a part of it. This is a depiction of a Trinitarian God capable of immense hospitality who calls the world to join the feast.[13]

The point here emphatically is not that Genesis 18 actually teaches the doctrine of the Trinity; rather, the point is that as Christians have read this story, it should not be surprising that their interpretation has moved on a distinct trajectory. We might put it this way. In reading Genesis 18 we encounter a surprising scenario in which Adonai sits down at the table, apparently capable of sharing not only in conversation and friendly debate but even in the full spread of a Middle Eastern feast. Subsequent rabbinic interpretation could affirm the nearness and communion-creating capabilities of God but shied away from the blatant anthropomorphism involved in portraying God as washing down calf and curds with a swig of milk. The

Qur'an takes this rabbinic trajectory a step or two further by carefully insisting that Allah makes no appearance; further, even God's angelic emissaries do not participate fully in fellowship with these earthlings. They do not, and presumably cannot, eat.

Meanwhile, over time Christians developed a reading of Genesis 18 that yielded a portrait of God's communing, fellowship-engendering, incarnate grace in Jesus Christ. Thus, in the Christian rendering of this narrative it is ultimately God, not the human, who actually provides the hospitality. This hospitality, this room for us at the table, flows directly out of God's communal nature as Father, Son, and Spirit indwelling one another in mutual love. It is into this communal, mutual sharing-together that the gospel proclaims humanity to be invited in the church's ritual meal, the Eucharist.

We are confronted in this variety of readings of Genesis 18, then, with the importance of the role played by the historical communities of faith and practice that have laid claim to Abraham's legacy. The rabbinic hesitation to portray God simply in human terms is readily understandable. Similarly, the Qur'an's version of the story exemplifies the theme of God's utter transcendence, certainly a dominant theme in Islam. And Christians—reading Genesis 18 through the lens of their conviction that the Word who was with God, and who indeed is God, became flesh and dwelt among us—found in this story foreshadowings of God's communal, triune nature. Indeed, in a real sense none of these traditions was able to read Genesis 18 in a simply literalistic way. The rabbis found their solution by speaking metaphorically (signaled by their use of the phrase "so to speak") of God's communing presence, a presence further qualified and attenuated by their interpreting the three visitors as angels. Christian interpreters understood all stories of divine presence or theophany (lit., "divine appearance") as manifestations or foreshadowings of the Logos who later, in the incarnation, became the human being Jesus Christ, God's Son. Thus, in fact, Christianity built upon the rabbinic imagery of the Shechinah to affirm in an even stronger, more decisive way that God has become present to, and present within, God's own creation. The Qur'an takes the exact opposite direction; its solution to anthropomorphism is to keep the story but change the characters (angels pay a visit, not God), and then to edit the story such that God comes out looking very Godly: transcendent, almighty, omniscient—and, in a sense, effectively outside the narrative picture.

It may well be that one's community of faith and practice will determine, at least to a considerable extent, which portrait of God—and which portrait of Abraham, for that matter—one finds to be the most truthful, the most compelling. We will most assuredly confront, again and again, these differing Jewish, Christian, and Muslim trajectories of interpretation in the chapters that follow.

2

PEOPLE OF THE TORAH, PEOPLE OF THE GOSPEL

Say: "O People of the Book, come to an equitable word between you and us, that we worship none but Allah, do not associate anything with Him and do not set up each other as lords besides Allah." If they turn their backs, say: "Bear witness that we are Muslims."

—Qur'an 3:64

It is widely known that Muslims historically have categorized Jews and Christians as "People of the Book." It is easy to assume that "the Book" of which Jews and Christians are "People" is the Bible. To an extent that is an appropriate assumption—but only to an extent. In this chapter we will explore the reasons for this.

First of all, we must appreciate that Jews and Christians, generally speaking, do not read the same Bible. It will surprise few people to read that the twenty-seven documents (or "books") in Christianity's New Testament are not included in the Jewish Bible. Indeed, the documents that compose the Jewish Bible were written and selected as canonical texts several centuries before Christian leaders made similar decisions in creating what is now called the New Testament. Christians by and large have abided by the decisions of Jewish leadership and tradition regarding the Jewish canon,[1] though the church settled on a designation for those books—"the Old Testament"—that the synagogue has never embraced or appreciated. It is, after all, a short step from calling something old to calling it outdated or obsolete, and Christians often have been sorely tempted to make precisely that kind of judgment about their Old Testament—and, more importantly, about Jews and Judaism, with tragic and even murderous consequences. Instead, in Jewish tradition the designation that evolved for its canon is Tanakh, an acronym formed by the consonants T-N-K. T is for *Torah*, or the five books with which both the Old Testament and the Tanakh begin; N is for *Nevi'im*, or the prophets, such as Isaiah, Jeremiah, Amos; and K is for *Ketuvim*, which means "writings" that include stories of Israel's kings as well as Jewish wisdom, poetry, and psalms.

The difference lies not only in the differing names that Jews and Christians give to this collection of books. Equally significant, if not more so, is the ordering of the books, particularly when it comes to the end of each collection. The church's Old Testament ends with a little prophetic book, Malachi, which concludes with a passage that Christians have interpreted as a prophecy regarding the Messiah to come: "Lo, I will send you the prophet Elijah before the great and terrible day of the LORD comes. He will turn the hearts of parents to their children and the hearts of children to their parents, so that I will not come and strike the land with a curse" (4:5). Thus, for Christians the Old Testament ends on a note of expectation, even of longing, in awaiting the coming Messiah whose way is to be prepared by Elijah—or at least by an Elijah-like figure such as John the Baptist, as early Christians argued. Christians read their Old Testament, then, as ending with "To Be Continued." This reading, naturally, leads immediately to the first book of the New Testament, the gospel of Matthew.

For Jews, it's a different story! The Jewish tradition's Tanakh ends with the books called 1 and 2 Chronicles—but packaged as a single book—which are also in the church's Old Testament but are located much earlier in the arrangement of texts. The Chronicler's story ends with King Cyrus of Persia issuing a decree permitting all Jews who had been taken into Babylonian captivity to return to Jerusalem to help with the rebuilding of the temple. This conclusion corresponds perfectly with the books of Ezra and Nehemiah, which are also packaged as a single book in the Tanakh and immediately precede the Chronicles. The salient point is that the scribes Ezra and Nehemiah not only led in the project of rebuilding the Jewish temple but also led their people in a renewal of their covenantal relationship with God as described in the Torah. Thus, while Christianity's Old Testament ends with prophetic anticipation of a dramatic messiah figure, Judaism's Tanakh ends with scribes who teach the Jewish people the Torah and lead them in renewing the covenant into which their ancestors had been called under the leadership of Moses. By ending the Tanakh with this narrative sequence, Jewish leaders opted not so much for a yearning for the coming Messiah as for a relatively settled confidence that God has already accomplished the divine purpose by entrusting the Torah to the people of Israel to study, interpret, and obey. If the Old Testament ends in anticipation of a coming Messiah, the Tanakh concludes with the recognition, even the celebration, of the role of the scribe, or rabbi, in the ongoing life of the Jewish community. There is a "To Be Continued" here too—but the cliffhanger ending is gone, and the "continued" is expected to flow in far greater continuity with the story of the scribal renewal of the Jewish covenant.

Christians historically have not sufficiently appreciated this difference between their Old Testament and Jews' Tanakh. Instead, much of Christian tradition has tended to read these texts as an arsenal of prophecies about the Messiah-to-come. The Israeli philosopher David Hartman, in his lively and insightful book *A Living Covenant: The Innovative Spirit in Traditional Judaism*, acknowledges that the scribal labors of Ezra and Nehemiah, in their rallying of the returning Jews to rebuild the temple and reaffirm the covenant, did not match the more dramatic messianic expectations of some of the Hebrew prophets. The return of the Jews from Babylonian exile was not an especially triumphal event; it was, in fact, a relatively humble accomplishment. Hartman writes, "Just as Nehemiah and Ezra did not emulate Joshua by entering the land at the head of a victorious army, they were not the mediators of a new and greater covenant than that given through Moses at Sinai. Instead, as the closing chapters of Nehemiah relate, they organized the Great Assembly of the people [i.e., the first great gathering of scribes] to renew the existing covenant."[2] This difference will become especially significant later in this chapter; for now, the point is that the synagogue's Tanakh ends dramatically differently from the church's Old Testament.

If the Jews' and Christians' holy books are not the same—and we have seen that they are not—then what does the Qur'an mean by this designation, "People of the Book"? What is this single Book? After all, the Qur'an itself appears to reflect the differences we have been exploring by associating Jews with the Torah (*Taurat*) and Christians with the Gospel (*Injil*). So the Qur'an recognizes that the Torah and the Gospel are different books, not the same, not "the Book" per se. Indeed, in Q 9:111 we read of "a true promise from [Allah] in the Torah, the Gospel and the Qur'an," implying an equally revelatory validity among these three "books." So again we must ask, what is "the Book" that somehow unites the "books" that Muhammad identified as the Torah, the Gospel, and the Qur'an?

By splicing together several brief phrases in the Qur'an, Muslim interpretive tradition has developed an answer to this question with an intriguing doctrine of "the Book." In Q 85:21–22 we read of "a glorious Qur'an, in a Well-Preserved [or 'guarded'] Tablet" and immediately have to wonder precisely what "tablet" is being "preserved," and where? Similarly, Q 56:77–80 alludes to "a noble Qur'an" that is "in a hidden Book, that only the purified shall touch," and this Book is described as a "Revelation from the Lord of the Worlds." But the most significant of all such references, to be sure, is the phrase "the Mother of the Book" (*Umm al-Kitab*). Found several times in the Qur'an, the phrase "the Mother of the Book" is generally taken by Muslims to refer to a heavenly archetype of the Qur'an—the Perfect Original, one might say, of the Book.

I will examine this notion of "the Mother of the Book" more thoroughly in chapter 4. The important idea for us to consider now is that, in Muslim tradition, this heavenly book really is the "mother" or origin of any and all revelations that God communicates to human beings. To put it another way, there is a Heavenly Recitation (*Qur'an*) that is the eternal, archetypal source of all divine revelation. The implication of this, simply, is that all of God's revelation throughout all of history to all prophets has been essentially *the same message*.

Thus, for all of their differences, Jews and Christians can be deemed "People of the Book" because these two communities, the Qur'an proclaims, did in fact originally receive pure and essentially identical revelation that poured forth from this heavenly archetype of revelation, "the Mother of the Book." As we shall see, the Qur'an also insists that, over time, both the Jewish and Christian traditions have not only disobeyed but also intentionally misinterpreted and distorted their respective revelations. The pure Torah and pure Gospel, then, are no longer available. In their present state they do not represent (i.e., they do not *re-present*) the Mother of the Book. The Qur'an, on the other hand, is believed by Muslims to be a perfect representation of the pure heavenly Book; hence, the Qur'an is "the Manifest Book," made "an Arabic Qur'an" by God "that perchance you may understand" (Q 43:2, 3). But it is in Arabic not simply—or even primarily—in order that Arabic-speaking people might be able to understand it. Rather, as the same passage continues, "it [the Arabic text, presumably] is in the Mother of the Book, with Us, lofty and wise" (Q 43:4). A pair of Arabic translators has written that "producing an English text of the meanings of the Qur'an which achieves the same degree of excellence as the Arabic text is a task far beyond human endeavor. The Qur'an is Allah's book and no man can aspire to express Allah's message as He Himself has done"[3]—a message that is in Arabic. This may help us to appreciate the heavenly and miraculous power that Muslims associate with the recitation of the original Arabic of the Qur'an. For Muslim faith, the Qur'an alone has been, and continues to be, a faithful offspring of the Mother of the Book. Certainly the rank-and-file Muslim believes it to be the pristine, pure, and clear communication from God.

One thing that certainly *is* clear in the Qur'an is that Muhammad was deeply troubled by the arguments between Jews and Christians, whose spiritual ancestors, he believed, had been recipients of the same pure revelation from God. "The Jews say: 'The Christians follow nothing [substantial]' and the Christians say: 'The Jews follow nothing [substantial],' while both recite the Book" (Q 2:113). It vexed Muhammad that both of these communities appealed to their scriptures to argue over who were the true children of Abraham. The fact that both groups had at least some of their scriptures in common must have been especially bothersome; again, "both recite the Book." This is not an insignificant point. If indeed one does assume some notion of divine inspiration for the Bible, it might be troubling that Jews have a Tanakh while Christians have an Old Testament: different orderings of texts, divergent readings of those texts, and radically differing conclusions. The Qur'an observes that both Jews and Christians could appeal to their scriptures and even argue over the same texts; the inherent ambiguity of such a social and religious situation can be deeply troubling to any person, in any era, who seeks absolute certainty. It is not difficult to assume that, historically speaking, this unsettling situation contributed to Muhammad's search for a revelation that would settle these differences.

On the other hand, there is ample evidence in the Qur'an that Muhammad increasingly came to expect these differences among Jews and Christians to be intractable in this life. In the very passage cited in the above paragraph, the Qur'an continues, "Allah will judge between them [the Jews and the Christians] on the Day of Resurrection regarding what they differ on" (Q 2:113). Even if these arguments could not be settled in the present age—especially when it became obvious to Muhammad that most Jews and Christians were not going to warm up to his revelation—there would come a Day, Muhammad insisted, when all these arguments would be solved, all differences settled. This is not an uncommon hope for people of faith, and not just Muslim faith: the yearning for a scenario in which ambiguity and uncertainty are entirely banished is understandably common. No arguments are possible when The Truth is unambiguous and obvious to everyone. No issue is left for debate when there is no need for interpretation—of anything. So if the Qur'an in the present could not squelch religious arguments, the least it could do was to imagine or project a future state of affairs where no question will be left unanswered, no debate left in the air.[4]

Muhammad seemed to have been especially inclined to fault the Jewish community for being argumentative and creating a situation of religious uncertainty. Jews didn't need to have Christians around to have a good fight over a text! It is true that the Jewish style of learning the Torah is to a great extent a matter of developing arguments over how to interpret a given text. The amassed wealth of rabbinic commentary, debate, argument, and counterargument called the Talmud—which inscripts a tradition already well developed before Muhammad's time—makes all of this abundantly clear. Jewish textual study is, to put the matter mildly, *dialogical*, and often the dialogue is pitched at a fairly high volume. The divine voice in the Qur'an, however, displays no pleasure in all this discussion and disagreement: "We have given Moses the Book, but it was the subject of controversy" (Q 41:45). For the Qur'an it is a great irony that divine revelation—which is (supposed to be) simple, plain, and clear—has instigated argument among the people of Israel. The text then continues, mysteriously, "Had it not been for a Word that preceded from your Lord, a decision between them would have been made"—meaning, perhaps, that since the Jewish people had received the Torah from God as an arbiter, God would not call upon Muhammad to settle their differences? (The qur'anic text cries out for interpretation here.)[5] In any case, Muhammad reiterates that God's revelation had not cleared up differences of opinion: "Yet they are, with respect to it [i.e., the revelation given through Moses], in disquieting doubt" (Q 41:45). One might readily reply that no revelation, regardless of its pristine origin or purity, could avoid instigating differences of interpretation—and thus of creating doubt. History has made it plain that the Qur'an and its interpreters provide no exception to this rule. We human beings who would be revelation's recipients remain limited, frail, flawed creatures, radically situated in place and time. This condition leads inevitably to ambiguity and relative uncertainty. To borrow the apostle Paul's phrase, in this world "we see through a glass, darkly" (1 Cor. 13:12 KJV).

The Qur'an's preferred world, however, is one of clarity and light:

> He has enacted for you as a religion that which He charged Noah with and that which We revealed to you, and what We charged Abraham, Moses and Jesus with: "Perform the religion and do not diverge therein.". . . They did not split up except after the Knowledge came to them out of contention among themselves. . . . Indeed, those to whom the Book was bequeathed, after them, are in disquieting doubt concerning it. (Q 42:14)

It is safe, then, to assume that Muhammad, troubled by the often-contentious nature of textual interpretation and theological debate, longed for a revelation that would overcome the conditions of ambiguity we experience. Jews and Christians argued with one another and argued among themselves; surely divine revelation should quiet all such debates! One is reminded of the Abraham story in Genesis 18 and Surah 11, examined side by side in the previous chapter of this book. Recall that in Genesis we read that Abraham stood toe to toe, as it were, with God, arguing about the morality involved in destroying whole cities that might well have righteous people within their walls. Abraham had put the immortal question to his Maker, "Shall not the Judge of all the earth do justly?" Remember too that the qur'anic version tends to suppress such dialogue, to say nothing of friendly debate, between God and Abraham—"The Command of your Lord has come and an irreversible punishment shall surely smite them." Israel means "God wrestles," or "God-wrestler." Islam means "submission." Therein may lie great differences.

If Israel is a wrestler with God, then it is not surprising that rabbinic Judaism developed self-consciously as a wrestling with holy texts, and a wrestling with one another over how to interpret and live by those texts. The wrestling is unavoidable because no text, no sentence, no word—indeed, no moment or experience of our lives—bears an immediately obvious or self-evident meaning. Interpretation is demanded of us, and demanded all the time.

Perhaps Muhammad imagined and hoped for a different situation. If there is a "Mother of the Book"—a pure, heavenly, and perfect Revelation—then one might hope for some kind of immediate access to its clear truth. (It is undoubtedly the case that a goodly number of Christians make a similar assumption about the Bible. It is equally obvious that this hope is never fulfilled in either Christianity or Islam—or anywhere else.) Indeed, Muhammad assumed that all divine revelation has that character, and that the earlier "People of the Book" had distorted, whether intentionally or not, that pure revelation. One of the Qur'an's harsher judgments against Jews and Christians is found in Surah 5:

> Allah made a covenant with the Children of Israel, and . . . on account of their violating their covenant, We cursed them and caused their hearts to harden; they take the words out of their context and forget part of what they were enjoined, and you do not cease to find them treacherous, except for a few of them. Yet pardon them and forgive; Allah surely loves those who do good to others. (5:12–13)

This sort of criticism against the Jews was not wholly original with Muhammad. Sadly enough, Christians had been perfecting the *adversus Judaeos* ("against the Jews") rhetoric of Jewish hardheartedness and rebellion for several centuries before Muhammad. But now Christians' own sharp weapons of the tongue and the pen could be wielded against them, as well as against Jews. The passage above dealing with the People of the Torah wastes no time moving immediately to the People of the Gospel:

> And with some of those who say: "We are Christians," we made a covenant; but they forgot part of what they were reminded of; so we stirred up enmity and hatred among them till the Day of Resurrection. Allah will let them know what they did. O People of the Book, Our Messenger came to you to show you much of what you used to conceal of the Book and to pardon a great deal. Indeed, a light and a clear Book has come to you from Allah. (5:14–15)

It should be noted that the Qur'an first acknowledges that separate covenants were made by God with the Jewish people and, later, with believers in Jesus. In both cases, however, these two peoples have proven unfaithful to their God-ordained covenants.[6] These failures, presumably, are their own responsibility, that is, a matter of their having chosen to turn away from the God of the covenants. God, in response, has added divine insult to human injury, causing the Jews' "hearts to harden" and stirring up "enmity and hatred" among Christians—the latter in itself providing a sad commentary on the fragmented state of the church in Muhammad's (to saying nothing of our own) time. Thus on the one hand there is recognition of human responsibility in these covenants; on the other hand there is an assumption that God ultimately controls all outcomes, such that even human hardheartedness becomes an expression of God's mysterious will. It is also significant that, according to the Qur'an, in both cases their covenantal failures reap serious consequences specifically for Jews' and Christians' reading of their scriptures. Jews "take the words out of their context and forget part of what they were enjoined"; likewise, Christians "forgot part" of the revelation given to them. But God is merciful, having sent Muhammad to unveil what Jews and Christians had concealed; hence, "a light and a clear Book has come to you from Allah."

A seemingly unavoidable implication of the Qur'an's judgments regarding Jews and Christians is that Muslims, too, exist in a kind of religious precariousness: if other peoples have failed to live in accordance with the revelation granted them, what guarantee exists that Muslims will not follow suit? Granted, Muslims understand the Qur'an to be the perfect earthly copy of the heavenly Mother of the Book, but that in itself provides no certitude that Islamic tradition can perfectly interpret it or obey it. Similarly, Muslims confess Muhammad to be the "seal of the prophets," the final and ultimate human messenger from God. But why would this preclude the possibility that later prophets might be needed, if the Qur'an were to become extensively misunderstood or disobeyed? Yet Muslim tradition insists that beyond Muhammad the final prophet and the Qur'an given to him, no other revelation is needed or to be expected. The final Day of Judgment will bring no new revelation but only make plain and obvious to all people that the Qur'an's message is the perfectly true one.

But, again, what would ensure Muslim faithfulness to that revelation in the time between Muhammad and the end of the world? Undoubtedly part of the answer lies in the fact that Muhammad appears to have expected an imminent end of the world, a theme I will address in this book's ending chapter. If the time remaining is short, then there is less opportunity for widespread, radical failure to occur. Yet as history stretches out over centuries, the question becomes more pressing: what precludes a covenantal failure comparable to the one the Qur'an lays at the feet of Jews and Christians? Finally, it can only be the power and will of Allah that can circumvent such apostasy—and this conclusion, in turn, raises critical questions regarding the nature of divine power in the world.

David Hartman, the Israeli philosopher cited earlier in this chapter, explores how the early generations of rabbis wrestled with this very question of human faithfulness—and human failure—within the vagaries and vicissitudes of history. As Hartman indicates, centuries earlier the Hebrew prophets interpreted the Babylonians' destruction of the temple and exile of the Jews as God's punishment for Israel's unfaithfulness to the covenant. But many of those same prophets also proclaimed that the great God of mercies would in the future restore Israel's land, people, and fortunes. This, though, only raises a new question: What would prevent the Jewish people from failing again in the future, thereby becoming endangered, again, by divine retribution? How to avoid the vicious cycle of human unfaithfulness, followed by divine punishment and restoration, from repeating itself? This, according to Hartman, is where the prophecies especially of Jeremiah and Ezekiel addressed a deeply felt need: God, proclaimed Jeremiah, promised to place the Torah *within* the Jews, inscribing it in their hearts (Jer. 31:32); similarly, Ezekiel envisioned a day when God would remove their "heart of stone" and replace it with a "heart of flesh," even giving them God's own spirit to "make you follow my statutes," (Ezek. 36:26–27).

It is noteworthy that Christian tradition has been drawn to these prophecies, arguing their fulfillment in the coming of Jesus and, through Jesus, the gift of the Holy Spirit to Christian believers. Hartman, however, suspects these prophets of promising too much. Hartman argues that a thoroughly *covenantal* understanding of God's relationship with creation includes God's willingness to accept and even embrace the creaturely limitations of the people Israel and, by implication, of all people.[7] According to Hartman, the rabbinic interpretation of God's labors in the world, taking its primary cues from this covenantal understanding, tended to make a lot of room for human agency, judgment, and limitations. Jeremiah and Ezekiel, on the other hand, seem to have been yearning for a divine short-circuiting of human freedom and responsibility: "I will put my spirit within you, and *make* you follow my statutes." If taken too far, such a promise does indeed sound as though God, ultimately distrustful of human agency, would finally transform the Jewish people—and again, by implication, all people—into automatons in order to guarantee their compliance with God's commandments.

In the prophecies of Jeremiah and Ezekiel, then—at least as Hartman interprets them—we encounter once more the understandable desire for a world of certainty, all ambiguity and risk having been cleared away. On the other side of the ledger, we find one of the better-known rabbinic maxims, "Everything is in the hands of heaven except the fear of heaven." Freely rendered, this would mean something like: Everything is in God's hands, except for whether or not human beings will respect and obey God. And that turns out to be a rather considerable exception.

Ideas such as those espoused by the rabbinic tradition, I suspect, are lurking behind some of Muhammad's theological frustrations with the Jews he encountered. In fact this saying, "Everything is in the hands of heaven except the fear of heaven," could conceivably be the sentiment that instigated Muhammad's disdain in Q 5:64: "The Jews say, 'Allah's hand is tied.'" Many commentators tend too quickly to assume that, at least in Muhammad's perception, Jews were claiming that God "is not generous in blessings" or has "suspended his generosity."[8] This, I suspect, is far too simplistic a reading. For one thing, all of Jewish liturgy, including the daily blessings Jews are instructed to recite over virtually every facet of life, is predicated on the wealth of God's goodness and blessing. It is highly unlikely that Jews in Muhammad's milieu were accusing God of miserliness. For another thing, the Qur'an proceeds with a curse in kind: "May their own hands be tied and may they be damned for what they say." If we interpret the image of tied-up hands as implying a lack of generosity, then we have this somewhat odd curse from Muhammad in reply: "May the Jews themselves not be generous!" It lacks punch, as far as curses go. Finally, the Qur'an then adds, "His Hands rather are outstretched; *He grants freely as He pleases.*" The issue here seems not to be so much divine generosity as divine freedom and power. The Qur'an, in this case, seems to be proclaiming God's ability to do as God pleases. Given these considerations, it is possible that the dictum "Allah's hand is tied," attributed by the Qur'an to Jews, does not imply a denial of God's generosity or kindness; rather, the statement more likely involves an attempt to take seriously the role of human agency in God's world.

Are there ways in which God's hands, so to speak, are tied?

Popular piety—and not just among Muslims—would immediately answer "No!" It sounds far more religious to insist, with Muhammad, that God does whatever God wants and "grants freely as He pleases." I heard a faculty colleague not long ago preach in university chapel, "What God wants, God gets!" It is difficult not to be sympathetic with this sentiment; it is, after all, *God* that we're talking about. Often there is also, I think, a subtle fear of offending God's honor by speaking too lowly of the divine. But it is precisely here that the genius of the Jewish tradition asserts itself perhaps most creatively: Abraham debates God, Jacob wrestles God, psalmists lament before God, prophets challenge God. Through all of this covenantal push-and-pull with God, a new understanding of divine power emerges. This is dramatically demonstrated in a passage from the Talmud that has become widely quoted in contemporary Jewish theology:

> Rabbi Joshua ben Levi said: "Why were they called men of the Great Assembly? Because they restored the crown of the divine attributes to its ancient completeness. Moses had come and said: 'the great, the mighty, the awesome God' [Deut. 10:17]. Then Jeremiah came and said: 'Aliens are frolicking in His temple; where then are His awesome deeds?' Hence He omitted the word 'awesome' [in Jer. 32:18]. Daniel came and said: 'Aliens are enslaving His sons; where are His mighty deeds?' Hence he omitted the word 'mighty' [in Dan. 9:4]. But [the men of the Great Assembly] came and said: 'On the contrary, therein lie His mighty deeds that He suppresses His wrath, that He extends longsuffering to the wicked. Therein lie His awesome powers, for but for fear of Him, how could [our] one nation persist among the nations?'" (Yoma 69*b*)

Hartman writes that this rabbinic passage "gives an exegesis of 'Ezra blessed the Lord the *great* God' (Neh. 8:6) that explains why 'the *Great* Assembly' was the name given to the assembly of the people called by Nehemiah and Ezra to renew the covenant."[9] Ezra and Nehemiah were leaders of the Great Assembly of covenantal renewal because they found a way to reaffirm God's attributes. In order to make this point, the rabbinic tradition (here summed up in reflections attributed to Rabbi Joshua ben Levi) offered what from our perspective could be considered an artful, perhaps even playful, reading of Tanakh texts. The rabbis noticed that Deuteronomy describes God as "great, mighty and awesome" but that Jeremiah describes God as only "great and mighty" (Jer. 32:18). Where's the "awesome"? What most readers today likely would dismiss as an accident of history, a thoroughly inconsequential difference between two biblical passages, rabbis assumed to be of critical theological importance. In their reading, Jeremiah felt obligated to omit the adjective *awesome* from his description of God because the Babylonians were desecrating the temple; where is God's awesomeness in that? Likewise, a little later Daniel, writing from his experience as a Babylonian captive, called God "great and awesome" (Dan. 9:4). Where's the "mighty"? The rabbis supposed that Daniel was constrained to omit that attribute given the situation of Jewish exile; where, after all, is God's might in that? But then later in the Jews' return from exile, Ezra and Nehemiah "restored the crown of the divine attributes" to God essentially by *reinterpreting* the ideas of divine might and awesomeness. For the Great Assembly, said the rabbis, God's power is expressed in allowing human beings real freedom, even the freedom to desecrate and destroy; similarly, God's awesomeness is demonstrated in the historical fact that despite the Babylonians' violent misuse of their power in destroying the temple and taking many Jews into captive exile, the people of Israel persisted. This is divine power understood in a new, much more subtle way—a way that *does not* insist that God's power should be obvious, or that this power is such that everything that happens in the world is the perfect expression of God's will.

This striking talmudic passage, moreover, is not quite finished. The text immediately raises the question "But how could [Jeremiah and Daniel] abolish something established by Moses?" How dare they play fast and loose with the Torah? How could they simply drop *awesomeness* or *might* from the Torah's listing of divine attributes? Rabbi Eleazar, the passage continues, was the one who offered the answer: "Since they knew that the Holy One, blessed be He, insists on truth, they would not ascribe false things to Him" (Yoma 69*b*). The rabbis, in other words, said that in our theological reflections it is more important to be faithful to the hard facts of experience than to traditional, time-honored concepts. Jeremiah and Daniel, said the rabbis, preferred to speak truthfully about God rather than simply to honor God with their lips in empty adulation. They accordingly toned down their accolades for God. It was left to the scribal tradition of Ezra and Nehemiah, of which the rabbis were heirs, to reinterpret creatively these traditional attributes of divine power and sovereignty. In Hartman's words, "They saw their God now manifesting His power through 'mighty' patience and 'awesome' compassion. With this bold and ingenious reinterpretation, they shifted the focus of the notion of divine power from external victorious power to the inner power of God's patience with human beings."[10]

The Qur'an too testifies to Allah's patience with human beings (Q 16:127), so Muhammad was no stranger to this concept. Of course, there is an appreciable difference between saying that God is patient, even long-suffering, and saying that God's hands are tied. Assuming there were Jews in Muhammad's milieu who actually were saying this, or something like this, perhaps we can assume that they were claiming that God is limited by human choices. While I do think that this is an important first step in understanding the rather unexpected theological claim that Muhammad attributes to Jews of his time—"Allah's hand is tied"—it is possible to take a second step. In order to do so we must undertake a creative and imaginative reading of another passage in the Qur'an, but it will be worth the effort.

In Q 9:30 we read of another notion attributed to the Jews, a notion even stranger than that of God's tied hands: "The Jews say: 'Ezra is the son of Allah,' and the Christians say: 'The Messiah is the son of Allah.' That is their statement, by their mouths; they emulate the statement of the unbelievers of yore."[11] This last phrase undoubtedly means that by associating some kind of divine offspring with God, Jews and Christians are repeating the polytheistic idolatries of the Arabic peoples, both in Muhammad's own time and in the history that preceded him. As we will explore more fully later, for Muhammad and subsequent Muslim tradition such association of anything with God is *shirk*, idolatry, the most serious sin. Indeed, the Qur'an immediately adds, "May Allah damn them; how they are perverted!"

Of course the Christian claim that "the Messiah is the son of Allah" is not at all surprising and will merit further reflection in a subsequent chapter on Jesus and in another on the doctrine of the Trinity. But what are we to make of this charge: "The Jews say: 'Ezra is the son of Allah'"? Heribert Busse, a contemporary German scholar of Islam, considers the possibility that Muhammad was aware of a Jewish sect that had elevated the figure of Ezra to angelic, perhaps even semidivine, status on the basis of the speculations of a noncanonical document called 4 Ezra (or 2 Esdras). In fanciful narrative typical of apocalyptic literature, this document, dating from the late first century, imagined Ezra as having been taken up into heaven, without dying, after fulfilling his mission among his fellow Jews. Such a story might easily inspire a deep reverence, shading toward worship, of the Ezra figure as an angelic mediator between the heavenly and mundane realms. But Busse quickly rejects this relatively obscure reading of the figure of Ezra in favor of a simpler explanation: "Muhammad, in the heat of debate, wanted to accuse the Jews of heretical doctrine on a par with the heresy of the Christian doctrine that teaches the divine nature of Jesus. In doing so, he could take advantage of the high esteem granted to Ezra in Judaism."[12]

In Judaism, Ezra and his scribal helpers are acclaimed as the figures who first "read from the book, from the law of God, with interpretation. They gave the sense, so that the people understood the reading" (Neh. 8:8). They were, in other words, the figures who were the fount of the rabbinic tradition. No wonder, then, that Ezra was, and is, accorded great honor and significance. Certainly, rabbinic estimation of Ezra was high: "Ezra would have been worthy to have made known the law if Moses had not come before him" (*Sanhedrin* 21:2). Contemporary Jewish scholar Lawrence Schiffman writes, "Ezra . . . is often credited with having created postbiblical Judaism. With less exaggeration, one can say that he established the *basis* for the future of Judaism: from here on, the Torah, the Five Books of Moses, would be the constitution of Jewish life. By pointing postbiblical Judaism on the road of scriptural interpretation, Ezra insured the continuity of the biblical heritage."[13] However, as Busse has rightly argued, we need not assume that Jews in Muhammad's milieu were actually worshiping the figure of Ezra or were even according him the title "son of Allah"—at least in any mystical or unique sense. For in fact the language of sonship, applied to the entire people of Israel, is not unusual in the Tanakh (e.g., Hos. 11:1; Exod. 4:22–23). Further, the Judaism that developed out of Ezra's renewal of the Sinai covenant was a religious community quite willing to embrace the title "son." In the setting of rabbinic discussion, the title "son" tended to suggest the image of a Jewish interpreter who, like Abraham arguing with God, is bold in undertaking the divinely entrusted burden of textual interpretation.

There is a passage in the Talmud, of considerable significance for Judaism, that dramatically illustrates this particular sense of sonship. In this famous rabbinic story (*Baba Mesia* 59*b*), a charismatic teacher named Eliezer is attempting to persuade a group of his colleagues of his position in a debate regarding certain purity laws. As the story proceeds, Eliezer tries to convince his fellow rabbis that he is right, and they are wrong, by performing several miracles of nature: he causes a tree to be uprooted and to fly through the air (traveling "a hundred cubits out of its place—though some say it was four hundred cubits"); at his word, a stream reverses its directional flow; even the very walls of the house of study demonstrate their support for Eliezer by leaning as though they might collapse. But Eliezer's opponents are unmoved. Unlike the walls surrounding them, they refuse to lean under the pressure of his arguments. Hence, Eliezer finally appeals to heaven to settle the argument. "Suddenly a heavenly voice went forth and said to the sages, 'Why are you disputing with Rabbi Eliezer? The Halakhah [legal ruling] is in accordance with him in all circumstances.'" Such a phenomenon might be expected to have been just the trump Eliezer needed to emerge victorious, but the narrative turns out otherwise. Instead of conceding the debate to Eliezer, Rabbi Yehoshua stands to his feet and simply quotes from Deuteronomy 30:12, "It is not in the heavens." Like Abraham in Genesis 18, Yehoshua stands up to God and argues against the viability and legitimacy of God's having the final word in the argument! That is chutzpah.

But what is the nature of Yehoshua's counterargument? What is it that is not in the heavens? *The Torah.* The word or commandment of God is not out of reach, not beyond human comprehension or application, "not in the heavens," but down here on earth. Indeed, the Deuteronomy text continues, "No, the word is very near to you; it is in your mouth and in your heart for you to observe" (Deut. 30:14). The word, *God's* word, dwells in the human realm; it is fitted to, and relevant to, the capabilities of the people of Israel. Yehoshua's reply to the divine interruption, in other words, is an appeal to Moses' own description of the Torah as being God's covenantal word entrusted to the people of Israel to read, interpret, and obey. No further appeals to heaven can be made, precisely because *it is not in the heavens.* Perhaps this is a tying of God's hands, so to speak?

But the story is not over in the Talmud. The narrative immediately shifts to a subsequent encounter between a certain Rabbi Nathan and the long-departed prophet Elijah, who apparently had returned to earth to fulfill some divine mission. (Elijah could function readily as an intermediary between earthly and heavenly realms in such stories as these because he was a prophet who, according to 2 Kings 2:11, had been taken up into the heavens in a fiery chariot without having died. Indeed, Elijah's mysterious departure from this world would provide a precedent for the later speculations about Ezra, mentioned briefly earlier in this chapter.) Nathan asks Elijah, by this time a veteran resident of heaven, about that debate between Eliezer and the other teachers that ended with Yehoshua's declaration from the Torah. The rabbi wants to know, "What did the Holy One, blessed be He, do at that time?" Elijah's reply is classic, for it suggests that God has a good-natured sense of humor as well as a willingness to abide by the "rules" of textual interpretation and debate. God, reports Elijah, "laughed, saying: *'My sons have defeated me, My sons have defeated me.'"* God is portrayed as having appreciated Yehoshua's nerve, as well as his rabbinic skills in textual argument. Hartman writes that this talmudic passage "signifies God's self-limiting love for the sake of making His human covenantal partners responsible for intellectually developing the Torah," such that "students of the Torah are called upon to exercise human initiative and creativity."[14] So perhaps God ties God's own hands, according to the rabbis, in order that the Jews—and perhaps by implication all people—might mature spiritually, intellectually, morally, and aesthetically.

To the extent that this recognition of responsibility and call for creativity can be attributed to Ezra as the founding textual scribe of Judaism, we see what kind of "son of Allah" Ezra is. Ezra is a covenantal partner of the God of Israel, and by his bold renewal of the Torah covenant against overwhelming circumstances when the Jews returned to Jerusalem to rebuild the temple, the people of Israel become God's son(s)—that is, maturing children. Ezra's innovative leadership provides the path toward maturity as responsible agents. If Ezra and the historical stream of scribal leaders who flow from him are God's "sons," then it is also important to note just what sort of Parent, in this case, God is thought to be: God is a Parent-figure who entrusts to the teachers of Israel the responsibility for interpretation and application of the Torah and even displays no disappointment at being defeated in talmudic disputation. This is a deity who can smile and say, "My sons have defeated me."

It is highly likely that one of the purposes of this rabbinic story was to downplay (if not to deny altogether) the role of miraculous events as providing proof of God's presence or approval. This would have been important, perhaps among other reasons, as a rebuttal to Christianity's claim to validity on the basis of Jesus's miraculous deeds. The rabbinic impulse, instead, is to turn to the holy text and to undertake the hard labor of arguing over that text in order to discern God's will and work. How much easier would it be simply to seek, or at least to hope, for a secure sign from God! We can speculate at length as to the power dynamics that would inspire rabbis to tell this story, but we should not overlook its implicit realism. Miracles and signs—divine evidences that would imply a purely divine inbreaking, a unilateral act—generally are not abundantly available. Ambiguity, however, is—and in great abundance. If Ezra is indeed a "son of Allah," this ambiguity inevitably implied by the burden of interpretation may well be his message.

"It is not in the heavens." It is interesting that the apostle Paul, in his letter to the Romans, quotes the same text from Deuteronomy as Yehoshua does in this talmudic passage. While throughout this book we are mostly laying the Bible and the Qur'an side by side, in this instance it will be instructive to lay the Tanakh and the New Testament side by side:

Deuteronomy 30:11–19	Romans 10:6–9
Surely, this commandment that I am commanding you today is not too hard for you, nor is it too far away.	But the righteousness that comes by faith says,
It is not in heaven, that you should say,	"Do not say in your heart,
"Who will go up to heaven for us,	'Who will ascend into heaven?' (that is,
and get it for us and so that we may hear it and observe it?"	to bring Christ down)
Neither is it beyond the sea, that you	Or
should say, "Who will cross to the other side of the sea for us,	'Who will descend into the abyss?' (that is,
and get it for us	to bring Christ up from the dead).

40

Deuteronomy 30:11–19	Romans 10:6–9
so that we may hear it and observe it?"	
	But what does it say?
No, the word is very near to you;	"The word is near you,
it is in your mouth and in your heart	on your lips and in your heart"
for you to observe.	(that is, the word of faith that we proclaim);
See, I have set before you today life	because if you confess with your lips that Jesus is Lord
and prosperity, death and adversity . . .	and believe in your heart that God raised him from the dead,
Choose life so that that you and your descendants may live . . .	you will be saved.

For Paul, writing a few decades after the time of Jesus, the divine word that "is not in the heavens" is "the word of faith that we proclaim"—the gospel—and it is not in the heavens because "it is on your lips and in your heart . . . that if you confess with your lips that Jesus is Lord and believe in your heart that God raised him from the dead, you will be saved" (Rom. 10:8–9). This dramatically marks the point at which the People of the Torah and the People of the Gospel part ways. While for Ezra and his rabbinic heirs the divine word is the Torah entrusted to Israel ("that you may observe it"), for Paul and the other apostles the divine word is the gospel of Christ. New Testament scholar Richard Hays concedes that the rabbinic interpretation of the Torah passage above "may appear to be closer than Paul's to the original sense of the words in Deuteronomy" but nonetheless proceeds to assert that "[both] . . . presuppose the legitimacy of innovative readings that disclose truth previously latent in Scripture."[15] True; yet Hays appears to overlook a more fundamental point: it is precisely *because* "it is not in the heavens" that both the rabbis and Paul could *rightly* presuppose the legitimacy of their innovative readings. God does not "step in and settle the argument" between the rabbis and Paul, or between the Jewish and Christian paths that would flow from their writings, any more than God settles the dispute between Eliezer and his opponents—or, for that matter, between Muslims and the other "People of the Book." At least according to the Jewish tradition, therefore, God's word "is not in the heavens" but instead is entrusted to fallible, historically situated interpreters. This in turn strongly implies that divine revelation inevitably is ambiguous, multivalent, and, we might say, arguable.

"It is not in the heavens." This deceptively simple statement from Deuteronomy has been taken by the Jewish tradition to mean that God entrusts the Torah to the Jewish people—who live on earth, not in the heavens—to internalize through study ("in your heart"), to recite ("in your mouth"), and to obey ("for you to observe"). Meanwhile, Paul has taught the church to interpret the statement to mean that the gospel proclaims the near approach of God to creation through Jesus Christ, the Son of God *and* the son (or descendant) of David (Rom. 1:3). In Paul's reading, "it is not in the heavens" precisely because Christ has truly lived among us as a fellow human being on earth. Again, let us bear in mind that a revelation that is "not in the heavens" but truly in the midst of human history, frailty, and situatedness is inevitably vulnerable to the differences produced by the act of human reading (i.e., interpretation). But of course, it would not be *revelation* if the message did not enter truly into this human realm. It is at least a mild irony that the Qur'an, on the other hand, makes reference to a heavenly "Mother of the Book," "well guarded" against the differences inevitably created by human reading. For traditional Islam it is that Book that precisely *is* "in the heavens," we could say—and at least in the ideal religious milieu for which Muhammad yearned, the Qur'an is the perfect earthly *incarnation*, we might also say, of that perfectly preserved heavenly Text.

Meanwhile, differences abound: Jews still differ among themselves on how to interpret their texts and traditions; Christians still differ among themselves regarding markedly similar issues; Jews and Christians still differ with each other over the identity and mission of Jesus and a host of other related matters; Muslims still differ with both Jews and Christians and, obviously, among themselves as well. No claim to divine revelation—whether the Torah by Jews, the gospel by Christians, or the Qur'an by Muslims—has either settled or silenced those differences. Apparently it is still not in the heavens! However, even this situation—one that might easily be perceived as theologically problematic, perhaps even threatening—can be made somewhat bearable if it can be attributed to God. This is indeed the case in the Qur'an; here, the religious differences among human beings are attributed to the will and working of God: "To each of you, We have laid down an ordinance and a clear path; and had Allah pleased, He would have made you one nation, but [He wanted] to test you concerning what He gave to you. Be, then, forward in good deeds. To Allah is the ultimate return of all of you, that He may instruct you regarding that on which you differed" (Q 5:48).

It is conceded in the above passage, then, that religious differences and diversity are unavoidable and in fact attributable to God, who could have willed the world to be otherwise. This is an interesting possibility for the "true believer" in any religious tradition to entertain; indeed, the stronger one's doctrine of divine sovereignty (God's "in charge-ness," as one of my students once defined it), the greater the challenge presented by religious traditions other than one's own. If God is indeed "in charge," then presumably God is in charge of the religion-making business as well. At the very least, one would have to admit that God apparently allows a vast amount of religious difference to exist in the world. (Is God's hand tied?) Given the strong doctrine of sovereignty in the Qur'an, then, it is not surprising to find on its pages precisely this fascinating theological position: the plurality of religious traditions (convictions, practices, liturgies), in some mysterious way, exists by the will and work of God as a "test . . . concerning what He gave" to each community. We all shall ultimately return to God—who alone is able to "instruct [us] regarding that on which [we all] differed." In the meantime the Qur'an calls Muslims, Jews, Christians, Zoroastrians, and "Sabeans"[16] to be "forward in good deeds," to "compete" or "vie with one another in good works."[17] Surely there is a profound wisdom in this admonition. If only we strove to outdo one another in works of goodness and compassion, rather than to prove that "we" are correct and "they" are wrong!

There is something noticeably realistic, finally, about the position that the Qur'an espouses regarding religious differences: "The believers, the Jews, the Christians and the Sabeans—whoever believes in Allah and the Last Day and does what is good, shall receive their reward from their Lord. They shall have nothing to fear and they shall not grieve" (2:62). To be sure, even this text can be interpreted with varying degrees of latitude toward non-Muslims; the most that can be claimed is that the kinder, gentler reading offers a relatively minimal set of expectations for biblically rooted monotheistic faith communities. (On the other hand, we must admit that there is nothing here especially encouraging to Buddhists, Hindus, Taoists, etc.)

Yet in the end, the Qur'an insists, only God knows the human heart and motives. In Q 22:17, Muhammad expands the list of religious traditions to include Magians (Zoroastrians, most scholars believe) and even idolaters, stating that "Allah shall decide between them on the Day of Resurrection. Surely, Allah is a witness of everything." This sounds hauntingly similar to some of Paul's words: "God, through Jesus Christ, will judge the secret thoughts of all" (Rom. 2:16). Only God knows the heart, so in the end only God can judge the quality of our character. To employ the traditional Muslim phrase, *Allahu a'lam*—God knows best.

But what if Yehoshua is right? What if even *God* says, "It is not in the heavens"?

3

THE CREATIVE WORD OF GOD: *BE!*

> In the creation of the heavens and the earth; in the alternation of
> night and day; in the ships which sail in the sea with what profits
> mankind; in the water which Allah sends down from the sky in
> order to bring the earth back to life after its death and disperses over
> it every type of beast; in the continuous changing of winds; and in
> clouds which are driven between heaven and earth—surely in these
> are signs for people who understand.
>
> —Qur'an 2:164

At first glance, it might seem that a doctrine of creation is something that
Jews, Christians, and Muslims share alike. In one sense that is true. All of
these traditions affirm that the Power they mean by "God" is the Creator of
the world. The Jewish Tanakh and the Christian Old Testament both begin
with "the beginning" of Genesis, in which "God created the heavens and the
earth" (Gen. 1:1). Similarly, the Qur'an repeatedly insists that the One to
whom it bears witness is "the All-Knowing Creator of . . . the heavens and
the earth" (Q 36:81), which is to say the "Creator of everything" (Q 40:62).
This certainly sounds much like the opening of the Apostles' Creed, recited
regularly by millions of Christians: "I believe in God the Father Almighty,
Maker of heaven and earth."

45

Perhaps we should take a moment to appreciate what this common confession, to the extent that it *is* common to these traditions, implies. It means for Jews, Christians, and Muslims that not only our planet but the entire universe, unimaginably immense, finds its ultimate source and meaning in the One to whom we pray. It means that our lives here in this world are imbued with a meaning and a purpose—for we are created by God and for God's purposes, even if we are sometimes unclear about the particulars of those purposes. It means we come from Someone and, presumably, are ultimately returning to that Someone in one way or another. Our lives may be difficult and exceedingly short by the standard of the immense age of the universe, but we are more than a passing vapor. Our lives, and all lives and things in the universe, have a purpose because there is One to whom we may pray who is our Maker. Life has meaning beyond whatever small meanings we may generate in our strivings for security and happiness.

If the conviction that all of reality is *creation*—a product of divine labor, the handiwork of a Creator God—provides a sense of meaning and direction to those who embrace and live it, this need not at all imply that the meaning is identical for Jews, Christians, and Muslims. Indeed, there is very good reason to suspect that the meanings differ appreciably, since the doctrine of creation is not primarily an abstract principle; rather, it is rooted in the specific narratives, confessions, and practices of each tradition (as well as in other traditions, of course). The question I shall attempt to explore in this chapter is, How does each of these great traditions describe God's creative activity? What differences may be discerned among them—and what difference might these differences make?

First, in the Qur'an we find a distinctive emphasis upon the sheer and utter power of God's commanding speech in the act of creation. Its formulaic statement runs along the lines of Surah 36:82–83: "His Command is indeed such that if He wills a thing, He says to it: 'Be,' and it comes to be. Glory, then, to Him in Whose Hands is the dominion of everything and unto Whom you will be returned" (cf. Q 16:40, 40:68). God's creative word, as described in the Qur'an, is absolute command rooted in omnipotent authority. In the words of commentator Abdullah Yusuf Ali, "He is not dependent on time or place or instruments or materials" in the act of creation.[1] While Ali's remark may seem to claim more than the qur'anic text itself does, his logic is sound. In Surah 16:3 we read, "He created the heavens and the earth in truth; may He be exalted above what they associate [with Him]." In other words, Muslim conviction regarding God is that God is *God alone* and there is nothing that can be associated with God. There is no room for a statement that would begin "God *and* . . ."—because nothing goes with God. To associate anything with God, to think anything in company with God, and of course to offer worship to anything or anyone or any power alongside of God is to commit the deeply serious sin of *shirk*, or idolatry.

Of course, many biblical passages make the same sort of claim for God. The writings gathered under the name of Isaiah the prophet, in particular, place a distinct emphasis upon the creative power of God. "I am the LORD, who made all things, who alone stretched out the heavens, who by myself spread out the earth" (Isa. 44:24). "I am the LORD, and there is no other. I form light and create darkness, I make weal and create woe; I the LORD do all these things" (45:6–7). Such statements have a distinctly Qur'an-like ring to them.

Likewise, the idea of God's creating things by the act of *speaking* should be familiar to Bible readers. The Qur'an insists repeatedly that God says "Be!" and a thing is, and we encounter a similar (if not identical) notion in the very opening of our Bibles. Several times in Genesis 1 we read the formulaic statement "And God said, 'Let there be . . .' and it was so." With each new development within the creation sequence of the Bible's opening chapter, in fact, it is God's act of speaking that calls all things into existence.

It may be instructive, however, to compare the Qur'an's emphasis upon the simple command "Be!" with the tenor of the language in Genesis 1. The "Let there be" of Genesis 1 is written grammatically in the jussive voice of the Hebrew language. The jussive voice has a "softer" tone, we could say, than that of the imperative, the language of command. One can certainly overstate this distinction, but allow me to venture that the jussive voice is more like a tone of permission, of invitation, and not especially of unilateral command. The jussive communicates desire, or what one wishes might be the case. In this light, might it be possible to interpret the divine word of Genesis 1 as less like a command and more like an invitation? That perhaps God is, in a certain sense, "making space" for creaturely existence to occur, rather than coercing creation into being with irresistible commands?

One could easily overstate this argument. Even so, I do think at least this much can be ventured: when in Genesis we read, "Let the waters bring forth swarms of living creatures," or "Let the earth bring forth living creatures of every kind," we may hear the Creator inviting the creaturely realm to share in the playful labor of creation. It isn't God's solo act; the earth itself is called upon by God to contribute its energies and possibilities to God's creative activity. There are Hebraic puns in the passage that may reinforce this idea of creation's creativity: the earth is called upon by God to "put forth" (*tadshe*) vegetation (*deshe*), and the waters are called upon to "bring forth" (*yishretsu*) swarming creatures of the sea (*sherets*). *Tadshe Deshe*—the earth, we might say, is called upon to produce produce, to implant itself with plants. *Yishretsu Sheres*—the seas, we could say, are called upon to swarm with swarms of swimmers. Creaturely elements are invited to contribute their distinctive capacities to God's creative labors; indeed, God's creative labors are expressed precisely in this invitation to the creaturely realm. Reading Genesis 1 in this way does not lead us to a God who simply "says 'Be!' and it is" but to a Maker who invests creation with creative powers. The portrait of divine creating that arises out of such a reading of Genesis 1 is that of a Maker who creates the world by inviting it to be, and by the power of this divine invitation empowering the world to be creative—and not so much that of an irresistible Power that unilaterally commands everything into existence.

It might be tempting to contrast these two models, as though to suggest that the Bible always espouses a cocreative portrait of God's activity and the Qur'an always that of the unilateral divine command to "Be!" Of course, it is not so simple. I have already noted that the Bible, too, can portray God's creative power as though it works unilaterally and irresistibly. Similarly, the Qur'an employs other images for God's creative activity besides the simple command to be. For example, it repeatedly insists that human beings are created out of "sperm-drops" or comparable speckles of fluid, rather than out of nothing. We read, for example, in the opening of Surah 96—traditionally called "The Clot" and believed by Muslims to have been the first revelation given to Muhammad—"Recite, in the Name of your Lord, Who created: He created man from a clot" (Q 96:1–2). Here is an at least slightly different nuance from "'Be!'—and it is." One of the more dramatic examples of an apparently gradualist, naturalistic rendering of divine creativity occurs in Surah 40. "It is He Who created you from dust, then from a sperm, then from a clot. Then He brings you out as infants; then allows you to come of age, then to become old men" (Q 40:67; cf. 23:12–14). Here the creation of the human being by God is described in relatively empirical terms; God creates in and through natural processes and materials. Yet we can also read in the same surah, immediately after, that "it is He who brings to life and causes to die. Then, if He decrees a certain matter, He only says to it: 'Be,' and it comes to be" (Q 40:68).

We should not assume that the models of divine command ("Be!") and gradual development (or even evolution) are mutually exclusive. Even if God simply says "Be!" and the human then "is," that same human nevertheless develops over time from a fertilized egg and must be nourished and cared for in order to grow, eventually, toward maturity. We don't pop into existence out of thin air, dropping vertically into the world from the outside somewhere due to some omnipotent, transcendent decree. Everything we can observe in the world around and within us has a history—and a very long and complicated history at that. The Qur'an's repeated imagery of development out of a blood clot or semen clot underscores the observable, gradual processes involved in all living, material creatures in our world. At the same time, the authoritative command "Be!" underscores, presumably, that even the rough material itself is commanded into being by God. Indeed, it implies that the long and complicated history of creaturely existence hangs always by the thread of this divine command.

In the mainstream thinking of Judaism, Christianity, and Islam, the strong tendency has been to assert that God the Creator has called creation into being *ex nihilo*, out of nothing. This is essentially a logical deduction: if God created the universe out of something instead of out of nothing, where did that something come from? Was it a something that God did not create? If so, would that not imply that this something is coeternal with God, coexistent with God, and thus in some sense coequal with God? Most believers in all three traditions have shied away from such a scenario. For a classic example, *Genesis Rabbah* records a conversation between the famed Rabbi Gamaliel and a pagan philosopher in which the latter provocatively states, "Your God was indeed a great artist, but he had good materials to help him." When Gamaliel asks what materials the philosopher has in mind, the reply is gleaned directly from the opening of Genesis: "Unformed space, the void, darkness, water, wind and the deep." The philosopher thus attempts to argue on the basis of Gamaliel's own scriptures that God's act of creation was essentially a matter of organizing already existing energies and materials. Gamaliel's reply is spirited: "May your spirit burst! All of those are explicitly described as having been created by God!"[2]

Despite Gamaliel's protestations, it is not clear at all that the Bible teaches *creatio ex nihilo*;[3] nevertheless, the alternative is unattractive (and generally unacceptable) because it compromises on the sovereignty and power of God. Anything but *creatio ex nihilo* seems especially out of place in a treatment of the Qur'an's teaching about creation, because of its recurring insistence upon God alone as the self-existent, sovereign Power. Accordingly, in David Burrell's words, "What seems to be central to the Qur'an is what follows from affirming the oneness of God (*tawhid*): that God has no competitor in originating the universe or in carrying out the divine purposes within it."[4] To believe that Allah created from anything more than nothing would seem to veer toward *shirk*.

In the following pair of classic creation texts, though, neither the Bible nor the Qur'an seems particularly insistent upon the doctrine of creation from nothing. There are strong traditions for reading them in that direction but nothing in the texts themselves that insists upon such an interpretation.[5] We should say that the issue likely was not the most pressing of questions motivating the creation of either text. In any event, the structural similarities between the two passages, *creatio ex nihilo* or not, are striking:

The Bible	The Qur'an
Genesis 1:1–2, 6, 20, 14	*Surah 21:30, 32*
In the beginning when God created the	Have the unbelievers not beheld that the
heavens and the earth, the earth was	heavens and the earth were
a formless void . . .	a solid mass,
And God said, "Let there be a dome in the midst of the waters, and let it	
separate the waters from the waters." . . .	then We separated them,
And God said, "Let the waters bring forth swarms of living creatures . . ."	and of water We produced every living thing.
	Will they not believe, then?
And God said, "Let there be lights in	And We made the sky a well-guarded
the dome of the sky to separate the day	canopy,
from the night; and let them be for signs	and they still turn away from its signs.
and for seasons and for days and years . . ."	

It should be noted, too, that the Qur'an in several other passages echoes the creation story of Genesis 1 by proclaiming God's creation of all things in six days. "Truly, your Lord is Allah Who created the heavens and the earth in six days, then He sat on the Throne controlling all things" (Q 10:3; cf. 11:7). We must hasten to add, however, that the six days of creation have a function in Genesis 1 that they do not have in the Qur'an. A careful reading of the structure of the poetry of Genesis 1 reveals a systematic progression and arrangement for the created order, with days 1, 2, and 3 providing the basis and setting for days 4, 5, and 6, respectively. (See Gen. 1 table, p. 51.)

Meanwhile, we find nothing comparable in the Qur'an. In it, the six days are alluded to but never recounted in any detail. There is, however, an understandable reason for this silence. Most biblical scholars read Genesis 1 not as a literal or historical description of the first week of creation, as though this chapter could be consulted for scientific information about our world's beginnings. Rather, they read it as having provided a rationale for the Jewish observance of the sabbath. In Genesis 1:1–2:4, the six days of creation lead up to the sabbath, the day of rest, on which even God took a breather. Predictably (and again, understandably) the Qur'an is uneasy with the notion that God would need a rest after six days' worth of labor—or after anything, for that matter. What sort of deity would need to rest? Thus, in the Qur'an after Allah created everything in six days, "then He sat on the Throne

Day 1	Day 4
Creation of light, which is separated from the darkness. The light is called day, and the darkness night.	Creation of "lights" to separate the day from the night—a "greater light" and a "lesser light," as well as the stars.
Day 2	**Day 5**
Separation of the waters (above) from the waters (below) by an "expanse" or "firmament" or "dome"—the "heavens."	The waters below are commanded—invited?—to "swarm" or "teem" with creatures, and birds are created to fly in the expanse of the sky.
Day 3	**Day 6**
Separation of "the waters below" (the seas) from dry land, which permits earth to "bring forth" vegetation and trees, i.e., to "produce produce."	The earth is commanded—invited?—to "bring forth" land creatures—and then humanity as the male and female is created in God's image to "have dominion" in creation. The plants are given "for food" to all the other creatures of land and sky.
Day 7	
God rests, and blesses and hallows the seventh day.	

controlling all things" (Q 10:3). God, in other words, got right to the work of exercising sovereignty. In the Qur'an, then, there is no pressing need to narrate the details of six days' worth of creating, since there is no sabbatical goal in sight for its narrative. In fact, the Qur'an explicitly addresses the theological problem inherent in claiming that God requires rest: "Indeed, we have created the heavens and the earth and what is between them in six days, and We were not touched by weariness" (Q 50:38). A God "not touched by weariness" certainly has no need for rest.

This difference between the Qur'an and Genesis, moreover, helps us to appreciate the distinctive nature of the Jewish narrative. God not only rested on the seventh day, that first sabbath, but also "blessed and hallowed" it—in other words, set it apart as a distinctive and unique day—for human observance. The rabbinic logic tended to operate in this way: God's rest on the seventh day is not so much a theological statement about God being tired as God's example given to the people of Israel to imitate.[6] In the Torah, sabbath observance by the Jewish people is also connected to their gracious deliverance from Egyptian bondage; both creation and redemption, we might say, are celebrated and even to some extent conjoined in the Jewish observance of the sabbath day.

Further, this should help us to appreciate that the fundamental point of Genesis 1 is not to offer its readers *inform*ation about the beginning of creation in any historical or scientific sense but rather to provide a kind of sabbath *formation* of the Jewish people. If Genesis 1 was formulated in the historical setting of the Babylonian exile, as most scholars believe, then sabbath observance would have been a particularly important habit of life for shaping Jews in exile into a distinct people, providing a means of resistance against assimilation with the surrounding pagan culture and its perceived idolatries. Fittingly, then, Genesis begins with the proclamation that the God of Israel is in fact the Creator of all things—and thus none of the idolatries of Israel's captors or neighbors (e.g., worship of sun, moon, stars, kings) should be imitated. The fundamental practice whereby the Jewish people were called to worship and serve only the Creator, and not creatures, was the weekly sabbath observance rooted in the creation story of Genesis 1. While of course the Qur'an offers its own potent critique of idolatry, the particularities of the Jewish situation are not part of the qur'anic milieu. The Qur'an, therefore, does not encourage observance of the Jewish sabbath and really would have no reason to do so.

But let us return to the notion of God's creative speech. Certainly the Qur'an's repeated insistence upon God's authoritative command *Be!* complements and coincides with what we have already seen of Islam's emphasis upon God's transcendence and sovereignty. On the other hand, I have touched on the possibility of reading the creative, commanding word of Genesis 1, *Let there be*, as bespeaking divine invitation and cooperation with the elements of earth. Indeed, in the Genesis narrative not only does God issue an invitation for the land to produce produce and the seas to swarm with swarming swimmers; there is the further element that at each step in the way of creation—and, not surprisingly, on seven different occasions—Genesis proclaims that "God saw that it was good" (1:4, 10, 12, 18, 21, 25, 31). God calls to creation in invitation; creation responds with fitting activity; God responds in divine pleasure, seeing creation's goodness in its replies to the Creator's calling. While it would be an overstatement to claim that this kind of "call and response" dialogue between God and creation is altogether absent from the Qur'an, it certainly does seem muted there.

Christian teaching, however, goes even further in the direction of God's dialogue with creation, hedging toward the idea of divine vulnerability vis à vis creation.[7] It does this by identifying God's creative word, spoken at creation, with the person of Jesus Christ. This identification occurs most clearly in the opening of John's gospel, where we find an obvious echoing of the words of Genesis 1 ("In the beginning God created the heavens and the earth . . ."). John's opening statement is "In the beginning was the Word, and the Word was with God, and the Word was God"—or, closer to the Greek construction, "whatever God was, so also was the Word" (1:1). It is this Word that "became flesh and lived among us" (1:14) as Jesus Christ, according to John. Later, it was this Word-become-flesh who knelt to wash his disciples' feet (John 13) and soon thereafter was crucified. Radical vulnerability marks this Word-become-human. "He came to what was his own," John's prologue proclaims, "and his own people did not accept him" (John 1:11).

This idea of a preexisting divine word was already a part of the author's cultural inheritance by the time the gospel of John was written. "By the word of the LORD the heavens were made," proclaims Psalm 33:6, and it became natural for Jewish interpreters well before Jesus's era to assume that this divine word possessed some sort of existence as an actual thing or being. Particularly as Jews interacted with concepts of wisdom widespread in Hellenistic culture, this notion of God's *word* became readily interchangeable with *wisdom*. So, for example, we find in Proverbs 8 that wisdom has become personified as a playful female child.

> Does not wisdom call,
>> and does not understanding raise her voice? . . .
> The LORD created me at the beginning of his work,
>> the first of his acts long ago.
> Ages ago I was set up,
>> at the first, before the beginning of the earth.
> When there were no depths I was brought forth,
> when there were no springs abounding with water . . .
>> when he established the fountains of the deep,
> when he assigned to the sea its limit,
>> so that the waters might not transgress his command,
> when he marked out the foundations of the earth,
>> then I was beside him, like a master worker [or *little child*],
> and I was daily his delight,
>> rejoicing before him always,
> rejoicing in his inhabited world
>> and delighting in the human race. (vv. 1, 22–24, 28–31)

Similarly, in the apocryphal Wisdom of Solomon—one of the documents of the Septuagint, included in Catholic Bibles but not in most Protestant versions—we find an even stronger and more distinct personification of wisdom. In this fascinating text, Woman Wisdom is virtually indistinguishable from God; it is Wisdom who has accomplished mighty deeds of salvation in the world, such as the exodus (Exod. 10–15), and who in fact is described in terms that sound reminiscent of none other than God: "Wisdom . . . because of her pureness pervades and penetrates all things. . . . For she is a reflection of eternal light, a spotless mirror of the working of God, and an image of his goodness . . . while remaining in herself, she renews all things; in every generation she passes into holy souls and makes them friends of God, and prophets" (7:24, 26–27).[8]

It was a short leap indeed for Jewish readers to associate this divine Wisdom with the Torah, God's gift to Israel for wise living. In *Genesis Rabbah*, the accumulation of rabbinic commentary on the book of Genesis, we read that "the Holy One, blessed be he, consulted the Torah when he created the world"—a reading of Genesis aided by the passage from Proverbs 8.[9] If the Torah actually provided the plans—perhaps even the "blueprint"—for creation, then this Torah-Wisdom must be of foundational, even eternal, significance. Wilfred Cantwell Smith helps us to better understand this notion by suggesting that "the idea of pre-existence"—that is, that the Torah, or later the Qur'an, dwelled in some "bookish" form with God even prior to creation—"was a Semitic time-related way of saying something regarding the supremacy and non-contingency of certain matters in human life discerned as transcendingly valuable."[10]

So we encounter repeatedly this widespread notion of a preexisting divine Word or Wisdom—whether the Jews'Torah, the Christians' Christ, or the Muslims'"Mother of the Book" (*Umm al Kitab*). In every case it is a Word from God to human beings that issues forth so directly from the very heart and mind, so to speak, of God, and is so thoroughly representative of the character and will of God that it is virtually indistinguishable from God. While the structural similarity among these concepts—preexistent Torah, eternal Christ, and heavenly Book—is not difficult to discern, it is of course only Christianity that understands such divine communication to have become an actual human being who lived among us on planet Earth.

On this basis of identifying the word God spoke in creation with the person of Jesus—"the Word become flesh"—we may begin to understand the rather difficult statements of the apostle Paul (or of one of his students) to the effect that God created the world "through" Christ (e.g., Col. 1:15–17). Jewish, Christian, and Muslim traditions all have gladly confessed and affirmed that God created the world "in wisdom"; only Christianity took it a step further and came to equate this divine wisdom with a person. But what does it mean, theologically, to say that God created *in* or *through Christ*? For example, Paul in 1 Corinthians 8:6 writes that God the Father is the One "*from* whom are all things"—and then adds that Jesus Christ, the Lord, is the One "*by* [or *through*] whom are all things." This is a critical point at which Christian and Islamic, along with Jewish, convictions radically diverge. Especially for Muslims, Christians are at this very point guilty of the sin of *shirk* or "association," that is, associating with God something from the creaturely realm. One of the classic surahs on creation, "The Bees," to which we will give further attention later in this chapter, emphatically makes this point: "He created the heavens and the earth in truth; may He be exalted above what they associate [with Him]" (Q 16:3). We have already seen that the prophet Isaiah's writings in the Tanakh make the point about Adonai as the Creator in quite similar terms: "I am the LORD, who made all things, who alone stretched out the heavens, who by myself spread out the earth" (44:24).

There are other affirmations in the New Testament of the role of Christ in creation similar to Paul's (e.g., John 1:3; Heb. 1:1–2), but it is not immediately obvious what such statements mean. Perhaps it would be easier to begin with what they do not mean. What they *cannot* mean, for the Christian, is that God was not (or is not) directly involved in the deed of creation. There is no need or reason for Christians to interpose an intermediate creator figure between God and the world if in so doing it is implied that God could not or did not become directly involved in the creating and sustaining of the material world. This was a problem that both the early Church and the Synagogue faced in the threat of Gnostic ideas that dismissed and devalued material creation, such that all physical bodies were deemed disgusting, far beneath the purity and goodness of God. The opening chapter in the Bible clearly proclaims not only that God is the Creator of all things ("heaven and earth") but also that what God creates is *good* and thus agreeable, presumably, to God.

The New Testament texts regarding Christ's role in creation, then, should not be read as suggesting that there is some uncrossable chasm between our material world and its spiritual origin such that God would have to "keep a safe distance." (Obviously, as we shall explore in greater depth momentarily, the Christian doctrine of the incarnation claims that in fact God initiated a decidedly *un*safe, radically near approach to the world.) The creation is not denigrated or belittled because it is of a material nature: seas and land, sun and moon, plants and stars, fish and fowl, female and male. None of this is so far "below God" in its materiality as to be beneath divine dignity, concern, or love. God pronounces creation to be *good* during each step of the creative processes described in Genesis 1. Indeed, in Genesis 2 the imagery employed to depict God's relations to the physical world is noticeably intimate and down to earth: Adonai forms the *adam* ("dirt creature" or "earthling") from the *adamah*, the dust of the ground, and plants a garden in Eden (vv. 7–8).

Thus, the Christian conviction that Christ is the mediator of creation does not and cannot mean that God is put off by materiality, or too distant, too spiritual to be Creator and Sustainer of the world. What, then, does it mean?

Perhaps we can follow the lead of the prologue of John's gospel (1:1–18) and connect the *logos* or Word, "without [whom] not one thing came into being" (1:3), with the spoken word by which God creates in Genesis 1: "Then God said, 'Let there be. . . .'" As I have suggested earlier, the Jews' Tanakh, the Christians' Bible, and the Muslims' Qur'an all consistently insist that God's Word is alive, active, and creative, accomplishing the effects that God intends. Even if Genesis 1 had not repeatedly affirmed the goodness of creation, Christianity, along with Judaism and Islam, would have to insist that creation is good since God the Creator is good. But beyond this confidence in the goodness of creation, grounded in the goodness of the God who speaks it into being, Christian faith follows the gospel of John in its surprising declaration that this same divine Word, whereby all things have been made, "became flesh and lived among us" (John 1:3, 14). The Creator has, in ways utterly beyond our ken, actually joined us as a fellow-creature, an earthling of flesh and blood. Again, we must acknowledge that this is the fundamental parting of the ways between Christians and Jews, certainly—but even more decidedly so, it seems, between Christians and Muslims. Thus, while all three traditions celebrate the goodness of creation as the work of a truly good Creator, that goodness is reaffirmed by Christians in a more profound, more radical, and certainly more surprising way: in God's ability, and willingness, to participate directly in the material life and processes of this world. This notion is not only utterly strange but in fact blasphemous as far as the Qur'an is concerned.

The apostle Paul explicitly makes the connection between creation and incarnation when he writes to the Corinthian church, "For . . . God who said, 'Let light shine out of darkness,' has shone in our hearts to give the light of the knowledge of the glory of God in the face of Jesus Christ" (2 Cor. 4:6). But beyond even this grand mystery of the incarnation of the Word, Christians press further to say that this Word-become-flesh "laid down his life for us" (1 John 3:16), thereby revealing that *God who creates by the Word is self-giving, sacrificial love.* God the Creator is outpouring and life-giving Love toward the creation in and through the Word incarnate and crucified for us (cf. 1 John 4:8, 16).

Finally, then, the contrasts begin to become pronounced; if God's Word is such that it can enter into, and participate in, creaturely existence as a human being in our midst, then that Word is heard differently in Christianity from what we encounter in the other Abrahamic traditions. For Muslims, for example, Allah's word (*Be!*) tends to be a transcendent and omnipotent power of unilateral effect. For Jews, God's word (*Let there be . . .*) in the opening of Genesis calls for creaturely cooperation in response to the divine invitation. While Christian faith recognizes the validity and the value of those understandings of God's creative word, it also insists that they do not encompass God's definitive Word in Jesus Christ: God's *logos* has become incarnate in a human being in a particular place and time. The Word became flesh and thus became bounded, bodily, finite, and vulnerable. This is a Word that can suffer, bleed, and die a criminal's death—a Word that is *humble*, even humiliated (John 13:1–17; cf. Phil. 2:1–11) in a world of his own making. Paul understandably called such teaching "foolishness to Gentiles" and "a stumbling block to Jews" (1 Cor. 1:23). It is no less than blasphemy to most (if not all) Muslims.[11]

Christian theologians of many traditions, especially during the past few decades, have argued that the uniquely Christian doctrine of the incarnation of the Word calls for a radical rethinking of divine power, including the nature of God's power exercised in creating the universe. A God whose Word becomes incarnate and thereby shares fully in creaturely realities and frailties is not sheer power conjuring a universe out of nothing like a magician producing a rabbit out of a hat; instead, the Word incarnate suggests a much more *involved* and *invested* process in God's speech-act of creating. If the Word whereby God creates, whereby God calls things into being, is a Word that is humbled even to the point of death on a cross, outpouring divine love and human blood for the sake of all creation, then perhaps we can understand why the New Testament would teach that "God is love" (1 John 4:8, 16). Thus we might understand God's act of creation to be a great outpouring of love through the Word that indeed became truly human and dwelt among us.

These are important differences, to be sure. They need to be respected. Let us not smooth over the distinctiveness of each of these models of divine creative power. Nonetheless, let us not overlook some significant similarities among the Muslim, Jewish, and Christian traditions regarding the doctrine of creation, nor the possibility that each may have much to learn from the others.

One of the distinctive emphases found often in the Qur'an is that the world is filled with "signs" of the Creator's hand. Here is one example, among a great many: "And it is He Who spread out the earth and placed therein firm mountains and rivers; and of each kind of fruit He created two pairs. He causes the night to cover the day. Surely in that are signs for people who reflect" (Q 13:3). Interestingly, "signs" is a translation of the Arabic term *ayat*, which is also used to refer to the verses of the Qur'an. Thus, just as the Qur'an is filled with *ayat* that point to God, so also the natural world is filled with *ayat* that point to God. The Qur'an, like creation itself, is a book filled with signs.

A notion like this is found also in the Bible, though it is not nearly so dominant and widespread there as it is in the Qur'an. One of the best examples occurs in Psalm 19, where David sings that "the heavens are telling the glory of God" and that "day to day pours forth speech, and night to night declares knowledge" (vv. 1–2). Though they are not able to utter a word, their testimony issues forth. Similarly, Paul later wrote to the Christians in Rome that "ever since the creation of the world [God's] eternal power and divine nature, invisible though they are, have been understood and seen through the things he has made" (Rom. 1:20).

Indeed, it is fascinating to note Paul's teaching in this passage that the root of sin lies precisely in the fact that while all people "knew God" through the evidences within creation, "they did not honor him as God or give thanks to him, but they became futile in their thinking" (1:21)—fascinating at least in part because it is such a dominant theme in the Qur'an that all people should indeed be able to recognize God's hand in creation and to offer up their thanksgiving. If in fact Paul argues that the universal and fundamental human problem of sin is rooted in a refusal to recognize or to acknowledge the Power made known "through the things he has made," then Paul and the Qur'an are on the same page. Further, the very argument of the Qur'an is predicated on the assumption that human beings can in fact acknowledge the Creator through the "signs" of creation. In the words of the eminent Islamic religious philosopher Mohammad Iqbal, "The Qur'an . . . constantly calls upon the reader to observe the perpetual change of the winds, the alternation of day and night, the clouds, the starry heavens, and the planets swimming through infinite space"[12] as empirical signs of the presence and power of God. Christians have not yet begun to consider seriously enough the implication of this testimony of the Qur'an, particularly if it is read essentially as the human testimony of Muhammad. The implication I mean is that in Muhammad we do indeed encounter a human who, to adapt Paul's words, profoundly did "honor [God] as God," who did in fact give God thanks. Further, his status as Islam's prophet means that his gratitude to the God of creation has been a fundamental paradigm for millions of Muslims across the centuries. Are there in the *ayat* of the Qur'an testimonies to the *ayat* of God's goodness and bounty in creation such that, in reading them, Muslims are led to "honor [God] as God" and to "give thanks to him"? If so, we might also wonder if the Qur'an has offered to its faithful practitioners over the centuries an antidote to the downwardly destructive cycle of human sin that Paul describes in Romans 1—a cycle whose origin lies in the refusal to acknowledge the divine power made known in the signs of creation.

For all of the importance of questions like these, perhaps they mean relatively little when any one of us—whether Muslim, Jew, Christian, or someone else—actually stands out in the midst of nature's wildness and feels the raw power and beauty of the world. There are at least occasional moments, and places, in nearly all of our lives when we encounter an unspeakable majesty, an irresistible grandeur, that reduces us to the status of silenced beholders of a Power and Glory far beyond our ken. Certainly I have felt it while walking in the cool, dark shade of the ancient redwoods of northern California, or while peering down into the vast, multihued abyss of the Grand Canyon, or while watching from San Diego's Sunset Cliffs as a brilliantly orange, blazing sun melts into the Pacific horizon. In such moments of inscrutable mystery and ineffable beauty, perhaps our religious traditions and designations fade into the background, at least for a little while, in deference to something deeper and more basic to human experience.[13]

Perhaps it is an experience of the world something like this that comes to expression in a pair of passages—one from the Jewish Psalms and one from the Qur'an—that will provide closure to this chapter on the doctrine of creation. The parallels between Psalm 104 (for many years now easily my favorite psalm) and Surah 16 of the Qur'an are remarkable. Both texts invite us to an ecstatic celebration of creation's bounties and goodness. Further, the similarities of both of these texts to an even more ancient Egyptian text (14th c. BCE), "Hymn to the Aton" or Sun-God, have not gone unnoticed by scholars. I shall note a few of the themes common to all of these moving hymns of praise, hopefully appreciating the experiences of elation, even ecstasy, that the natural world in all of its beauty and power can inspire within us.

The Bible	The Qur'an
Psalm 104:1, 5	*Surah 16:1, 3*
Bless the LORD, O my soul.	Glory be to Him and may He be exalted
O LORD my God, you are very great.	above what they associate [with Him]! . . .
You are clothed in honor and majesty . . .	
You set the earth on its foundations, so that it shall never be shaken.	He created the heavens and the earth in truth; . . .

Note first that both hymns begin with praise to the Maker of all things and that the Qur'an especially is careful to insist that nothing in all of creation can be rightfully associated with (i.e., equal to) the Creator. In both cases, too, God the Creator is the One who ensures that creation is orderly, relatively predictable, and at least generally amenable to human existence: in the Qur'an God created all things "in truth," or reliably; in Psalm 104 God has placed the earth, as it were, upon a solid foundation.

Psalm 104:10, 13–15	Surah 16:10–11
You make springs gush forth in the valleys;	It is He who sends down water from the sky;
they flow between the hills, . . .	from it you drink,
From your lofty abode you water the mountains; the earth is satisfied with the fruit of your	
work. You cause the grass to grow for the	and through it grow the plants on which you
cattle,	feed your cattle.
and plants for people to use, to bring forth food from the earth,	From it He brings forth for you vegetation,
and wine to gladden the human heart,	olives, palms, vines and all kinds of fruit.
oil to make the face shine, and bread	In that, surely, there is a sign for a people
to strengthen the human heart.	who reflect.

Here we find one of the many places in the Qur'an where its readers are encouraged to see a "sign" in the world around them, in this case in the great variety of vegetation on our planet. In both texts one senses delight in the delicious variety of tastes associated with "all kinds of fruit" and the other edible plants. The flowing waters necessary to the growing of all such plants is also celebrated in both passages as the ongoing labor of God.

We should note that both passages describe God's creative activity in the present tense. The Qur'an teaches us that God "brings forth for you vegetation," while Psalm 104 instructs us to pray to our Maker, "You cause the grass to grow for the cattle." It is an impoverished theology that would insist only that God made all things in some creative burst in the ancient reaches of our cosmic beginnings; if God "brings forth for you vegetation" and "cause[s] the grass to grow for cattle," then God is doing something in this very moment by way of continuing the activity of creation.

These biblical and qur'anic propositions, though, clearly should not be misconstrued as somehow competing with scientific explanation. "God causes the grass to grow" is profound—even if simple-sounding—theology. However, it provides little insight for someone attempting to understand the natural processes a botanist describes. In that case, one would need to talk about the importance of light, adequate soil, nutrients, sufficient water, a healthy root system, and photosynthesis (among other things, I suspect). "God brings forth for you vegetation" is a significant theological proposition, but it simply will not suffice as science. Hopefully, this relatively simple example illustrates why the sorts of statements about the natural world that we are examining in the Bible and the Qur'an should not be read as competing against scientific explanations and descriptions. The claims of Holy Writ regarding God's creation are of a different order from the claims of science about nature, and each type of language has a rightful and proper place in discourse about the world we humans inhabit. As Muslim scholar Jamaal al-Din M. Zarabozo has written, "Although [such] verses may not add much to one's body of knowledge concerning nature, they bring about a new perspective on nature, a perspective that reminds one of Allah in the surrounding nature and of His greatness and supreme knowledge."[14]

Psalm 104:19–20, 24	Surah 16:12–13
You have made the moon to mark the seasons;	And He has subjected to you the night and
the sun knows its time for setting.	the day, the sun and the moon . . .
You make darkness, and it is night . . .	
O LORD, how manifold	And what He created for you in the earth is
are your works!	of multifarious colours; in that there is,
In wisdom you have made them all; the earth is full of	surely, a sign for a people who are mindful.
your creatures.	

Again the signs! Both the surah and the psalm revel in the vast diversity of shape and hue, form and texture, size and color within creation, the Qur'an more explicitly finding in this sensory wealth another sign of the Maker. Creatures and colors, sounds and smells, sights, tastes, and textures are constantly flowing into our awareness through our sensory connections with our marvelous environment. The Egyptian celebration of creation and Creator, "Hymn to the Aton," sings it this way: "How manifold it is, what You have made, hidden from view! O sole God, like whom there is no other! You created the earth—all people, cattle and wild beasts, whatever is on earth, going upon feet, and what is on high, flying with wings!"

Psalm 104:26	Surah 16:14
	And it is He Who subjected the sea, so that you may eat from it tender meat and bring out from it jewelry for you to wear;
There go the ships . . .	and you see the ships cruising therein.

The Egyptian hymn, too, mentions ships that "sail upstream and downstream." All these ships bring to mind the joy I experience in being a professor at a university that is perched on cliffs overlooking the breathtaking Pacific horizon. I often take classes outside—though not as often as my students would like!—to learn under a warm sun, breathing together the crisp, briny breezes blowing in off the ocean. At such times, it is not uncommon for us to peer westward and see great ships go sailing silently by. Some of us actually spot a whale out there now and then—perhaps identifiable with the "leviathan" mentioned in Psalm 104, formed by God "to sport in [the sea]" (v. 26).

Psalm 104:27–30	Surah 16:17–18
These all look to you	Now, is He Who creates like him who does
to give them their food in due season;	not create? Do you not take heed?
when you give it to them, they gather it up;	Were you to count Allah's Blessings, you
when you open your hand, they are filled with good things.	will not exhaust them.
When you hide your face, they are dismayed; when you take away their breath, they die and return to their dust.	
When you send forth your spirit, they are created,	Allah is truly All-Forgiving, Merciful.
and You renew the face of the ground.	

In these verses in Psalm 104 we find a beautiful celebration of God's ongoing, moment-by-moment, active, and dynamic relation to the world. Not only does the text claim that God feeds all creatures, human and nonhuman alike, but also that God is constantly involved in the even more fundamental act of "breathing life" into all creatures. God's Breath/Spirit animates all creatures, stirring up new life and instigating vitality. Both the Qur'an and the Bible celebrate the dynamic, ongoing, present-tense nature of God's creative activity. God's renewing of the face of the earth, expressive of the ongoing nature of God's creative act, is rooted in God's great mercy. "The LORD is good to all, and his compassion is over all that he has made" (Ps. 145:9). In the very midst of the prophet's lamentations over the destruction of Jerusalem and the Babylonian exile of the Jewish people, he could maintain hope in this mercy: "The steadfast love of the LORD never ceases, his mercies never come to an end; they are new every morning; great is your faithfulness" (Lam. 3:22–23). The rabbinic tradition drew upon this radical affirmation of trust to teach that "every morning" is itself a testimony to God's sustaining mercies, renewing all of creation as a gift of grace. Thus we find in the first blessing of weekday mornings in Jewish liturgy, "In mercy you give light to the earth . . . , and in your goodness you renew the work of creation each day continually."[15] Similarly, it is noteworthy that all but one of the Qur'an's 114 surahs begin with the formula "In the name of Allah, the Compassionate, the Merciful."

We should recall, too, that in the Hebrew, Arabic, and Aramaic languages—as well as in several other related dialects—the term for "mercy" or "compassion" is the plural form of the word *womb*. For all of the peoples who have spoken in these tongues, to feel and to share in compassion for a fellow creature is to be like a mother who bears, nurtures, and protects her unborn child. It evokes a feeling of deep connection to another, particularly to the weak and vulnerable. We might say, then, that divine mercy, God's own "wombishness," is what births the world "every morning" and in every moment. Perhaps too often in our debates regarding the doctrine of creation we lose our sense of the divine compassion that gently holds us in being; perhaps it is time to rekindle our sense of radical awe before the mystery of finite being's sustenance in the Infinite Mercy. Nevertheless:

Psalm 104:35	Surah 16:25
Let sinners be consumed from the earth, and let the wicked be no more.	So let [the doubters] on the Day of Resurrection bear in full their burdens and some of the burdens of the ignorant whom they lead astray. How evil is that which they bear!

Despite their celebration of the marvels and goodness of the deeply graced world we all inhabit—or perhaps precisely because of that celebration—both of these texts also bring a word of judgment and threat against those who, we might say, "spoil the view." God's wombishness apparently has its limits! Psalm 104, like many other psalms, yearns for a decisive moment of judgment in which the "sinners" and "wicked"—those who live in rebellion against the Maker and Molder of this beautiful world—might be no more. Similarly, the Qur'an envisions a day in which those who doubt creation's signs pointing to God will receive their just deserts in the world to come. It is in fact a prominent theme in the Qur'an to link God's act of creation with that of the resurrection; after all, the resurrection of that which has died is itself an act of new or renewed creation. But the expectation of a general resurrection of all people (if not of all creation) also raises the stakes for evildoers; while Psalm 104 can only hope for their extinction, the Qur'an, written at a later period in the history of ideas regarding death and afterlife, can threaten with more than extinction.

I will explore further the eschatological ideas of resurrection and final judgment in the final chapter of this book, but in the context of this chapter on creation perhaps I should mention this much: both the Bible and the Qur'an proclaim that there is a Creator of all things who has also undertaken to communicate with human beings regarding how they are to live. To spurn such communications is, at least to some extent, to undermine the goodness and compromise the integrity of creation. Both books also provide assurances that the day will come when the Creator will judge with righteousness those who by their sins have brought despoilment to God's good green earth.

4

THE REVEALING
OF THE WORD OF GOD

It is He who has revealed to you the Book, with verses which are precise in meaning and which are the Mother of the Book, and others which are ambiguous. As to those in whose hearts there is vacillation, they follow what is ambiguous in it, seeking sedition and intending to interpret it. However, no one but Allah knows its interpretation. Those well-grounded in knowledge say: "We believe in it; all is from our Lord"; yet none remembers save those possessed of understanding!

—Qur'an 3:7

Divine revelation is one of the most important theological issues in both Islam and Christianity, and thus of course also in Muslim-Christian conversation. The questions can be overwhelming: Can God communicate with human beings? Has God done so? How? When? How often? How clearly? Assuming some kind of satisfactory reply can be mustered for those questions, another quickly follows: *What is it* that God has communicated?

We have already noted that the Qur'an is explicitly self-referential, repeatedly presenting itself as *the* flawless communication from God. Indeed, it offers itself as the very speech or recitation of God given to Muhammad through a "Spirit" that Muslims traditionally have identified with the angel Gabriel (Q 2:97). In words addressed to Muhammad, "And this is the revelation of the Lord of the Worlds, brought down by the Faithful Spirit upon your heart, so that you might be one of the warners, in manifest Arabic tongue" (Q 26:190–95). For Muslims, then, when the Qur'an is recited it is truly God who speaks.

Indeed, Muslims typically insist that to hear the Qur'an recited "in manifest Arabic tongue"—if done with faith and expectation—is to *know experientially* that its claims for itself are true. This appeal to experience, I should add, is encouraged by the Qur'an; repeatedly the challenge is issued for someone, anyone, to compose a recitation that could match its power and majesty (e.g., Q 2:23, 10:38). The Qur'an inevitably adds to that challenge, however, its own assurances regarding the outcome of such a contest. "Say: 'Were men and jinn to band together in order to come up with the like of this Qur'an, they will never come up with the like of it, even if they back up one another'" (Q 17:88).

As we discovered already in chapter 2, the Qur'an's alleged absolute uniqueness and perfection as divine revelation led Muslim scholars to speculate as to its nature and origin—if for Muslims it could properly be said to have had an origin at all. Indeed, just as Christian theologians debated in the fourth and fifth centuries of the Christian era regarding the nature of Christ as the Son of God, so also—and at roughly the same historical stage of development—Muslim thinkers argued over whether the Qur'an was "created" or "uncreated." Perhaps not surprisingly, the two traditions eventually arrived at similar conclusions. The doctrine that the preexistent Logos, or Son of God, is eternal and uncreated—and thus shares in the very nature and being of God—became the orthodox Christian position particularly through the deliberations of the ecumenical councils of Nicaea (325 CE) and Chalcedon (451 CE). Likewise, a similar claim regarding the Qur'an—that it is the material, earthly representation of the heavenly, uncreated "Mother of the Book"—became the dominant Muslim position during the fourth century of the Islamic era (i.e., the tenth century of the common era).[1] In both cases, certainly a significant factor was the concern to undergird and support believers' confidence that it is *truly God* who has drawn near to the world in the act of revelation. For Christians, this act occurred supremely in the person of Jesus Christ, the eternal Son who, to employ the language of the Nicene Creed, was "begotten, not created" and who "for us and for our salvation . . . became man." For Muslims, this act occurred supremely in the angel Gabriel's flawless recitation of the Qur'an to the prophet Muhammad.

I have earlier noted that the Jewish tradition, several centuries before the advent of Christian faith, had come to make comparable claims regarding the Torah, identifying it with the Divine Wisdom whereby God created the world. Indeed, I mentioned in chapter 3 that at least some Jews imagined God as having created the universe by using the Torah as a blueprint. In this case the Torah becomes functionally equivalent to God's Mind, or at least the quintessential expression of the Divine Mind. We find a comparable process occurring in Islam in regard to the Qur'an. This is not surprising; in the words of Michael Cook, "as a way to enhance the canonical status of a text, it is hard to trump the doctrine of its eternity."[2] I need not belabor the fact that Christians have not tended to make the same kind of claim for their Bible; I need only to reiterate that there is a very good reason for this. Christianity has not developed a notion of a preexistent or eternal Book precisely because that is the role—the "metaphysical place," we might say—of the figure variously identified as the eternal Son, the Logos, the preexistent Christ, the second person of the Trinity. While the preexistent Word for Jews ("Torah") and for Muslims ("Mother of the Book" or "heavenly Qur'an") became text, for Christians the preexistent Word "became flesh and lived among us" (John 1:14).

The Christian conviction that the eternal Logos, God's very Son, became a particular human being at a certain place and time is, of course, called *the doctrine of the incarnation*. It should be obvious that Muslims do not embrace a doctrine of incarnation; however, something comparable to an incarnation is believed to have occurred when the "Mother of the Book" was recited to Muhammad and eventually was committed to the written page. The Heavenly Book became an earthly book, the Qur'an. Thus it has become a truism in comparative theology that the functional equivalent to the Qur'an, for Christians, is not so much the Bible as it is Jesus Christ. We might put it like this: both Muslims and Christians believe that "long ago God spoke to [the people of Israel] in many and various ways by the prophets" (Heb. 1:1), but while Christians proceed to confess that God "has spoken to us by a Son" (Heb. 1: 2), Muslims insist that God "has spoken" the full, final, and authoritative Word in the Qur'an.

Each of the traditions, in other words, has to some degree and in some fashion affirmed a preexistent, eternal, divine status for its revelation. In that sense, God's Word—whether conceived as "the Mother of the Book," "the eternal Son of God," or "Divine Wisdom" (or Torah)—is believed to exist in a pure, unsullied form far removed from the ambiguities and imperfections of history. In the heavenly realm, the divine Word is untouched by creaturely limitations. The obvious issue for each of these traditions then becomes the extent to which it is willing to acknowledge a historical dimension, or what we might call a "human element," as a part of the revelation once it is communicated to and received—and in its reception always and inevitably interpreted—by human beings. Is there room for the human element in divine revelation?

I have already cited the strongest, or at least the most straightforward, claim for the incarnation in the Christian canon: "In the beginning was the Word, and the Word was with God, and the Word was God . . . And the Word became flesh and lived among us" (John 1:1, 14). The opening verse of John's gospel affirms the eternal, preexistent nature of this Word or Divine Communication. Verse 14 makes the always-startling claim that this Word truly has entered into creaturely modes of existence ("flesh") and made its dwelling among us human creatures. Nonetheless, it has been difficult for Christians through the centuries to maintain a sure grasp on the profoundly human element implied in the very doctrine of the incarnation. A most common and recurring tendency has been to picture Jesus as having had a human body but within that body a divine mind. Christians both ancient and contemporary have often tended to assume, for example, that Jesus was omniscient—knowing all things as God knows all things. But such a supposition does not take at all seriously Jesus's true humanity, nor the description of Jesus's boyhood and adolescence in the gospel of Luke: "Jesus increased in wisdom and in years, and in divine and human favor" (2:52). The unacceptable alternative, presumably, would be to assume that Jesus the infant knew all things—or, for that matter, that as a prenatal child in Mary's womb he was cognizant of his eternal identity as the Logos.

Fortunately, when those kinds of implications arose from the theory regarding Jesus offered by the fourth-century theologian Apollinaris, his Christology (or doctrine of Christ) was roundly rejected during the ecumenical council at Constantinople in 381. Apollinaris had suggested that in the incarnation the Eternal Logos essentially replaced the functions of what would have been the human mind of Jesus. Hence, Jesus was a human body that provided the outer casing, so to speak, of the Divine Mind. Apollinaris's odd portrait of Jesus inspired one of the most famous rejoinders in the history of Christian theology, offered by Gregory of Nazianzus: "If anyone has put his trust in [Christ] as a man without a human mind, that person is himself really lacking a mind. . . . For that which [Christ] has not assumed he has not healed; but that which is united to his Godhead is also saved."[3] At its best and wisest, the church has followed Gregory's suit. In so doing, it has seen fit to claim that Jesus's sharing in the divine nature does not negate or compromise his truly human status. Likewise, Jesus's sharing in what it means, essentially, to be a human being does not preclude or exclude his truly divine status. In other words, God and humanity are not mutually exclusive categories. The divine nature and the human nature can be united without compromising the identity or the integrity of either.

This is an amazing way to think about God, all too often unappreciated by Christians themselves. For this doctrine of the incarnation strongly implies that God is both able and willing to interact profoundly and intimately with the creaturely realm, even to the point of entering into and sharing in its modes of being. God can "assume"—take on, shoulder, live with and within—creaturely existence.

It should be obvious by now that the Muslim doctrine of God vehemently disallows such a notion. The most obvious example of the Muslim rejection of the human or creaturely element in revelation is the traditional insistence that the Qur'an is the flawless recitation of Divine Speech. No room is allowed for the possibility of Muhammad's own contribution to the creation of the Qur'an. Not only is the Qur'an traditionally believed to be the very recitation of God, but most Muslims also believe that Muhammad was illiterate. Clearly, to insist that Muhammad could neither read nor write functions to accentuate the thoroughly divine character of the qur'anic text. If Muhammad is understood to have been essentially a passive recipient of revelation, only a receptacle for divine speech, then any attempt to interpret the Qur'an as a historical document created within and as a response to particular social-historical settings will be strongly discouraged if not censored entirely.

Islamic scholar Fazlur Rahman (1919–88) offered an insightful and sophisticated analysis of how the Qur'an itself presents Muhammad's role in the revelatory event. In one instance, Rahman cited Q 75:16–19: "Do not wag your tongue with it [i.e., the divine recitation] to hurry on with it. It is incumbent upon Us to put it together and to recite it. Then, when We recite it, follow its recitation. Then, it is incumbent upon Us to expound it clearly." Rahman's comment:

> That the Prophet actually mentally "heard" words is clear from 75:16–19. . . . It is also clear that, in his anxiety to retain it or to "anticipate" it in a direction different from that of his Revealing Spirit, the Prophet moved his tongue of his own ordinary human volition, the intrusion of which was repudiated by God. This necessarily implies the total "otherness" of the agent of Revelation from the conscious personality of Muhammad in the act of Revelation.[4]

Rahman, however, immediately proceeded to clear some theoretical space for the role of the human nature, so to speak, of Muhammad:

> But it is equally clear that the words heard were mental and not acoustic, since the Spirit and the Voice were internal to him, and there is no doubt that whereas on the one hand, the Revelation emanated from God, on the other, it was also intimately connected with his deeper personality. Thus the popular

traditional accounts of the utter externality of the agency of Revelation cannot be accepted as correct.[5]

Note Rahman's attempt, in the above, to affirm the divine initiative and content in the gift of qur'anic revelation—*and also* to acknowledge the "deeper personality" of Muhammad with which this revelation was "intimately connected." Not surprisingly, many Muslims have found Rahman's phenomenology of Muhammad's revelatory experiences to be objectionable. Nonetheless, such a description bears a structural similarity to the centuries-old attempt of Christian theologians to accord proper recognition to the divine and human natures of Jesus. The danger that both traditions have often perceived is that in giving such an acknowledgment to the human role—whether conceived in terms of spiritual maturity, or receptivity, or sensitivity, or another such quality—there often follows a corresponding devaluation of the utter graciousness of God, thoroughly unmerited, in drawing near to humanity through the act of revelation. The more attention or credit that is given to the human, some fear, the less is given to God.

Perhaps many Muslim believers would prefer to set aside Rahman's attempt to give even limited recognition to the human element of Muhammad's "deeper personality" in the event of qur'anic revelation. Even so, there remains a factor within Islamic tradition that bears significantly on the issue at hand. From very early in the history of interpretation of the Qur'an, careful attention has been given to what Muslim exegetes have called the "occasion" or "situation" for the revelations Muhammad received. In other words, there has been a tacit—indeed, an explicit—recognition that the words of the Qur'an are directed to specific historical settings and events. Thus, on the one hand we encounter the conviction that the Qur'an is the perfect and flawless echo of the eternal and utterly ahistorical "Mother of the Book"—and on the other hand that its revelations are fitted to specific questions, struggles, or situations in Muhammad's life and prophetic ministry. In the Muslim tradition, according to Daniel Madigan, "the Qur'an is presented as already complete in the realm of eternity; the text is preserved on a heavenly tablet (Q 85:22) and transmitted to Gabriel, who in turn parcels it out to Muhammad according to the situation in which he finds himself." Madigan proceeds to suggest that the motivation for holding to this notion of a preexisting, eternal Divine Word that is perfectly reproduced in the text of the Qur'an "seems . . . to arise from a sense within the [Muslim] community that its scriptural canon must be fixed and complete by its very nature as the utterance and decree of God."[6]

One of my concerns in this book is to offer the humble suggestion—admittedly as an outsider to Islam—that perhaps revelation need not be conceived as so thoroughly excluding the human element. Again, it is not as though Christians themselves have never struggled over this issue. We have, and many still do—some vehemently so. Nonetheless, the heart of Christianity lies precisely in the conviction that God has become incarnate within the very processes of human history and creaturely realities. Those processes, admittedly, compose a messy realm filled with partial meanings and lurking uncertainties, ambiguities abounding. For Christianity, revelation is ultimately and supremely a human being, a first-century Jew from Nazareth in Galilee—one who shared and shares in all that is implied by the vicissitudes of history. Indeed, the New Testament opens with four different, and very often noticeably divergent, testimonies regarding the ministry of that human being. Those four testimonies—the gospels of Matthew, Mark, Luke, and John—cannot be blended into a single, smooth, streamlined story. Their differences cannot be ironed out or glossed over. In the words of Protestant theologian William Placher, "Conflation of the Gospels . . . would muddle the ways in which each Gospel narrative develops such matters in a quite different way. . . . The different stories stand in their odd juxtaposition. Reading them pulls us into a complex dialectic between their narrations and the world of our experience."[7] Such reading demands care, effort, and a willingness to bear the burden of interpretation.

Admittedly, not all Christians would agree with this rendering of revelation, and more than a few would be unhappy to think about the gospel(s) in this way. But it seems not only the most faithful accounting of the facts before us but also the most consistent outworking of the doctrine of the incarnation. If the Divine Word truly became flesh—truly entered into and participated in creaturely reality—then a Christian doctrine of revelation cannot be afraid to acknowledge its profoundly historical and human elements. Of course, an argument from the Christian doctrine of the incarnation really carries no weight in an appeal to Muslim interpreters to acknowledge and embrace the possibility—nay, the presence—of a truly human element in the Qur'an. Many if not most thoughtful Muslims would be unmoved. Indeed, it is a fairly typical criticism of Christianity by Muslim apologists that sometimes there are glaring differences in detail and narrative among the four gospels of the New Testament. This argument reaches back at least as far as the eighth-century Muslim scholar Ibn Kathir, who wrote, "It is said that the Gospel was transmitted from Jesus in four versions: Luke, Matthew, Mark, and John. Among these four gospels are many differences with respect to each version, many additions, and many deletions."[8] For the Muslim tradition, these differences testify clearly to the human element in the gospels, rendering questionable their status as divine revelation.

Given the traditional Islamic assumptions regarding the nature of divine revelation—purely divine, unsullied by historicity, presumably unambiguous—this criticism is understandable and legitimate. On the other hand, given the Christian understanding of revelation as reaching its fullness in the Word who "became flesh and lived among us" in the midst of history and nature, shrouded in ambiguity and multiple perspectives, the criticism falls harmlessly to the side. It is probably even worthy of note that we Christians owe our doctrine of the incarnation, and its attendant view of divine revelation as occurring in the very person and ministry of Jesus, primarily to the gospel of John (and to the three letters traditionally attributed to the same author).

John is of course only one gospel of the four we cherish as canonical—and its teaching about the incarnation of the Logos (John 1:1, 14; 1 John 1:1–4) is not a clear and unambiguous teaching in the other gospels, though certainly one can argue for its implied presence there. The point is, Ibn Kathir was correct in his pointing out the differences among the gospels, not to speak of Paul and other lesser New Testament authors. But Kathir was incorrect in supposing that "the Gospel was transmitted from Jesus in four versions," since there were in fact many more than four—though only four were accepted into the church's canon—and none of them can be said to have been directly "transmitted from Jesus." Let me repeat it: revelation in Christianity is inevitably and inescapably a messy and ambiguous phenomenon. Further, it is readily arguable that one does not have to dig too deeply to find the same kinds of ambiguities and open-endedness in other religious traditions, including Islam.

Perhaps my point is best stated this way: as I discover and present in this book what I consider to be compelling evidence of direct Jewish and Christian influences upon Muhammad's thinking—and, further, as I assume that his and, likely, others' thinking was indeed an important and indispensable element in the creation of the Qur'an—my argument will *not* be that such factors as these, in and of themselves, necessarily compromise or undermine the Qur'an's status as divine revelation. If the reigning traditional model of revelation in Islam is essentially that of a "vertical," downward intrusion of God's Speech as essentially alien, divine recitation, I will be working throughout this book with a different model of revelation that might well be applicable to the Qur'an. I will assume that revelation is better and more accurately conceived to be a historical, "horizontal" dynamic in which God is patiently laboring to communicate and to commune with humans. I will further assume that God accomplishes such work not in spite of, but precisely in and through, human communities of faith and discourse over time, including and perhaps especially in those communities' interactions with one another. This model obviously does not assume that divine revelation must bypass or negate the human and historical elements; indeed, it assumes quite the opposite. In the words of Roberto Tottoli in his *Biblical Prophets in the Qur'an and Muslim Literature*: "Even those who consider the Qur'an the word of God cannot ignore the fact that the Qur'an was revealed in a particular historical period and had to be comprehensible to Muhammad and his contemporaries. In this sense therefore the contents of the Qur'an can be considered as a reflection of the traditions and stories with minor or major affinity with the homologous Jewish and Christian versions, which must have been current in Arabia at the end of the sixth century."[9]

It is not as though all Muslim commentators would disagree entirely with Tottoli's point. Rahman, for instance, readily assumes that Muhammad did indeed hear of biblical stories and lore from both Jewish and Christian sources. "Muhammad insisted, nevertheless, that they were revealed to him," Rahman adds. "He was, of course, right. For, under the impact of his direct religious experience, these stories became *revelations* and were no longer mere tales."[10] Indeed, we have seen already that even the most conventional approaches to interpreting the Qur'an place significant emphasis upon the "occasion of revelation" for each surah, so the door is already opened—even if only a crack—to recognizing the historical element in the Qur'an. However, those same traditionalist readings also insist that the Qur'an is the earthly version of the "Mother of the Book," the "heavenly tablet" that exists eternally, utterly independent of human and historical considerations. In addressing this paradox, Michael Cook alludes to one solution that many Muslims find attractive: one can affirm both the eternity of the Qur'an and the reality of each surah's concrete historical setting precisely because God knows all things from eternity.[11] This would mean, essentially, that the Qur'an can fit perfectly with contingent historical situations because for God, all of history is immediately known in a kind of "eternal now." Further, the Qur'an itself offers a self-commentary on this issue: "It is a Qur'an which We have divided into parts that you may recite it with deliberation, and We revealed it piecemeal" (17:106). That is, the Qur'an exists, in eternity with God or within God's mind, as a whole and complete Book; but God divided it into a number of distinct recitations, possibly that it might be more readily committed to memory, and certainly so that its eternal truths might be more readily applicable to Muhammad's immediate circumstances. It is, after all, helpful to remember that it is first of all a recitation, or a series of recitations, that would have been spoken and heard in specific situations. The Qur'an is a set of oral performances, at least on this earth—even if in the heavens above it is also, for Muslims, a completed heavenly tablet.

For Muslims, then, the Qur'an is divine speech recited for human hearing and repetition; however, this is not the case for the Qur'an alone. We saw in chapter 2 that according to the Qur'an, Moses received a Torah and Jesus received a Gospel that were equally revelatory, equally representative of the Mother of the Book in heaven. Any significant differences that may now exist between the Qur'an and these books of the Jews and the Christians are attributed to the latter groups' having distorted and even intentionally perverted the message of revelation. This may be the appropriate place to expand our considerations beyond that *Taurat* and that *Injil* to Islam's broad yet fundamental affirmation of multiple revelations given to a host of prophets. "We have sent you forth in truth as a bearer of good news and a warner," Muhammad hears. "There is no nation to whom a warner has not come and gone" (Q 35:24).[12] Of course, for the Qur'an all of these revelations were, at least in original form, like pages lifted from the Mother of the Book, the well-guarded heavenly tablet. Hence, all revelations given to all true prophets are in essence the same revelation. Allah's recitation toward Muhammad invariably sounds the proposition "We never sent a Messenger before you to whom we did not reveal, 'There is no God but I; therefore serve Me'" (Q 21:25).

While the particular occasions of revelation to every prophet might require certain nuances or emphases in one prophet's message lacking in another's, the underlying conviction of the Qur'an is that the message has been the same throughout the centuries. In Surah 2, known as "The Cow," we read of a sentiment voiced by the competing Peoples of the Book: "They say: 'If you become Jews or Christians, you shall be well-guided.'" To reply to their claims, Muhammad is instructed, "Say: 'Rather, we follow the religion of Abraham, who was upright and no polytheist.'" Since Abraham predated both Moses and Jesus, the Qur'an argues, a revelation given to him possesses a kind of primordial and originary character. But Muhammad does not stop simply by claiming Muslim lineage to Abraham. Rather, all of the prophets stand in this lineage. "Say: 'We believe in Allah, in what has been revealed to us, what was revealed to Abraham, Ishma'il, Isaac, Jacob and the Tribes, and in what was imparted to Moses, Jesus and the other Prophets from their Lord, making no distinction between any of them, and to Him we submit'" (Q 2:135–36).

Indeed, the title prophet (*nabi*) is assigned to a considerable number of men by the Qur'an, including not only some figures from the Jewish Tanakh who are not generally considered prophets within Judaism but also some nonbiblical figures whose names and stories were part of the Arabic folkloric milieu. Among the names familiar to most biblical readers, in addition to Abraham, Moses, and Jesus, are Noah, Ishmael, Isaac, Jacob, Aaron, David,

Solomon, Elijah, Lot, Joseph, and Zechariah. Even Adam is often honored as a prophet in the development of Muslim tradition; at most, however, the Qur'an identifies Adam as the genealogical head of a chain of prophets that culminates in the "house of 'Imran," the family of Mary the mother of Jesus. The nonbiblical prophets of the Arabic region—whose names and exploits presumably were at least somewhat familiar to Muhammad and his audience—were Hud (who preached to the people 'Ad), Salih (prophet to the Thamud), and Shu'ayb (whose people were the Madyan). The Qur'an certainly is consistent: most of the stories associated with these prophets revolve around the call to submit to the one true God, a warning of punishment for those who refuse the call, and finally the punishment that had been threatened. Of course, often the rehearsal of these earlier prophets' message, falling generally on deaf ears, functioned as the background and precursor for Muhammad's own prophetic experience. Just as Muhammad was maligned, ignored, and rejected, so too were most of the prophets before him. The recitation of the fates of all these hardhearted peoples of earlier times, then, would have been intended to encourage a more receptive response among Muhammad's audience. The Qur'an repeatedly issues just such a warning. Tottoli helps to make this point about how the experiences of the earlier prophets provided a meaningful context for Muhammad's own difficulties: "These stories of punishment were revealed when the prophet Muhammad was a Meccan, and thus in the first phase of his prophetic mission, when his message was openly derided and rejected by the majority of his fellow citizens. The vivid description of the efforts and the fruitless proclamations of Noah, Abraham, Lot and Moses . . . mirrors the substantial lack of success of Muhammad among the pagans of Mecca."[13]

In subsequent chapters we will explore some of these prophetic figures from the Bible and observe more closely the extent to which their experiences are framed in terms highly suggestive of Muhammad's own controversies as a prophet among often recalcitrant people. One of the many fascinating facets of reading the Qur'an, in fact, is to give attention to the variety of objections and criticisms that some of Muhammad's listeners apparently threw his way. I conclude this chapter with a few of the more common catcalls, all of which offer us glimpses into that social world, along with brief comment:

- "This is nothing but fables of the ancients" (6:25).

This criticism, in effect, was that Muhammad was not offering anything particularly new. "We've heard all this before." But "fables of the ancients" goes a step further and implies that Muhammad simply is repeating stories— presumably biblical and otherwise—with which everyone was familiar. Of course, there is a good deal of truth in this criticism; after all, the Qur'an itself regularly quizzes its hearers, "Have you not heard?" to introduce a biblical narrative. Obviously, much of this book is predicated on the Qur'an's fascinating retelling of biblical stories. Thus, the point of the Qur'an could not be that it is *not* reciting "fables of the ancients" but that it is putting those "fables" or tales to a very specific purpose. That purpose is to be a "book of guidance" to humanity.

- "Allah has not revealed anything to a mortal" (6:91).

This objection bears a more distinctly theological or philosophical tone. It is a straightforward denial of divine revelation. The obvious implication is that any prophetlike figure, including Muhammad, is either lying or deluded. It is a denial not of God but of the *kind of God* that would actually devote significant attention or energy to communicating with human beings. Of course, it would not be difficult to combine these first two criticisms: "God doesn't send anything down to us, and you don't prove otherwise since all you do is repeat the old stories." But allow me to reiterate a central idea of this book: such a bifurcation between divine revelation and human history and cultures is unnecessary and, in my opinion, religiously and theologically naive. As Alan Dundes has put it, "The presence of ancient fables in the Qur'an (and in the Bible) in no way diminishes the religious or moral value of these great sacred documents. Quite the contrary, the presence of folklore is a guarantee of their basic humanity, and, if one chooses to believe so, their divine character."[14] If divine revelation does occur, it cannot occur otherwise than in and through the gritty historical realities of human thought, language, and lore.

- "We will not believe, until we are given the like of what Allah's Messengers have been given" (6:124).

It is difficult not to feel some sympathy for this one. "Why should I believe that *you* received a revelation? Why can't God talk to me as you say God talks to you?" This is a difficult objection and reaches into the heart of any religious tradition's claim to having received a unique revelation from a divine source. In the words of Mohammad Iqbal, "Are we in possession of a test which would reveal [a religious experience's] validity? If personal experience had been the only ground for acceptance of judgment of this kind, religion would have been the possession of a few individuals only."[15] Further, the phrase "the like of what God's Messengers were given" points, presumably, toward an experience of divine communication that the recipient *could not deny*—not, at least, during the experience itself. Thus, in a sense Muhammad's objectors, with this challenge, were insisting upon a self-validating communication experience from God. Such an experience would presumably move the recipient from a standpoint of faith to a standpoint of sure knowledge—but on a radically individualistic basis. It is much like the atheist on the street insisting that he will not believe in God unless and until God shows up at his front door. Yet a troubling question remains: How could anyone know for certain that any supposed experience of God truly is an experience of God? Could there be a self-validating experience that reduces all doubts, ambiguities, and questions to dust and ashes, à la Job?

Perhaps more importantly: Would any human being really, truly covet such an experience?

5

ADAM: WHAT DOES IT MEAN TO BE HUMAN?

> We have revealed it as an Arabic Qur'an and expounded therein in detail some of our warnings, so that they may fear God, and so that it may be a reminder for them. Exalted be Allah, the True King. Do not hasten the Qur'an before its revelation to you is complete, and say: "Lord, increase me in knowledge." And We commanded Adam before, but he forgot, and We found in him no firm resolve.
>
> —Qur'an 20:113–15

I sat in a small, unpretentious office at a table with three other men. One, Ziwa, was my guide—"the best guide in town," he called himself. Another, Muhammad, served as translator. The third was Shekh, the imam or clerical director of the Muslim Studies Center where I was visiting. It was the summer of 2004, and I was in the Kenyan coastal town of Lamu, a thoroughly charming fishing village on the Indian Ocean. On this unforgettable Saturday morning, I had been granted an audience with the imam to talk about the Qur'an—and especially about its portrayal of the primal human, Adam.

"Are you familiar with how the story of Adam is told in the Bible, in the book of Genesis?" I asked.

No, they shook their heads. Apparently it was not their practice to read the Bible and the Qur'an side by side.

"Let me tell you a little about it."

They seemed amenable to my proposition. They were not threatened; they did, after all, have the home-field advantage in our little dialogue.

"In the second chapter of Genesis, it says that God first made Adam alone. Then, after seeing that it wasn't a good thing for the human to be alone, God said that he would make a partner, a helper, for this human."

My listeners sat unfazed.

"So God began to make all the other animals out of the dirt of the ground, everything—bears, lions, giraffes, gazelles, and so on—and brought them to the human. Genesis says that God brought them to the human to see what he would name them—"

I figured that would get a reaction. I was right. If God brought the animals to the human being "to see what he would name them," the lurking implication is that God did not yet know what names the human would invent. The very hint of the notion that God would not know with absolute certainty every detail of the world, including details regarding the future, had them looking at me askance.

"—and Genesis says that whatever name the man gave to each creature, that was its name. God apparently was interested to see what the human would name them, but whatever name he came up with for each kind of creature, that was its name, no questions asked." (I wasn't sure how Muhammad our translator would render that last phrase, but felt confident he'd find something roughly equivalent.)

My new acquaintances now looked at me like I was crazy. They were shaking their heads as if to say, "That cannot be right. Allah is nothing like this story depicts."

I told them that in this Genesis story it seems as though it was only after God created all these creatures, and Adam gave them names, that God recognized that none of these creatures could really be the human's life-partner. Only then did God create the woman, Eve, out of a rib that God removed from the man while he was in a deep sleep.

"What do you think of this story?" I asked them. "I know how the story goes in the Qur'an, so how do you think they compare?"

Their reply was simple enough: my Bible story was a fabrication. It was wrong, and was unworthy of Allah.

I will soon attempt a careful intertextual study of the story of Adam as narrated by Genesis and the Qur'an. Before that, however, it surely cannot hurt to try to get a feel for Genesis 2 as the story was heard by my African Muslim hosts. Not unlike what we have already encountered in Genesis 18 as explored in chapter 1 of this book—the story of God's sit-down meal with Abraham—this story of Adam offers a radically anthropomorphic deity. In Genesis 2 God, like a potter, molds the *adam* (from *adamah*, "ground"), or human, followed by the rest of the animals, out of dirt; God, recognizing the human's need for companionship, ushers all these animals into his presence to find out what he would name them; finally, God makes the companion female from a rib of this solitary *adam*. It is no wonder that a vast number of Jews and Christians have seen fit not to read this story as a literal or straightforwardly historical depiction of the earliest human beings. Surely the story itself begs to be read metaphorically or symbolically.

This is not to deny that there are certainly a great many Christians, and probably a fair number of Jews, who insist that these ancient stories of humanity's creation are historically factual accounts. However, among academically trained theologians and Bible scholars such people are exceedingly rare. I for one (among many others) certainly avoid a literalist interpretation of the early chapters of Genesis. This of course does not at all necessarily entail that these stories do not contain great and deep truths about God the Creator, as well as about human beings in their relations to God, one another, and the rest of creation. Just as it is not necessary for Jesus's parables to be historical depictions of things that really happened and of people who actually existed in order for them to depict the nature of the kingdom of God, so we may similarly approach the creation stories of Genesis. Deep truths are given to us in these stories, but they are not the truths of scientific knowledge.

I mention this in order to emphasize that when we compare the Bible's and the Qur'an's stories of Adam's naming of the animals, the point is not to decide which story is the more historically accurate—even though there are Christians today (and probably some Jews) who would insist precisely on this point as the virtue of Genesis 2, just as there are many Muslims who would make the same claim of factual exactitude for the Qur'an's description in Surah 2 of God's creation of the first humans. Our intent will be to ponder the stories not as historical descriptions of long ago events but as theological narratives. Our purpose is to reflect theologically on the stories, to ask about how God is construed, how human beings are depicted, and perhaps most importantly how the relationship between God and creation is imagined, in these stories. I will then attempt to trace out of these stories some of the fundamental theological convictions of Islam, Judaism, and Christianity regarding what it means to be human. And so, back to the texts:

The Bible	The Qur'an
Genesis 1:26	*Surah 2:30a*
Then God said, "Let us make humankind [*adam*, "earthling"] in our image, according to our likeness; and let them have dominion over the fish of the sea, and over the birds of the air, and over the cattle, and over all the wild animals of the earth, and over every creeping thing that creeps upon the earth."	Behold, your Lord said to the angels, "I will create a vicegerent [*khalifa*] on earth."

Most of our story, as far as the Bible goes, is found in Genesis 2. However, in order to appreciate fully the dynamics of these texts, we must begin with the opening chapter of Genesis. In verse 26 God (*elohim*) announces the divine intention to create humanity, male and female, in the divine image. Of course, a lot of ink has been spilled in the history of Jewish and Christian interpretation regarding the meaning of humans' having been created in God's image or likeness. We should note immediately that the Qur'an and subsequent Muslim tradition have avoided this language, most presumably because it could readily lead to the conclusion that God is a physical being and thus possesses an "image" that humans could represent. Indeed, such a possibility lies not far from the language of the Genesis text. The weight of contemporary biblical scholarship suggests that the phraseology of "in our image, according to our likeness" reflects the practice of ancient political rulers' erecting statues of their likeness in the faraway reaches of their empires—precisely as a reminder to the locals of who was in charge. The language of Genesis 1 appears to draw upon common knowledge of this practice in order to portray human beings as the functional images of the Creator within the realm of creation itself, representing or standing in for their Maker.

It is clear, then, that in Genesis 1 the purpose of creating *adam*, male and female, is that these creatures might "image God," or reflect the Creator, within and toward the rest of creation. Human beings are given the responsibility of exercising divine rule and care for all of the other creatures. The point is that the "image of God" is not about humanity providing a physical resemblance of the Creator; rather, "image of God" denotes a function, a vocation, of re-presenting or standing in for God in the created order. This becomes most obvious in Psalm 8, a hymn celebrating the human role in God's creation: "You have given them dominion over the works of your hands; you have put all things under their feet, all sheep and oxen, and also the beasts of the field, the birds of the air, and the fish of the sea, whatever passes along the paths of the seas" (Ps. 8:6–8). To exercise "dominion" is to undertake the divine task of ruling in God's behalf, of further ordering God's created order.

When the biblical language of "the image of God" is interpreted in this way, we find that it is virtually identical to what the Qur'an teaches: the human is a "vicegerent" or designated representative (*khalifa*, or caliph) for the Creator. "Have you not seen how Allah has subjected to you whatever is in the heavens and on earth . . . ?" (Q 31:20). The biblical and qur'anic traditions, accordingly, emphasize the ennobling yet sobering responsibility of human beings to represent the very presence and rule of God toward all other creatures. While these traditions (especially the biblical[1]) have often been criticized for having given license to human beings to rule over creation with an iron fist—that is, to treat the earth and its resources rapaciously, consumptively, and destructively—there certainly is no good reason to think that either Genesis or the Qur'an should be interpreted in this way. One could just as readily argue that (1) if humans are called by God to function as God's vicegerent or representative, it is obvious that they do not occupy a position of absolute rulership or ownership but instead one of responsibility to the Creator to maintain the beauty and goodness of the creation; and (2) if these holy writings portray God as One who not only creates but also loves and possibly even enjoys the creation, then for humans to "image" or reflect this God would require of them to nurture God's creation, to practice a life-sustaining ecology in their attitudes, actions, and habits of living. In Seyyed Hossein Nasr's words, "Human beings must be perfectly passive toward Heaven as the servant or slave of God, and active toward the world around them as God's vicegerent on earth. To be truly human is to receive in perfect submission from God and to give to creation as the central channel of grace for the created order."[2] All of creation ultimately belongs to God, and not to human beings, into whose care planet Earth is entrusted.

Surah 2:30b

They said, "Will You place therein one who will make mischief therein and shed blood?—While we do celebrate Your praises and glorify Your holy name?" He said: "I know that which you do not know."

This slice of narrative stands alone in the Qur'an, for in the opening chapter of Genesis there is no explicit mention of angels. While we shall examine this fact more closely later, it is important to recognize that angels do appear in rabbinic interpretation of Genesis 1 precisely in order to deal with the problem of the One God's saying something like "Let us make humanity in our image . . ." It helps to have someone to whom God can address such words as these!

The angels of this qur'anic passage uncharacteristically raise some unsettling questions about the wisdom of creating this *khalifa* to stand in as Allah's representative in the earth—a representative who, the angels correctly anticipate, will not represent the Creator to creation well at all but instead "will make mischief therein and shed blood." Meanwhile, Allah's angels protest that they are already much better muslims (i.e., submitters to God) in their faithful worship of God than these proposed human beings will be.

It is noteworthy that the shedding of blood is specifically mentioned by the angels as the sort of deed that Allah's proposed representative-creatures will commit. Judaic studies scholar John Reeves writes, "A major question generated by this formulation of the text is whether the Qur'an envisions a specific narrative event or sequence of such events when it represents the angels condemning humanity for its impending 'corruption of the earth' and the 'shedding of blood.'"[3] But perhaps there is no great mystery here; after all, the Qur'an essentially follows the Genesis narrative in telling the story of Cain's primordial murder of his brother Abel.[4] Thus, the shedding of blood is not far down the road. Even so, Reeves's observation is noteworthy, for it is precisely in the sense that Cain's murder of his brother is a primordial or foundational deed that it functions as the wellspring of the long history of human rivalry and violence. Simply put, the angels would seem to have a point.

Indeed, there is at least a hint of rivalry already here in the qur'anic passage. I do not mean, however, the rivalry among humans but the implicit one between the Creator and the angelic beings. If they seem a bit put off by Allah's intentions, Allah's rejoinder is an assertion of his superior knowledge: "I know that which you do not know." In terms of the qur'anic narrative structure, this divine reply obviously sets up the next part of the story, while at the same time indicating decisively the unquestionably superior wisdom of God.

The Bible	The Qur'an
Genesis 2:18–20	*Surah 2:31a*
Then the LORD God said, "It is not good that the man [*adam*] should be alone; I will make him a helper as his partner." So out of the ground the LORD God formed every animal of the field and every bird of the air, and brought them to the man to see what he would call them; and whatever the man called each living creature, that	
was its name. The man gave names to	And He taught Adam the names of all
all cattle, and to the birds of the air,	things.
and to every animal of the field; but for the man there was not found a helper as his partner."	

In the text of Genesis, we have now moved from the first to the second chapter. More significantly, we have moved from one creation story to another. The indications of two distinct stories are many, obvious, and commonly assumed among biblical scholars. For example, in the first narrative (1:1–2:4a) God is identified as *elohim*, in the second as *yahweh elohim*. In the first, God creates by the sheer power of speaking, "Let there be"; in the second, God is portrayed much more as a down-to-earth artisan, planting a garden and fashioning Earth's creatures out of the dirt. In the first, God crowns each day's work with the divine satisfaction of "it is good" and the story culminates in the sabbath; in the second, there is no succession of days at all, let alone mention of a sabbath, and it is not long before God announces that something is *not* good: "It is not good that the man [*adam*] should be alone" (Gen. 2:18). Again, we find that many of the biblical passages that give evidence of having come from what scholars call the *yahwist* source—passages that explicitly identify God by the name Yahweh—tend to portray God in strong anthropomorphisms. So it is here. Yet I have also pointed out (in chapter 1) that this name *yahweh* (or *YHWH*) has been deemed by Jewish tradition to be God's unspeakably holy name, so sacrosanct as to be unspeakable by human lips. Hence, the Hebrew term *Adonai*, generally translated as "Lord" (and in most English translations styled "Lord"), has functioned as the acceptable replacement term. (So shall I also utilize Adonai throughout the remainder of the chapter, and generally throughout the book when signifying the divine holy name.)

The folksy contours of the creation story in Genesis 2 make it all the more attractive to read it symbolically instead of literally—how long, for example, would it have taken the *adam* to name all those creatures, freshly dredged up out of the earth? In fact, it is both inviting and fruitful to read it as a picturesque commentary on the kind of activity that is characteristic of us humans. We have developed languages to help us to communicate with one another, but also and equally to *name our worlds*—to bring order to our experience of the world with classifications, labels, defining characteristics of things. This is not a task undertaken by a solitary human in a single day; it is the ongoing labor of us all as we strive to comprehend the wonderful and mysterious world in which we live. Particularly when we recognize the importance of the act of bestowing names in the ancient Near Eastern cultures, the fact that this biblical narrative consciously recognizes naming as a uniquely human task is worthy of attention. To name is to assign meaning, to read into a thing its function and destiny; it is profoundly to bring order to, and make sense of, those things that become named. As Harvey Cox wrote in *The Secular City*, "The passage [in Genesis 2] indicates that man has a crucial part to play in the creation of the world. The world is not really finished, not really 'the world' until its components are 'named.'. . . Here is a truly exalted view of man. God does not simply insert man into a world filled with creatures that are already named, in relationships and meaning patterns already established by decree. Man must fashion them himself."[5]

Indeed, Genesis 2 announces not only that God has given to human beings the task of naming the world and its creatures; there is also that delightfully evocative detail that Adonai brought the creatures to the human *to see what he would name them.* We sense here more than a hint of divine curiosity about what humans will do, and of course this narrative detail points the reader toward a sense of openness about the future. Such a future is not a fixed series of events, even for God. God offers the task of naming the elements of creation to the human, giving *adam* such room and freedom as to make, and keep, the human project in the world an open vista. In Genesis 2 there are no "right" names, no divinely prescribed meanings for the world and its creatures; there is instead a radically human vocation to contribute to God's activity of creation by the acts of observation, discovery, naming, and meaning-making.

We should bear in mind that in the qur'anic version, God's act of teaching the human the properly divine names of things—the utterly correct names— follows God's confident reply "I know that which you do not know" to the murmuring angels. Indeed, God's superior knowledge is demonstrated on two levels: God knows the true and proper names for each and every thing, and God knows that God can (and will) instruct Adam regarding these names. "Allah knows best," as the Qur'an teaches Muslims to confess—and the narrative world construed by this text dramatically demonstrates Allah's certain knowledge. Further, it is possible that Allah's reply functions to assure the angels (and us) that, even while acknowledging that humans will "make mischief" and "shed blood," God knows more, knows better, that there are other values made possible by their creation.

It is obvious that this pair of narratives from the Bible and the Qur'an create differing theological trajectories. In Genesis, Adonai appears all-too-human—but this portrayal also connotes the human powers of intellect, creativity, and language. Given such powers to name and to shape the world, the future becomes open to a rich set of possibilities; even the world's Maker is interested in seeing how things will develop. In the Qur'an's version, on the other hand, it is precisely the greatness and superior knowledge of God that find expression.

Let us remember what this difference would entail for the dominant interpretive tradition within Islam. Since all revelation that God has bestowed through the prophets is essentially *the same,* and since the Qur'an is the final and authoritative arbiter of all religious disputes, it is obvious that when the Bible and the Qur'an diverge, it is the Qur'an that is the correct book, the corrective for all religious error. The unavoidable assumption for the traditional Muslim reader is that, in its original form as divine revelation, the story in Genesis must have been very much like (if not identical to) the version of the story in the Qur'an. Further, this would nudge one toward the conclusion that at some point in history prior to Muhammad, there were Jews who had perverted the story of Adam into the form in which we now have it in Genesis 2. Why would such distortions have been foisted upon the text? Presumably to defame God, to blight God's majesty and power—and at the same time to aggrandize the human being's role in the world.

Surah 2:31b–34

Then He placed them before the angels, and said, "Tell Me the names of these if you are [so] right." They said: "Glory to You! We have no knowledge, except what You have taught us. In truth it is You who are perfect in knowledge and wisdom." He said: "O Adam! Tell [the angels] the names [of the creatures]." When he had told them, Allah said: Did I not tell you that I know the secrets of heaven and earth, and I know what you reveal and what you conceal?"

And behold, We said to the angels: "Bow down to Adam," and they bowed down, except for Iblis. He refused and was haughty, and he was of those who reject faith.

Again, there is in Genesis no passage corresponding to God's challenge to the angels as described in the qur'anic passage above. The Qur'an's emphasis lies on the angels' confessed inability to render the correct names for all the creatures God places before them: "Glory to You! We have no knowledge, except what You have taught us." Once more the Qur'an proclaims God's power, knowledge, and unsurpassability. All the more surprising, then, that God would then command the angels to bow in prostration before Adam. Such obeisance, presumably, would rightly be directed only toward God. However, given that the angels had earlier been quick to voice their doubts about the wisdom of making such a creature to be God's caliph or vicegerent upon the earth, in God's demand that the angels now bow before Adam perhaps a sort of poetic justice is served.[6] The point in the Qur'an's version of the story is to magnify God's honor and wisdom and to serve as a reminder that God "know[s] what you reveal and what you conceal."

In the light of the Qur'an's telling of Adam's story, it may not be entirely surprising that Christian theologian A. Christian van Gorder would write that in Islamic teaching "humanity is uncreative and has no capacity to fashion anything separate from God. Orthodox Islam condemned the *Qadariyya* [or 'Qadarites'], the only sect in Muslim theological history who held that individuals had some power to innovate. If humanity is creative in any way, then there would be other 'Creators.' This is impossible within the framework of Islamic theology."[7] .

The great Muslim thinker Fazlur Rahman, on the other hand, writes of the same story that God "brought about a competition between angels and Adam, asking the former to 'name things' (to describe their natures). When the angels could not do so, Adam could. This demonstrated that Adam possessed the capacity for creative knowledge that angels lacked, whereupon God asked all the angels to prostrate themselves before him to honor him."[8]

While I am not without sympathy for Rahman's proposed reading of the passage, it is difficult to find in the Qur'an's telling of the story of Adam any significant affirmation of humanity's "capacity for creative knowledge." It may well be found in other passages, but is exceedingly difficult to discern here. For in this passage we read that Allah *taught* the human the right names of the creatures; all that Adam needed to be able to do was to "recite" what he was taught. Adam is as passive in this story as Muhammad is believed to have been during the process of receiving revelation, at least as that process is understood by most traditional Muslims. Consider, again, these words of the angels: "We have no knowledge, except what You have taught us. In truth it is You who are perfect in knowledge and wisdom." Since God is perfect in knowledge and wisdom, only God can give the correct names to things, for only God knows what each thing truly is. "In Islam, . . . Adam is the father of the prophets," Isma'il Ragi al Faruqi wrote. "He received his learning directly from God, and in this he was superior to the angels to whom he taught the 'names' (i.e., essences, definitions) of the creatures."[9] Just as the angels "have no knowledge, except what [God has] taught" them, so also it is for Adam in this story. Contrary to Rahman's more human-centered reading, there is no clear indication here of a "capacity for creative knowledge that angels lacked"; the only difference that the qur'anic narrative marks between angels and humans is that God was pleased to teach Adam the names of everything.

It likely is preferable to find a happy medium between van Gorder the Christian and Rahman the Muslim. Surely it is not correct to say with van Gorder that Islam has thoroughly discouraged the spirit of human adventure and creativity. Surely too it is a stretching of the Qur'an to argue that in this story we encounter a clear testimony to human creativity and freedom. Perhaps a mediating position is found in the insightful reflections of Mohammad Iqbal. In *The Reconstruction of Religious Thought* Iqbal first argues that "the point of these verses is that man is endowed with the faculty of naming things, that is to say, forming concepts of them, and forming concepts of them is capturing them."[10] Not surprisingly, in his modernist leanings Iqbal desires to portray—or, perhaps truer to his title, to reconstruct—Islam as a tradition that validates human conceptual and linguistic capacities. In his interpretation of the Adam story in Surah 2, Iqbal affirms and even celebrates human creativity. Yet later in the same book Iqbal betrays a different reading of the story, writing of "Adam's superiority over the angels in remembering and reproducing the names of things."[11] To *re*member, to *re*produce, is not to create but to imitate. In this second allusion to Adam's naming of things, Iqbal gravitates toward the portrait of the human as passive recipient rather than creative actor. It is as though Iqbal cannot consistently uphold such a celebration of human freedom and creativity as he would like; the gravity of a more traditionalist Islamic position, rooted in the Qur'an's retelling of Adam's story, is more than he can resist. In Iqbal, then, we detect an important tension in Islamic interpretation of the Qur'an—a tension between the celebration of human ability and the subjugation of the human before the utterly sovereign God. Certainly the latter has received the far greater emphasis in Muslim tradition. As Sayyid Abul A'la Mawdudi has written, "The nature of man's knowledge is such that he acquires information of different things through their names. Hence it might be said that the sum total of man's knowledge consists of the names of things. To teach Adam the names of all things means, therefore, imparting the knowledge of those things."[12]

Mawdudi's assertion that we acquire information about things through their names is debatable. It certainly appears to overlook the fact that most names of things are created, at least to some extent, as a result of certain observable characteristics or functions. In other words, names do not carry information nearly so much as information suggests names. However, if one were to assume that in fact names bear a certain priority, and were to assume further that God taught Adam the names of all things, then it would indeed be the case that God "impart[ed] the knowledge of those things." Knowledge in this case would not be a human achievement or project gleaned through observation and collective experience over time; it would instead be imparted to humanity in word-packages that God has imparted. One encounters a similar, indeed even more radical, sentiment in Mawdudi's rhetorical question: "Who has harnessed countless powers and energies for the service of man, oil and electricity, sunlight and atomic forces—man or God?"[13] Of course, the expected reply to his rhetorical question is "God"—but in fact it is human beings who have undertaken to learn how to "harness" these and other energies "for the service of man." Presumably God the Creator does not "harness" energies at all; that sort of activity is left to us.

Were I pressed to choose the version of the story that I believe better coincides with—and sheds truer light upon—human history and the human task in the world, I would not hesitate to opt for Genesis. One need not (and, I think, should not) take the story literally in order to appreciate its ancient, and recognizably primitive, portrayal of human responsibility, creativity, and need for companionship. By the same token, its construal of God as limited in knowledge, a Creator who is uncertain regarding the world's immediate future, should not be read simply at face value. Indeed, we must first appreciate the real differences between the two creation stories that together provide the genesis of Genesis. Unlike *elohim* of Genesis 1, by whom everything in creation is judged to be "good," *yahweh* of Genesis 2 can say of something in creation, "It is not good" (2:18). In this second creation story Adonai brings the creatures to the *adam* in order to see what he will name them, and it is only after this naming exercise is complete that it becomes obvious to all—including Adonai, apparently—that none of these nonhuman creatures will be able to function as an adequate life-partner to the *adam*. This may be the most fitting place to invoke the rabbinic proviso "Had Scripture not written [this], it would not have been permissible [for us] to say this."[14] No wonder my African Muslim acquaintances shook their heads in bewilderment at the yarn that is woven in Genesis 2. And yet what a lovely narrative rendering of God's openness to new possibilities, perhaps even to surprises, in our world of human creativity and open futures.

I believe it difficult to avoid the likelihood that in this story of Adam's naming of the animals we confront another case in which subsequent Jewish interpretation of the story helped to pave the way for the Qur'an's version. A general schema of the relation among these texts would go like this:

The Genesis story → gives rise to a body of interpretation → that influences the Quran's retelling of the story.

I must reiterate that, from my perspective, the above scenario should not—or at least need not—be seen as dismissing the Qur'an or denying its revelatory potential. Nevertheless, Muslim tradition mitigates against this scenario on two counts: first, its dominant understanding of revelation gives very little, if any, role to streams of human history or tradition that might be seen as having influenced Muhammad; second, the qur'anic version of any story is assumed to be *the correct and even infallible version* of the story. If the Qur'an has details the Bible does not, then the Qur'an is assumed to be correcting (or at least complementing) the biblical version of the story—even if it turns out that many of the Qur'an's extra details are found somewhere in the body of Jewish interpretive material that arose after the writing of the biblical text and prior to the time of Muhammad. So it is again with the story of Adam's naming of the animals. Let us return to the story, this time setting the qur'anic version alongside the body of rabbinic interpretive material, gathered and collated at least two centuries before Muhammad's time, called *Genesis Rabbah*:

The Rabbis	The Qur'an
Genesis Rabbah	*Surah 2:30a*
R. Aha said: When the Holy One, blessed be He, came to create Adam, He took	
counsel with the ministering angels,	Behold, your Lord said to the angels,
saying to them, "Let us make man."	"I will create a vicegerent on earth."

In the rabbinic commentary we find an attempt to solve the problem of the plural language of Genesis 1:26, "Let us make . . ." God, the rabbis said, was discussing the matter of creating humanity with "the ministering angels." To be sure, no angels are explicitly mentioned in the actual text of Genesis 1, but the rabbis, intent on solidifying Jewish monotheism, found this to be a relatively handy solution. This rabbinic speculation about the "let us" of Genesis as signifying God and the angels was later to gain canonical status, we might say, with the writing of the Qur'an. Thus: God announced to the angels God's intention to create human beings.

Genesis Rabbah	*Surah 2:30:b*
"What will be the nature of this man?"	They said, "Will You place therein one who
they inquired.	will make mischief therein and shed blood?—While we do celebrate Your praises and glorify Your holy name?"
"His wisdom will exceed yours," He said.	He said: "I know that which you do not know."

The structural similarities between the two passages are unmistakable and unavoidable. In both narratives, the angels ask God a pointed question about the proposed human creatures, and God replies sharply—perhaps even dismissing the question. In Jacob Neusner's analysis, God's answer as imagined by the rabbis "represents a stunning rejection of the angels and affirmation of man."[15] The qur'anic version has a stronger, more obvious suggestion of tension between the angels and God, to be sure—but it is not difficult to detect in it an elaboration of the tension already lurking in the rabbinic tradition. Further, in both *Genesis Rabbah* and the Qur'an the divine-angelic interchange serves structurally to set up the Adamic action to follow.

Surah 2:31a
And He taught Adam the names of all things.

Interestingly enough, while the Qur'an offers this significant detail regarding God as Adam's instructor, a notion to which I have already given extensive attention, the rabbinic commentary on Genesis—like Genesis itself—is silent. It is in the Qur'an that we encounter an Adam who is utterly dependent upon God's teaching, thoroughly passive as the recipient of the true names and natures of all things. We recall Nasr's words: "Human beings must be perfectly passive toward Heaven as the servant or slave of God, and active toward the world around them as God's vicegerent on earth. To be truly human is to receive in perfect submission from God."[16]

Genesis Rabbah	Surah 2:31b–32
What did the Lord do? He brought the animals, beasts, and birds before [the angels] and asked them, "What should be the name of this?" but they did not know; "and of this?" and they did not know.	Then He placed them before the angels, and said, "Tell Me the names of these if you are [so] right." They said: "Glory to You! We have no knowledge, except what You have taught us. In truth it is You who are perfect in knowledge and wisdom."

Again, here we find a significant structural similarity between the narratives, the only difference (as before) being the Qur'an's heightened sense of tension, even rivalry, between God and the angels. This heightened tension, in turn, fairly demands a more dramatic resolution of the tension in terms of the angelic response. "In truth," cry the qur'anic angels, "it is You who are perfect in knowledge and wisdom." We should note that this conviction regarding God's perfect knowledge is far from unique to Islam. It is readily discoverable in other biblical passages as well as in traditional Judaism and Christianity. The immediate point, however, is that the notion of God's possessing perfect knowledge of all things seems to be foreign to this particular biblical story of Adam's naming of the creatures.

Genesis Rabbah	Surah 2:33
Then He paraded them before Adam, and asked him, "What is the name of this?" "An ox." And this? "A camel."	He said: "O Adam! Tell [the angels] the names [of the creatures]." When he had told them, Allah said: Did I not tell you that I

Genesis Rabbah	Surah 2:33
And of this? "An ass." And this? "A horse." Thus it is written, "And the man gave names to all cattle," etc. (2:20). He said to him, "And what is your name?" "It is fitting that I be called Adam, because I was created from the ground [*adamah*]," he replied. "And what is My name?" "It is fitting for You to be called *Adonai* [LORD], since You are Lord over all Your creatures," was the answer.	know the secrets of heaven and earth, and I know what you reveal and what you conceal?"

In rereading the qur'anic version, we should recall that the Qur'an is given as "guidance" to humanity, as spiritual and moral instruction. In this case, the guidance is a solemn reminder that only God knows "the secrets of heaven and earth"—and thus, more importantly, only God knows the secrets of the human heart. The rabbinic extrapolation of Genesis, on the other hand, remains near to the Bible's narrative logic: Adam is asked to name the creatures, and does so. Further, the names Adam creates are "fitting," that is, appropriate to each creature. Adam even names himself, acknowledging that he comes from the *adamah*—though apparently the rabbis overlooked the problem of who named the ground! The point, though, is that their expansion of the Genesis 2 story underscores the truth that humanity is entrusted with the task of creating language, of crafting words appropriate to human experience of the world. Indeed, the rabbis go a bold step beyond Genesis by imagining that God even allows Adam the power and responsibility to give the Creator a name—"*Adonai*, since You are *Lord* over all Your creatures."

The profound observation in the rabbinic reconstruction of Genesis 2 is that, in fact, we human beings do create names for things, including ourselves—and even names for God, the Maker of all those things. The human task and art of theology is to engage in the quest to "name God" as accurately, as adequately, as we can. We may believe that God has given us help in this task through the gift of revelation. But as we have seen in earlier chapters, any help that God may give will inevitably be in the form of words from the stammering tongues of mere humans. In the qur'anic retelling of this rabbinic story, only God knows the true and best name for each thing; for Genesis 2 and many of the rabbis who reflected on its narrative, God bequeaths the task of naming—and of naming even God's own self—to those stammering human tongues. This is remarkable.

93

Genesis Rabbah

Then he paraded them again before him in pairs, [male and female]. Adam said, "Everyone has a partner, but I have none"; thus, "But for Adam there was not found a help suitable for him." And why did He not create her for him at the beginning? Because the Holy One, blessed be He, foresaw that [Adam] would bring charges against her; therefore He did not create her until he expressly demanded her. But as soon as he did, so, forthwith, "The LORD God caused a deep sleep to fall upon the man, and he slept" (2:21).

As the rabbis tell the story, God's making of the woman only after Adam's presumably arduous task of naming all the creatures is actually a piece of some wise planning. It is safe to assume that they did not deem it worthy of divine wisdom to imagine God operating by trial and error in the search for a suitable partner for Adam. Yet it appears on the first reading of Genesis 2 that God's creation of all the other creatures actually was in hopes of finding just that sort of partner for the *adam*. Taken literally, is not the story laughable? Surely sex differentiation in humanity, male and female, was no jerry-rigged afterthought on God's part! Surely God knew all along what God would do to address Adam's loneliness! Hence, these rabbis who did indeed take the story literally—even as they also took considerable interpretive liberties—were bound to add narrative details in order to render a more godlike portrait of God. Thus: "Why did He not create her for him at the beginning?" Because God "foresaw that he would bring charges against her," which is what occurs only a chapter later in Genesis. In response to God's interrogation regarding his having eaten of the tree of the knowledge of good and evil, Adam defensively replies, "The woman whom you gave to be with me, she gave me fruit from the tree, and I ate" (Gen. 3:12). Since he would so soon "bring charges against her," it was according to divine wisdom to temper Adam's latent talent for blaming others by allowing his loneliness to reach desperation level. Though the Bible does not report Adam as lamenting, "Everyone has a partner, but I have none," the rabbis attribute this plaint to him after his long labor of naming all those creatures—in female-male pairs, no less. By so proceeding, God succeeds in ensuring that the *adam* will actually be the one making demands for a partner. Thus, when in the divinely foreseeable future this man will blame the woman for his misdeed, he will also have to admit that, in fact, he asked for her.

Surah 2:34

And behold, We said to the angels: "Bow down to Adam," and they bowed down, except for Iblis. He refused and was haughty, and he was of those who reject faith.

94

The refusal of Iblis, or Satan, to bow prostrate before Adam is not found in Genesis Rabbah, our source for rabbinic commentary on Genesis. The story is, however, found in other strands of Jewish literature, most notably in *The Life of Adam and Eve*, roots possibly as early as the first century CE. This document identifies the serpent of Genesis 2 with Satan—an identification that would become common currency in Christian tradition—and speculates as to the reason for Satan's opposition to human beings. Centuries before Muhammad's time, *The Life of Adam and Eve* explains that the angels worshiped the image of God, Adam, but that Satan had refused to do so. God, in turn, cast out the rebellious Satan and his angelic followers from the realm of glory.[17] The point, again, need not be that the Qur'an is drawing directly upon this Jewish legend. It is sufficient to assume that the story, likely in several variations and versions, gradually became part of the Jewish interpretive milieu with which Muhammad would become familiar.

Genesis need not tell such a story of Satanic rebellion in heavenly glory, because in fact Satan does not appear anywhere at all in its creation stories. In the text of Genesis, the serpent is simply a serpent—"more crafty than any other wild animal that the Lord God had made" (Gen. 3:1)—and is never treated in the narrative as anything other or more than that. Its punishment from Adonai for having allured Adam and Eve was, apparently, to lose its legs and from then on to slither along on its belly (3:14). Of course, encounters with talking snakes are not an everyday occurrence, to put it mildly—all the more reason to read this story metaphorically, as a kind of allegory about the dynamics of human temptation in our alluring world, rather than literally. But the strand of Jewish tradition represented by *The Life of Adam and Eve* took another route, postulating a malevolent intelligence that "possessed" the serpent, enabling it to speak, so as to tempt and ruin these human beings whom God had crowned with such majesty and honor.

Speaking of temptation, it is tempting to postulate that the Qur'an's story of Satan's refusal to bow before the human developed historically out of the rabbinic story of God's conversation with the angels. If this is the case, then the angels' question of God, "What will be the nature of this man?" is only a mild precursor to the more active resistance that Satan would soon (in terms of the narrative's logic) pursue. This identification of Satan with the serpent was solidified in the New Testament book of Revelation (12:9), thereby becoming the normative reading in Christianity and, of course, later in the Qur'an as well.

Thus we encounter, again, the same problem for qur'anic hermeneutics touched upon earlier in this chapter. The Qur'an presents as pure and pristine revelation a story that is not in the Bible—but that *is* found in Jewish and

Christian elaborations on the biblical text. These retellings of biblical narrative predate the Qur'an by several centuries, and it can (and should) be readily assumed that they were elements in the formative milieu of Muhammad's culture. For the Muslim who reads the Qur'an as God's pure revelation, this presents a peculiar problem. Islam's general tendency is to assume that the Jews (and, later, Christians) received a pure and inerrant revelation that only later became corrupted. Yet the stories of God's consultation with angels before the creation of humanity, as well as of Satan's rebellious refusal to bow down before the human, are later developments or elaborations of the biblical texts. No biblical scholar who understands the history of these textual relationships would imagine for a moment that these stories were in the original Genesis text and were subsequently deleted. Rather, they are additions to the Genesis stories, elaborations that developed as Jewish (and, later, Christian) readers attempted to make sense of problematic textual details such as God saying "Let *us* make humanity in *our* image"—and a serpent saying anything at all. As I see it, there is no good reason to harden these playful elaborations into a harsh literalism of pure divine speech. That, unfortunately, is how the Qur'an's rendering of these stories functions for at least most Muslims.

Note how the Bible's and the Qur'an's stories of Adam naming the creatures actually mirror this issue for us. In Genesis, God brings the land creatures before Adam to see what he will name them, and whatever the human would name a creature, that was its name. The human in this story plays an active and creative role in the naming—the shaping and ordering—of God's world. The future is relatively open, such that new developments and unexpected interpretations may occur. Meanings are not preset or eternally determined in the mind of God. But in the Qur'an's telling, God teaches Adam the right names of each and every thing. Correspondingly, in Islamic teaching revelation is purely and entirely God's. There is little if any room for human naming, for human interpretation and elaboration. Whereas the Jewish or Christian scholar should in principle offer no resistance to the task of tracing historical developments in the Bible (not to mention rabbinic or other speculative interpretations like *The Life of Adam and Eve*), the Muslim understanding of the Qur'an as purely divine revelation tends strongly to inhibit—if not entirely to prohibit—historical considerations like these. Perhaps it finally comes down to the difference between the human's naming the creaturely elements of the world and God's teaching the human all the right names for those elements.

As we near the close of this chapter on what Genesis and the Qur'an mean for us as human beings, it is instructive to return to the central point of the Qur'an's telling of the story of Adam's learning the names of everything: we should recall and respect the Qur'an's self-description as a book of *guidance* for human thinking and behavior. The statement about Allah immediately preceding the story is "He has knowledge of all things" (Q 2:29); this proposition receives elaboration in the story itself when Allah says to the angels, "Did I not tell you that I know the unseen in the heavens and the earth, and that I know what you reveal and what you conceal?"(Q 2:33). If God knows the unseen realms and knows what is in the hearts of angels, then surely it is a simple thing to know human beings completely. And if God knows humans that well, then surely God knows what is good for them. Further, the Qur'an offers itself as the authoritative communication of that divinely intended good. This is the essence of Islamic anthropology, and so also of Islamic ethics.

The surah to which we have devoted our attention in this chapter bears the traditional name *Al-Baqarah*, "The Cow," because a sacrificial cow is mentioned in verses 67–73. It is by far the longest of the Qur'an's 114 surahs, containing a great deal of biblical material yet to be explored in this book. More pertinent to this chapter's conclusion, though, is that "The Cow" also contains the fundamental theological precepts of Islam: "Allah, the Last Day, the angels, the Book and the Prophets" (Q 2:177) and divine sovereignty. It also includes the "five pillars" or fundamental practices of Islam: the giving of alms to the needy (v. 177); the performance of the prescribed prayers (v. 177); fasting during the daylight hours of the month of Ramadan as a remembrance of the revealing of the Qur'an (vv. 185–87); pilgrimage to the holy city of Mecca (vv. 196–203); and, of course, as throughout the Qur'an, the confession that there is one true God (see esp. v. 284) and one final, authoritative messenger, Muhammad (v. 285).

I close with this listing of fundamental Muslim precepts and practices to underscore an exceedingly simple yet profoundly important point. For Islam, to be human is to be *muslim*—a human in submission to God, the one true God who is revealed perfectly in the words of the Qur'an. In so living, the human being fulfills the divine vocation of *khalifah*, being God's representative in and to the rest of creation: "to receive in perfect submission from God and to give to creation as the central channel of grace for the created order."[18]

6

Cain and Abel

THE COMMANDING WORD OF GOD

And recite to them in all truth the tale of Adam's two sons . . .

—Qur'an 5:27

Jews, Christians, and Muslims share in the understanding that the Creator of all things, generally identified by the term *God*, has not simply created the world and then let it go with that. Believers within these traditions all affirm, instead, that in some way(s) or another God not only makes us but also makes known to us God's will for how we should live. All of these traditions—as well as others—affirm that God's will is revealed perhaps most directly in divine commandments. The Ten Commandments (Exod. 20:1–17) provide an obvious example of this notion, but there are numerous other commandments found elsewhere in the Tanakh, the Christian Bible, and the Qur'an.

Given this fact, one of the primary aims of this chapter is to explore what I shall call *the logic of command*. Perhaps we could even call it a kind of *theologic*—the logic or line of reasoning that is implied in the common biblical and qur'anic notion that God issues certain commands to human beings. Since later in this chapter we shall reflect upon the story of Cain's murder of Abel, let us take for our example of a divine commandment the one that reads "You shall not murder."

What is the implicit logic of a commandment like "You shall not murder," under the assumption that this is an example of a command of God issued to the Israelites (Exod. 20:13)? There are several important considerations:

1. God's command that the children of Israel not commit murder implies, first of all, that it *is possible* for them to commit murder. There would be no reason for God to prohibit such a behavior were it not possible for them to pursue it.

2. God's command that the children of Israel not commit murder implies, also, that God does not will for murders to occur. To put it another way, to commit murder is to break a commandment of God, which is to disobey God's will. This implies, obviously, that it is possible for us humans to do what God does not want us do. Presumably, God would not prohibit murder if God did not desire that murders not occur.

3. These first two considerations lead to a third implication, namely, that those who are commanded by God not to murder actually are, to some extent or another, free. It is within their power both to commit murder and to refrain from murdering. Only in such a situation does God's prohibition of murder make any sense.

4. This leads to another important implication: it is possible for God not to "get what God wants" in creation. God desires that there be no murder and expresses that desire in a command. The fact that the command can be broken means that God's desires may, perhaps even frequently, go unfulfilled.

5. The command not to murder implies that God at the very least does not—and perhaps cannot—force the divine desire for a murderless world upon us human creatures. If God were simply to make us incapable of murdering—or at least make us refrain from murdering—there would be no need whatsoever to command us not to murder. But a command, even a divine command, not only cannot coerce its hearer but even implies that the hearer exercises a measure of freedom in relation to God and God's exercise of power in the world.

6. God's commanding the people of Israel not to murder makes sense only if God does not know whether or not murders, or at least what particular murders, will occur among the people. If God knows already what will occur, no commandments are necessary. To be sure, it may be argued that God knows that this command actually will affect certain future choices of people, such that fewer murders will occur because this

command is given. One might also argue that God's having issued the command makes people who do commit murders responsible for their actions and punishable by God. Hence, God could know all murders that will occur but prohibits them precisely so that murderers can be rightfully held responsible and judged. While I grant a certain logical force to such scenarios, I would argue that they dull the edge of divine commandment far too much. I will proceed on the assumption that if the future is already known by God, then there is in fact no reason for God to proceed with the charade of commanding humans to do (or not do) anything. In such a world as that, whatever will be, will be. If, on the other hand, *what God desires* is that no murders occur, this can be the case only if God does not know entirely what actually will occur. God's willing or desiring a certain state of affairs can make sense only if the future of the world is open, to a significant degree, to a variety of possibilities—depending, for example, upon whether or not people obey God's command not to murder (among a host of other factors).

7. If it were to turn out that any of the above implications was false, then in fact God's commandment "You shall not murder" is not truly a commandment after all. It would be a facade, a divine charade. God would only be playing at issuing commands. Divine reward and punishment would be utterly meaningless.

The preceding points, all flowing from a certain theo-logic of divine command, are of course not new with me. While they represent a minority position among Christians, Jews, and Muslims, they are not unheard of. For example, these ideas were espoused by the Mu'tazilite school of thought in Islam, a group of rationalist thinkers whose ideas actually attained a significant level of influence among many Muslims for several centuries (800s–1100s). Contemporary author Reza Aslan typifies the Mu'tazilite approach as having argued that "it would be irrational for God to behave so unjustly as to will belief and unbelief upon humanity, then reward one and punish the other."[1] Obviously, the argument holds in regard to any divine command or expression of God's will.

As has been the case also in the history of Christian doctrine, the status of any particular teaching often hinges precariously on prevalent political conditions; for example, Athanasius, the great fourth-century champion of orthodox Christology, was exiled (and recalled) five times during his life due to his teachings about Christ—mostly depending on who was occupying the emperor's throne. So also the Mu'tazilites enjoyed periods of ascendancy,[2] but by the end of the thirteenth century the Ash'arite, or Traditionalist, school became the dominant tradition of interpretation in Sunni Islam. From my perspective, the relative loss of influence by the rationalist Mu'tazilites is an unfortunate historical circumstance. It is at least mildly surprising to learn that among Muslim theologians who anticipated and contributed to the development of the Mu'tazilite tradition, some went so far as to claim that "God cannot know our actions until they occur"—"a notion," Aslan indicates, "that understandably offended the more traditionalist theologians, who believed the doctrine of tawhid [divine simplicity and unity] necessitated the belief in God's determinate power."[3] For my part, while admittedly not a Muslim, I applaud contemporary attempts to reopen discussion of the issues that divided the Rationalists and the Traditionalists.[4]

In the present chapter, the specific issue has to do with the theo-logic of divine command and the implications of this logic for how we think about the nature of divine sovereignty and freedom in relation to creation, and specifically in relation to human agency. Let us consider a couple more biblical illustrations to move our thinking along.

Uniquely in the gospel according to Matthew, Jesus on two different occasions quotes a sentence from the prophet Hosea: "I [God] desire mercy, not sacrifice" (9:13; 12:7). On both occasions Jesus expresses frustration that the Pharisees who are criticizing him have not really learned what this saying means. Jesus choruses Hosea's message that God desires mercy—that is, real, heartfelt, and practical compassion for others. By comparison, what God does not desire is sacrifice—that is, ritual offerings of worship that often may effect no change of heart or behavior for the worshiper. The fact that Jesus thinks his critics need to "go and learn what this means" immediately implies that what God desires of human creatures (mercy) is not what God is getting from at least some of them. Indeed, it seems clear that in both Jesus's time and our own, ritualized religion is as common as compassion is rare. But this is not the situation that God desires. From this reading of the Matthean text, one might even suggest that it cannot be entirely wrong to say that God *hopes* for greater compassion and less religiosity on planet Earth.

Later in the same gospel of Matthew, Jesus again is giving his opponents a serious tongue-lashing. Calling them "snakes" and "vipers" (23:33), Jesus announces that "all the righteous blood shed on earth, from the blood of righteous Abel to the blood of Zechariah" (23:35)—literally the blood of martyrs from A to Z—will come upon them. It is safe to assume, then, that the shedding of all of this "righteous blood" is not pleasing to God. It is contrary to God's will. Presumably, then, humans must be sufficiently free so as to disobey God's will for them. This further implies that the world is not necessarily at all as God desires, which—along with Jesus's own words— brings us to the primordial story of violence: Cain and Abel.

Adonai, we read in Genesis 4, inquires of Cain, "Why are you angry, and why has your countenance fallen? If you do well, will you not be accepted? And if you do not do well, sin is lurking at the door; its desire is for you, but you must master it" (vv. 6–7). Though in the narrative structure of the Tanakh this occurs long before the time of the gift of Torah at Mount Sinai, with its clear prohibition of murder, it is still evident in this primordial situation that God does not desire that murder should occur. Adonai does not say, "You shall not murder," but nevertheless does attempt to encourage Cain to take a different path than the path of violence he is considering. This divine visitation of Cain makes no sense if (a) God already knows what Cain is going to do; or (b) Cain has no real choice confronting him; or (c) there is a live possibility that God will simply force Cain to do God's bidding—to refrain from murder. But God *does* speak to Cain, does attempt to offer an alternative to violence against his brother—and yet God's attempt does not succeed. "And so," I once heard the late Israeli scholar Pinchas Peli conclude during a lecture in Jerusalem on the problem of evil, "Cain destroyed one-fourth of the human race, and God did nothing to stop him." But of course, God did do *something*. God attempted to reason with Cain, to warn Cain of the path he was taking. What God did not do was anything that would have forced Cain into compliance.

As we turn now to the story of Cain and Abel as narrated in the Bible and the Qur'an, we do well to note the context in which the story is told in the Qur'an. In Q 5:15 we encounter a call upon Jews and Christians ("O People of the Book") to heed this new revelation that unveils "much of what you used to conceal of the Book." This is an important subtext insofar as at least one Muslim commentator suggests that "the moral of this particular Biblical story—a moral which the followers of the Bible have been 'concealing from themselves'—is summarized in verse 32."[5] We will take a close look at Q 5:32 a little later in the chapter; for now, let us simply recognize that this is one of many instances in which Islamic interpretive tradition assumes that the qur'anic version of the story unveils certain aspects of the divine revelation that had been suppressed by its earlier recipients, the Jews. This detail will prove to be telling.

The Bible	The Qur'an
Genesis 4:2–7	*Surah 5:27a*
Now Abel was a keeper of sheep, and Cain a tiller of the ground.	And recite to them in all truth the tale of Adam's two sons,
In the course of time Cain brought to the LORD an offering of the fruit of the ground, and Abel for his part brought of the firstlings	

The Bible	The Qur'an
Genesis 4:2–7	*Surah 5:27a*
of his flock, their fat portions.	when they offered a sacrifice,
And the LORD had regard for Abel and his offering,	which was accepted from one,
but for Cain and his offering he had no regard.	but not accepted from the other.
So Cain was very angry, and his countenance fell. The LORD said to Cain, "Why are you angry, and why has your countenance fallen? If you do well, will you not be accepted? And if you do not do well, sin is lurking at the door; its desire is for you, but you must master it."	

The role that God plays in this story is much more muted in the Qur'an. Not only is there no conversation between Cain and God, but even the account of the sacrifices of the two brothers is rendered in the passive voice: "accepted from one, but not accepted from the other." God is implied but definitely remains in the narrative background. In Genesis, on the other hand, it is Adonai's rejection of Cain's offering that appears to instigate all the difficulties. Rabbinic interpreters, feeling some discomfort over this, shifted the story into "an account of human greed, arrogance and lust," writes Jacob Neusner, such that "God loses his role as precipitant of the murder."[6] By taking this interpretive route, the rabbis were then able, also, to accentuate Adonai's reconciliatory role: God's not an instigator but a peacemaker! Adonai draws near to Cain and begins probing him with questions, sounding almost like a divine therapist. Even if the questions are rhetorical, one suspects that their purpose is to get Cain to talk. Cain needs to open up, to talk about what's bothering him.

But he does not. God fails to get a conversation going. Cain walks away from the encounter. Violence ensues.

Genesis 4:8	*Surah 5:27b–29*
Cain said to his brother Abel, "Let us go out	The latter said,
to the field."	
	"I will surely kill you"; the other replied, "Allah accepts only from the God-fearing. Should you stretch your hand out to kill me, I will not stretch my hand out to kill you; for I fear Allah, Lord of the Worlds. I only wish that you be charged with my sin and yours and thus be one of the companions of the Fire; and that is the reward of the evildoers."

Whereas the conversation between the brothers is sparse and one-sided in Genesis, in the Qur'an both Cain and Abel speak freely. Cain's announcement of his intention is out in the open, a clear verbal threat; Abel, in response, virtually preaches a short sermon, and a hellfire one at that. It almost reads like a dare. Nonetheless, in Abel's reply the Qur'an offers a striking example of nonretaliation between brothers: "Should you stretch your hand out to kill me, I will not stretch my hand out to kill you, for I fear Allah, Lord of the Worlds." On the other hand, the qur'anic Abel might be accused of adding a little of his own fuel to the (hell)fire with his prophecy about Cain's final destiny—"and that is the reward of the evildoers."

Rabbinic interpreters speculated freely about the specific reasons for this brotherly feud—other than what Genesis actually states—and their guesses gravitated mostly toward two: (1) who would get what land and (2) who would get which woman. (Why is this not surprising?) Of course, within the framework of the Genesis story no women are yet on the scene except "the mother of all living," Eve. However, rabbis too had to field that eternal question "Who was Cain's wife?" (Need it be said that this is a troublesome issue only if the story is interpreted as a literal account of historical events?) Obviously, the rabbis deduced, there was a sister involved; indeed, there were two sisters, for God had provided a potential spouse for each of the brothers. They, however, fought over who would get whom. Neusner's observation that the rabbis tended to mute God's involvement in the sibling struggle, and to heighten the brothers' responsibility, finds support here. It is noteworthy that the Qur'an actually moves the narrative structure back toward the Genesis account, in which Cain is the aggressor and Abel a passive, perhaps even righteous, victim.

Given the fact that Abel says not a word in the Genesis story—only after his death does his "blood cry out" (see Gen. 4:10) to God from the ground upon which it has been spilt—it is not surprising that readers of this text wanted, and over time created, more details to the story. Inquiring minds do want to know! What did the brothers say to one another? Did little brother Abel put up a fight? The attempt to fill in the holes of a biblical narrative, to answer the questions the text leaves open, is called in Jewish tradition *midrash aggadah* (narrative interpretation). I have, of course, examined several instances of *aggadah* already in this volume and have suggested the likelihood that such traditions of interpretation bore an influence on the formulation of at least some of the qur'anic retellings of biblical narrative. The present story is no exception. We must at least in some instances, though, leave open the possibility that the Qur'an in turn influenced rabbinic midrash; much depends on how accurately and objectively we can assign dates and places of origin to ancient texts like these. In the main, however, we can be comfortably certain of matters of origin and, therefore, of likely directions of influence.

One of the great sources of Jewish midrash is the Targums, which are free interpretations of the biblical text from Hebrew into Aramaic, generously expanded and supplemented by the midrashic process. Targum Jonathan and Targum Yerushalmi "both provide a conversation between the two brothers, which though differing in its particulars from that given in the Qur'an, is similar in tone."[7] In these imaginatively rendered Aramaic versions of the story, Cain espouses an atheistic and noticeably nihilistic point of view. He announces that "there is no Judgment, no Judge, no world to come, no one who rewards the good deeds of the pious, and no one who requites the wicked. Neither was the world created in mercy, nor in mercy is it directed." Abel replies in kind, "There *is* a Judgement, there *is* a Judge, there *is* a world to come," and so on.[8] So in this stream of narrative interpretation, the struggle has become theological, ideological. It should also be noted that Abel's forswearing of violence toward his brother in the Qur'an—"Should you stretch your hand out to kill me, I will not stretch my hand out to kill you; for I fear Allah, Lord of the Worlds"—is absent in the Targums.

Genesis 4:8	Surah 5:30–31
And when they were in the field, Cain rose up against his brother Abel, and killed him.	Then, his soul prompted him to kill his brother; and so he killed him and became one of the losers. Then, Allah sent forth a raven digging the earth to show him how to bury his brother's corpse. He said: "Woe is me, am I unable to be like this raven and bury the corpse of my brother?" Thus he became one of the remorseful.

We have arrived now at one of the more fascinating midrashic passages in the Qur'an. Quite unexpectedly, a raven becomes important in the narrative, showing Cain how to dig a hole as a means of caring for his brother's corpse. Narratively speaking, this raven did not drop down out of the sky, out of nowhere. Jewish midrash contains similar narrative strands. While these materials are notoriously difficult to date, my guess is that they were around in various forms as oral tradition for centuries. We need not assume, necessarily, a direct line of influence in either direction, whether from Jewish midrash to Qur'an or Qur'an to Jewish midrash. It may be enough to acknowledge that this story, in one form or another, circulated among many communities of interpretation in the Middle East over several centuries. My assumption, admittedly, is that these traditions existed at least in oral form—and very often in written form—prior to the time of Muhammad.

Their function seems primarily to be etiological, that is, intended to explain some current feature or practice in the world by appealing to age-old stories. Why do we bury our dead in the ground? How did the first humans know what to do with a corpse? Thus we find in Midrash Tanhuma, a body of manuscripts notoriously difficult to date—it was first published in the early sixteenth century CE but contains midrashim attributed to a fourth-century rabbi, Tanhuma bar Abba—that "when Cain killed Abel, the latter's body lay cast aside for Cain did not know what to do. Then the Holy One sent him two pure birds, and one of them killed the other. Then he dug with his claws and buried him, and from him Cain learned. So he dug and buried Abel" (*Tanhuma Bereshit* 10). Varying somewhat from the Qur'an, *Tanhuma*'s version has a pair of birds virtually reenacting the Cain-Abel struggle. In the Qur'anic version there is only a single bird, identified as a raven, which scratches at the earth to suggest to Cain what to do with his dead brother.

In *Pirke R. Eliezer* (*Sayings of Rabbi Eliezer*), a work that contains Jewish interpretive material likely to have been roughly contemporary with the formation of the Qur'an, we find another version of essentially the same narrative. In this retelling, however, it is not Cain who is the funereal protagonist—possibly because this tended to cast the first murderer in an overly positive light? In this document, it is Abel's parents who learn what to do with a corpse. Note too that while the Qur'an and the *Midrash Tanhuma* both attribute the bird's pedagogical function to God, the Eliezer tradition makes no such theological claim, at least not explicitly:

> Adam and his companion sat weeping and mourning for [Abel] and did not know what to do with him, as burial was unknown to them. Then came a raven, whose companion was dead, took its body, scratched in the earth and hid it before their eyes; then said Adam, I shall do as this raven has done, and at once he took Abel's corpse, dug in the earth and hid it. (*Pirke R. Eliezer* 21)

Who knows when the story of the raven(s) first began to be told and circulated? The traditional approach to the Qur'an, still espoused by the overwhelming majority of Muslims, is that either (a) this was a detail revealed especially to Muhammad about Cain and Abel, which was subsequently borrowed by rabbis and incorporated into their interpretations, or (b) this was a detail that was originally in the Hebrew Bible, was for some reason excised from the text by the Jews (even if it survived in some rabbinic versions of the story), and subsequently was returned to its role in the story by the Qur'an. However, the story of the raven, it seems to me, is best understood as having evolved gradually in Jewish circles as a way to answer questions like "Whatever happened to Abel's body?" and "How did they know what to do with it?" and even "Why do we bury the dead?"

Genesis 4:9–10

Then the LORD said to Cain, "Where is your brother Abel?" He said, "I do not know; am I my brother's keeper?" And the LORD said, "What have you done? Listen; your brother's blood is crying out to me from the ground!"

In Genesis, unlike the Qur'an, God now returns to speak with Cain. Recall that prior to the murder, God attempted to initiate a conversation with Cain with a series of questions that got God nowhere. The conversation died—and then Abel died. In terms of the biblical narrative, the absence of God in between these conversations is palpable. In between God's warning in 4:7 ("[sin's] desire is for you, but you must master it") and God's question in 4:9 ("Where is your brother Abel?"), God is absent. Only Cain speaks, and that to Abel: "Let us go out to the field."

But God now reenters the narrative frame with yet another question to Cain regarding his brother. The second question is even more pointed, more poignant: "What have you done?" Let us return momentarily to the considerations with which this chapter began. God the Creator has drawn near to Cain to ask questions of him, to instigate conversation, to cajole Cain away from violence. Everything in the narrative suggests that God does not desire that violence be done to Abel. But God cannot—or at least does not—stop Cain from pursuing the path that leads to bloodshed. God attempts only to talk Cain out of it. Indeed, in the moment of murder God is effectively "absent" from the narrative action. It is as though Cain, by refusing to answer or even acknowledge God's initial set of questions, has so turned his back on God's presence that this bloodshed occurs outside of God's purview. Thus, when God now steps back into the narrative frame, God does so, again, by asking questions intended to spark a sense of responsibility in Cain: "Where is your brother Abel?" "What have you done?" Truly, this is a God of dialogue. And precisely as a God of dialogue, the God of this story is not the Power of unilateral causality, micromanaging the world or willing its every detail into being. This God asks questions; this God seeks to influence. To borrow the language of *Pirke R. Eliezer*, this may even be a God who, alongside "Adam and his companion," could sit "weeping and mourning for Abel."

It is precisely at this point that a most profound piece of theological and ethical reflection emerges from this ancient text. In *Mishnah Sanhedrin*, Jewish legal debate and rulings collected and collated several centuries before the time of Muhammad, we find a fascinating observation. Rabbis noted an unusual construction in the Hebrew text of Genesis 4:10, and—as the rabbis generally did—attributed considerable significance to this grammatical oddity. Their observation:

> We find it said in the case of Cain who murdered his brother: the voice of your brother's *bloods* cries out. It is not said here *blood*, in the singular, but *bloods*, in the plural, i.e., his own blood and the blood of his [would-be] descendants. Humanity was created single in order to show that to whomever kills a single individual, it shall be reckoned that he has killed the whole race; but to whomever preserves the life of a single individual, it is counted that he has preserved the whole race. (*Mishnah Sanhedrin* 4:5)

This is obviously a profound ethical interpretation of a simple, if unexpected, plural form! It is not simply Abel's blood that cries out from the ground but the *blood(s)* of all his potential descendants now lost to history—and, by interpretive extention, the blood of victims of murder throughout earth's long history. Innocent blood cries out to the Creator. It is a moving interpretation of a fine point of Hebrew grammar in the Genesis text—and it is replicated, virtually word for word, in the Qur'an:

Mishnah Sanhedrin 4:5	Surah 5:32
	For that reason, We decreed for the Children of
. . . to whomever kills a single individual,	Israel that whoever kills a soul, not in retaliation for a soul or corruption in the land,
it shall be reckoned that he has killed the	is like one who has killed the
whole race; but to whomever preserves	whole of mankind; and whoever saves
the life of a single individual, it is	a life is
counted that he has preserved the	like one who saves the
whole race.	lives of all mankind.

Islamic commentator Sayyid Mawdudi has written that it is "a pity that the precious words which embody God's ordinance are to be found nowhere in the Bible today," the implication being that they once were a part of the Genesis narrative. "The Talmud, however," Mawdudi admits, "does mention this."[9] His assumption, like that of virtually all traditional Muslim exegesis, is that this compelling principle—"whoever saves a life is like one who saves the lives of all mankind"—likely was in the original scriptures of the Jews but subsequently suppressed or removed. But of course, one would then have to wonder why later Jews, the rabbis of the Talmudic era, would insert these "precious words which embody God's ordinance" back into the story! There is a delicious irony here, and ignoring it does not serve the best purposes of telling the truth, in love, for the sake of honest friendship and scholarship.

The Qur'an, as we have seen especially in chapter 2 of this book, consistently affirms the validity of the revelations granted to the Jewish people and, through Jesus, to what would become the Christian community. However, the Qur'an also insists that those revelations have been perverted, misinterpreted, even suppressed. Jewish tradition, on the other hand, developed on the premise that just as God had revealed the Written Torah to Moses on Mount Sinai, so also did God reveal what was to become known as Oral Torah, that is, the long interpretive tradition winding its way through the complex arguments of the rabbis. This idea serves to underscore a notion of continuing revelation precisely through the history of rabbinic commentary and debate. The rabbis spoke of the "heaps of exposition" to be derived from the Written Torah, yielding, in the words of contemporary Jewish philosophical theologian Eugene Borowitz, "a near infinity of meaning" in the Oral Torah.[10] In this model, revelation is not fixed temporally, geographically, or textually; it is instead an ongoing historical process entrusted to the Jewish people. Divine revelation is not conceived to be a singular, vertical intrusion into the world; it is horizontal and historical. "It is not in the heavens."

Of course, it is precisely within this historical process of interpretation that rabbis weaved from the plural "bloods" the stunning idea that "to whomever kills a single individual, it shall be reckoned that he has killed the whole race; but to whomever preserves the life of a single individual, it is counted that he has preserved the whole race." And in the context of this very story of Cain and Abel, the Qur'an announces that it was God ("We") who so "decreed for the Children of Israel" that "whoever kills a soul . . . is like one who has killed the whole of mankind; and whoever saves a life is like one who saves the lives of all mankind" (Q 5:32). History—in this case, the history of texts and their relationships—makes it abundantly clear that if indeed God did so decree this marvelous principle, God did it in and through the rabbinic process of oral tradition. Ironically, then, the Qur'an actually (in this case) supports the traditional Jewish claim of divine authority, divine revelation, for the Oral Torah. Instead of a pristine revelation given in the Written Torah (the *Taurat* of the Qur'an) that is subsequently perverted or distorted by Jewish teachers, in Q 5:32 we actually encounter a moving validation of the rabbinic concept of divine revelation occurring through the ongoing rabbinic discussions and debates called Oral Torah.

All of this is important not because it reveals an embarrassing detail in the Qur'an; rather, it is important because it might nudge both Muslims and Christians toward a healthier, more full-bodied and historical notion of divine revelation. Clearly, what meanings certain rabbis long ago read into the odd detail of a plural form of *blood* cannot be supported, strictly speaking, by a historical-critical reading of the Genesis text itself. If we restrict revelation to what we take to be original meanings inherent in the text, then these "precious words" of Q 5:32 "which embody God's ordinance" do not actually qualify as revelation. But we should not restrict revelation so. There was an interpretive community that wrestled with this text, striving to wrest new meanings from the primordial story of two brothers. There is no good reason to assume that the God of Israel did not continue to reveal, precisely through the process of such interpretive moves as these made by the rabbis, how the people of Israel (and by implication, all people) were to live with one another.

This message from the Talmud and the Qur'an is one we desperately need to hear today: life is not cheap, and to save a life is to save the world. On the other hand, to murder is to destroy the world, to erode God's good creation. A further, grim implication of this message is that God does not intend to step in and stop us in our murdering, no matter its form or expression. God is more likely to ask us questions—indeed, perhaps, to *be* the Question that the faces of our brothers and sisters, our neighbors, even those who are "strangers" and "enemies," present to us in this very moment.

Whether we read it in the Talmud or the Qur'an, it has the ring of revelation.

7

KNOWING NOAH—OR NOT

And relate to them the story of Noah . . .
—Qur'an 10:71

If we were to tell the story of Noah, what story would we tell?

For Muslims, Noah is one of God's prophets. In the Qur'an, the office or function of the prophet is the quintessential religious role, the ultimate calling. Prophets are not highlighted for their individual characteristics or unique quirks; rather, their lives and words are presented in a virtually uniform way in order to underscore their similarity—both in their faithfulness to their prophetic calling and in the content of their preaching. Thus, like every other figure who is described as a prophet in the Qur'an, Noah is portrayed as a fearless and uncompromising preacher of the word of God. He is, like every other prophet, offered as a model for Muslims of the life completely submitted to God.

Not so with the Noah of the Bible, whose story is found primarily in Genesis chapters 6–9. Noah is never identified in the biblical text as a prophet per se. Indeed, in Genesis Noah actually is depicted as a silent and relatively passive figure. Despite the widespread portrayals of Noah as a bold preacher—portrayals found not only in the Qur'an but also in earlier noncanonical Jewish literature, briefly in the New Testament, and in many Christian sermons and Sunday school lessons—in the Genesis story Noah does not preach to anyone. Likewise, Genesis does not portray him as the object of his neighbors' mocking and derision as he builds his big boat prior to the flood, despite the enduring popularity of this image. Rather, Genesis simply reports that Noah "did all that God commanded him" (6:22). He was obedient to the will of God—a virtue, to be sure, among Jews, Christians, and Muslims alike. Yet, as we shall see, at least some of the early rabbis suspected that Noah was actually too passive, overly acquiescent, in his compliance with God.

Noah's story and prophetic example make numerous appearances in the Qur'an, many of them highly stylized and relatively brief. The most dramatic exception to this tendency is found in Q 11:25–49. Because of the length and detail of the treatment, this Noah narrative undoubtedly provides the most interesting and fruitful of qur'anic passages for reading alongside the biblical story. However, we begin the present chapter's intertextual reading of the Bible and the Qur'an with a passage from the Bible alone, for Genesis provides a setting for the Noah story that is not necessary—and indeed may be somewhat inimical—to the Qur'an's purposes:

The Bible

Genesis 6:5–8

The LORD saw that the wickedness of humankind was great in the earth, and that every inclination of the thoughts of their hearts was only evil continually. And the LORD was sorry that he had made humankind on the earth, and it grieved him to his heart. So the LORD said, "I will blot out from the earth the human beings I have created—people together with animals and creeping things and birds of the air, for I am sorry that I have made them." But Noah found favor in the sight of the LORD.

In the Qur'an, as I have mentioned, Noah's prophetic role is essentially identical to that of every other prophet—except for that dramatic flourish of a flood at the end of the story, vindicating his message. But there is no particular indication in the Qur'an that the times or the people of Noah were unique for their evil and rebellion. Noah's message is characterized as typical of all prophets: "O my people, worship Allah, you have no other god but Him. I fear for you the punishment of an Awful Day" (7:59). The fact that Noah's message in the Qur'an sounds very much like that of all the other prophets is significant precisely because in the Bible's account there seems to be much more at stake; in Genesis's rendition of Noah, all of creation hangs in the balance between humanity's universal evil and God's deep grief.

God's grief? Can God grieve? Indeed, is it any surprise that once again in Genesis, we encounter a notably anthropomorphic rendering of the God who goes by the name of *YHWH*, or Adonai (the LORD)? It is one thing for God to see the wickedness of human beings throughout the earth—but would not

God also have seen it coming? Given divine omniscience, would not God know human wickedness absolutely perfectly even prior to the creation of humans? And if so, how could Adonai have become sorry about having created human beings, let alone grieve about it? For that matter, could Adonai's plan to blot out all creatures, human and otherwise, in a great flood really be a matter of divine reaction—perhaps in fact an overreaction—to human evil gone wild? If God was reacting to the depth and breadth of human evil by sending a flood, then apparently God had not anticipated (let alone known eternally) that things would get so bad as this. At least on the face of it, the Genesis passage presents God as considerably taken aback.

Christians who insist on a literal reading of the Bible should themselves be taken aback. For those same readers most often will also insist upon divine attributes such as God's absolute knowledge of all things, including the future. But it is exceedingly difficult to read this passage from Genesis and garner any support for the notion that God knows all things perfectly and timelessly. God is portrayed as mulling over a situation that has gotten far worse than God had anticipated, even to the point of being "sorry" and deeply grieved over having created human beings.

Is it any wonder that there is no qur'anic parallel to this portrayal of God? Probably for most Muslims such a depiction would seem much less a portrayal, and much more a betrayal, of God. After all, "Allah knows best" in all situations; indeed, if the Qur'an included such a sense of deep regret in its rendering of Allah, the angels' protest explored in this book's earlier chapter on Adam—"Will you place one [on earth] who will make mischief in it and shed blood?" (Q 2:30)—would have been vindicated. The angels would have been right. But we recall that the point of the Qur'an's story of Adam naming all the other creatures is that God knows what we do not know, and all that we do know is taught us by God. "Did I not tell you that I know the unseen in the heavens and the earth . . . ?" (Q 2:33). The surprise and sorrow attributed to God in Genesis 6:5–8 simply is not worthy of Allah. Surely it is biblical passages such as this that contemporary Muslim writer Jamaal al-Din M. Zarabozo has in mind when he writes that "the distorted revelations in the hands of the Jews and Christians contain passages that are repugnant, for good reason, to the modern mind. Hence, mankind will never completely return to those sources and accept them as authoritative. It is the pure revelation, the Qur'an, that can rescue mankind"[1]—and so, according to Zarabozo, the Qur'an itself can function as a kind of textual ark, rescuing its readers from the floods of doubt and despair.

In the specific idea under consideration, let me repeat: the Qur'an "can rescue mankind" because it rescues humans from regarding God too anthropomorphically—as, in this case, a deity who can grieve, who can actually regret having made humanity in the first place. Such a God as described in Genesis 6 would not be the sort of God who knows all things perfectly, eternally, timelessly—and yet it is that sort of God that, through the centuries, most Muslims and Christians have assumed God to be.[2] Despite the weight of all that tradition, I must confess a preference for the God of Genesis 6, though (once again) I do not assume the text to be providing a literal or straightforward depiction of God. Even as we read the text metaphorically, the theological trajectory of Genesis 6 can (and I think should) be taken seriously for what it suggests to us about a lively, dynamic interaction between God and creation. We can appreciate the story's theological trajectory without having to read it as literal history.

Genesis 6:9–11; 7:5	Surah 11:25–26
These are the descendants of Noah. Noah was a righteous man, blameless in his generation. Noah walked with God. And Noah had three sons, Shem, Ham, and Japheth. Now the earth was corrupt in God's sight, and the earth was filled with violence . . . And Noah did all that	
the LORD had commanded him.	And We have sent Noah forth to his people; [he said:] "I am a plain warner to you, that you worship none but Allah. I fear for you the punishment of a very painful Day."

Noah is but one in a long series of "plain warners" whom God has sent to the peoples of the world—a series that comes to its end, its final fruition, in the calling of Muhammad to become "the seal of the prophets." In Islam, except for Muhammad's role as the final one, a prophet is a prophet is a prophet. Even so, there is a distinctive connection between Noah and Muhammad: while most of the prophets mentioned in the Qur'an are described in ways that tend often to mirror Muhammad's own situation and setting, this tendency is heightened in the Noah story. "In places," Neal Robinson writes, "the story has been adapted quite considerably in order to bring it into line with Muhammad's situation."[3] The "unbelieving dignitaries" among Noah's people reply to him, just as Mecca's civic and economic leaders initially responded to Muhammad, "We do not see in you [anything] except a mortal like ourselves; nor do we see in those who hastily followed you [anything] except the scum of our people" (Q 11:27). When Noah, prefiguring Muhammad, insists that his motives and message are pure, the dignitaries reply, "O Noah, you have disputed and disputed much with us. Bring us, then, what you promise us, if you are truthful" (Q 11:32). When Noah replies that "it is Allah who will bring it to you" (11:33), it is fascinating next to find the Qur'an virtually conflating

Noah's and Muhammad's critics: "Or will they say: 'He has forged it.' Say: 'If I have forged it, my guilt is upon me and I am innocent of the evil you commit'" (11:35). Muslim interpretive tradition seems correct to assume that "they," in this case, are Muhammad's pagan critics. Certainly the charge of forgery fits better with Muhammad's situation than anything Noah presumably would have experienced. And yet the little interchange occurs precisely in the middle of the Noah narrative! Noah's and Muhammad's prophetic personae are so thoroughly intermeshed here that Noah's story is becoming Muhammad's. That, of course, would tend to imply as well that Noah's warning is becoming Muhammad's: "I fear for you the punishment of a very painful Day" (11:26). In terms of the narrative logic of the Noah story, of course, what Noah feared has indeed already come and is long gone—which only underscores the pressing urgency for Muhammad's listeners not to repeat the obstinate refusal of Noah's people. Muhammad's message of repentance and obedience receives from the Noah saga all the rhetorical power of a fait accompli—if Noah's audience could not avoid the tumult of divine judgment, how could Muhammad's critics expect to avoid a soon-coming day of judgment?

Genesis 7:1	Surah 11:36–37
Then the LORD said to Noah, "Go into the ark, you and all your household; for I have seen that you alone are righteous before me in this generation."	And it was revealed to Noah: "None of your people will believe except those who have already believed, so do not grieve at what they do; and make the Ark under Our Eyes and with Our Revelation, and do not plead with Me regarding the wrongdoers; they shall be drowned."

In the Qur'an: not only does God not grieve, but God also commands Noah not to grieve. And, not unlike the qur'anic story of Abraham explored in chapter 1 of this book, Noah is further commanded not to "plead with Me regarding the wrongdoers." The interesting thing is that in the biblical version of the story Noah never is described as grieving the coming destruction, nor as pleading for the lives of the impending flood's victims. He is just following orders.

Genesis 6:27	Surah 11:38–39
Noah did this; he did all that God commanded him.	So he started making the Ark, and whenever a group of his people passed by him, they mocked him. [But] he would say: "If you mock us, we will mock you, as you are mocking. You shall surely learn who will be afflicted by a degrading chastisement, and will undergo a lasting punishment."

Perhaps surprisingly, Genesis does not describe any interactions between Noah and the people who would presumably have witnessed his big boat-building project. But it would be easy to imagine such interchanges—— those who heard or read the story of Noah would understandably have wondered about the details.

So Jewish midrash—creative, often highly imaginative retellings of biblical stories, with an eye for filling in the blanks and answering the questions left dangling in the text—happily provided such interchanges between Noah and his critics. One body of midrash, *Tanchuma*, reports that "they mocked and laughed at him in their words" (section Noah). *Genesis Rabbah*, the collection of rabbinic interpretation of the book of Genesis, states that people asked Noah why he was so busy with planting cedars and then later cutting them down. "Because the Master of the Universe told me that he is bringing a flood to the world" was his reply. Their retort, laced with ridicule, was that if such a flood really were coming, it would undoubtedly fall only upon Noah's home and family.[4] The legends grew of Noah's fearless faithfulness in the face of his mocking critics—though we should again note that if he was indeed such a preacher, Genesis does not tell us so. But the so-called *Sibylline Oracles* do, for there we read that Noah "entreated the peoples and began to speak such words: 'Men, sated with faithlessness, smitten with great madness, what you did will not escape the notice of God'" (see 1:127–31, 149–51).[5] The Noah story's proportions, then, grew increasingly grand; despite all criticism and opposition, the legend proclaimed, Noah persisted in his obedience to God and his fervent warnings to the people. So it was that the figure of Noah earned the honorific title "a herald [preacher] of righteousness" in early Christian writing (2 Peter 2:5)—without having preached a single word in the Tanakh. It seems obvious that the Qur'an inherits this midrashic development of the Noah story, clearly bestowing upon Noah a far more outspoken and charismatic persona than the reader detects in Genesis.

Genesis 7:11–16	Surah 11:40–41
In the six hundredth year of Noah's life,	And when Our Command came,
in the second month, on the seventeenth	
day of the month, on that day all the	and the
fountains of the great deep burst forth,	water gushed forth from the earth,
and the windows of the heavens were opened. The rain fell on the earth forty	
days and forty nights. On the very same	We said,

Genesis 7:11–16	Surah 11:40–41
day Noah with his sons, Shem and Ham and Japheth, and Noah's wife and the three wives of his sons entered the ark,	
they and every wild animal of every kind,	"Carry in it two of every kind,
and all domestic animals of every kind,	together with your family,
and every creeping thing that creeps on the earth, and every bird of every kind—	
every bird, every winged creature. They	except for those who have been doomed,
went into the ark with Noah, two and two	and [take] those who believe."
of all flesh in which there was the breath	
of life. And those that entered, male and	However only a few believers besides him
female of all flesh, went in as God had	were there.
commanded him; and the LORD shut him in.	And he said: "Embark on it. In the name of Allah will be its sailing and anchor. My Lord is indeed All-Forgiving, Merciful."

It is interesting to note the details where these two versions of the Noah story converge: there is the mention of waters gushing forth from the earth, and not simply rainfall; there is also the mention of two animals of every kind. Even in these details, however, the differences are noteworthy. Genesis actually does not say that the waters gushed up out of the earth per se as the Qur'an does but that "the fountains of the great deep burst forth." These "fountains of the deep" bear an obvious relation to Genesis 1, which speaks of God's breath-wind (Heb. *ruach*) blowing across "the face of the deep." It is clear—as clear as chaos can be!—that "the deep" represents the dark, mysterious, and massive waters of the sea (the Mediterranean, to be precise). In Genesis 1, it is these waters of "the deep" that God divides into waters "above" (whence falls the rain) and waters "below" (whence flow the springs). These waters, situated above and below the dry land called earth, are representative in biblical cosmology of the powers of swirling chaos, *tohu bohu*, that continually threaten the order of creation at its edges. In the flood narrative of Genesis 7, God is portrayed as unleashing these chaotic powers of destruction upon the earth, thereby reversing the act of creation as it is described in Genesis 1: the waters above and the waters below converge upon the land. Thus in the Genesis account, we encounter an act of divine *de*creation, God's undoing what was done in creation. Chaos is let loose from its boundaries above and below and gushes back in upon the dry land. The point is not that the Qur'an denies this portrayal of Noah's flood but that it mutes, if not altogether silences, the cosmic, even universal elements of the Genesis story.

Another difference between Genesis and the Qur'an regarding the story of Noah concerns the number of animals who made it on board. In this case, the difference very likely begins with varying traditions within the Bible itself. The Qur'an's mention of "two of every kind" echoes God's instructions to Noah in Genesis to bring "two of every kind," "of every living thing, of all flesh" (6:19). But Genesis includes another narrative tradition in which God commands that "seven pairs of all clean animals . . . and seven pairs of the birds of the air also" (7:2–3) embark on the ark. It becomes clear later that the greater number of kosher animals is necessary for the sacrifices that Noah would offer after the ark hit dry ground: "Then Noah built an altar to the LORD, and took of every clean animal and of every clean bird, and offered burnt offerings on the altar" (8:20). In other words, more than just a pair become necessary when Noah's story is told in a culture in which sacrificial animals are important; in such a setting one would be likely to ask how Noah would be able to offer sacrifices without a surplus of kosher creatures. The Qur'an, meanwhile, would have no need to bother with this issue, given the fact that sacrificial practices and concerns are virtually absent from its pages.

But of course it is not only animals that board the ark. A remnant of the human community is also delivered. At this juncture, though, the Qur'an includes a subplot that is absent from the Bible:

Surah 11:42–43

And as it sailed along with them amid waves like mountains, Noah called out to his son, who stood apart: "My son, embark with us, and do not remain with the unbelievers."

He said: "I will seek refuge in a mountain that will protect me from water."

He said: "Today, there is no protector from Allah's Decree, except for him on whom He has mercy."

Then the waves came between them and so he was one of those who were drowned.

There is no story like this one in Genesis, nor is it easy to locate anything comparable in the history of Jewish interpretation of this passage.[6] This may be entirely unique to the qur'anic revelation. In any case, it is a highly significant story line: whereas in Genesis Noah took his entire household—"you, your sons, your wife, and your sons' wives with you" (6:18)—in the Qur'an the humans who are saved are not necessarily all bound by family ties. Noah boards with family members who are believers and with others who have also believed in his proclamation. Further, one of his own sons, refusing to embark on the ark and seeking his refuge elsewhere, is drowned in the floodwaters. Robinson suggests that this fascinating detail may provide another point of identification between Noah's story and Muhammad's own prophetic experience, for it "probably mirrors the anguish of the Muslims who left relatives behind when they migrated [from Mecca to Medina]."[7] With this new twist in Noah's story, the Qur'an underscores the idea that Islam creates a new kind of social arrangement, a polis or social identity that is not dependent upon blood kinship but rather upon submission to Allah's will. Indeed, that spirit of submission is embodied in the next slice of the Qur'an's narrative:

Surah 11:45–47

Noah then called out to his Lord saying: "My Lord, my son is of my family; and Your Promise is surely the truth and you are the Best of judges."

He said: "O Noah, he is not of your family. It is an act which is not righteous, so do not ask Me about that of which you have no knowledge. I admonish you not to be one of the ignorant."

He said: "Lord, I seek refuge with You, lest I should ask You that of which I have no knowledge. For unless You forgive me and have mercy on me I will be one of the losers."

Noah's lament over his son is so quickly silenced that we might be tempted to censure the Qur'an's hardheartedness. Yet we should first at least recognize, if not appreciate, that the gospel testimonies about Jesus's ministry include some similar sentiments regarding the new kind of clan he was attempting to create. For example, the gospel of Mark reports that Jesus's mother and siblings, fearful for his sanity, had sought him out to take him home for a little rest from the maddening crowd. When they located him, he was teaching inside a packed-out house, with no way to reach him. "Standing outside, they sent to him and called him," so the crowd informed Jesus, "Your mother and your brothers and sisters are outside, asking for you" (Mark 3:31–32). But Jesus, gesturing to the crowd of listeners surrounding him, asked, "Who are my mother and my brothers?"—a question not likely to soothe his family's concerns for his mental well-being! He then answered his own rhetorical question, "Here are my mother and my brothers! Whoever does the will of God is my brother and sister and mother" (3:34–35). This is but the first of several such sayings of Jesus that decisively sever the natural family ties of blood in order to establish a new and different kind of social identity.

Both Jesus and Muhammad were undertaking a radical step, interrupting our evolution-driven momentum to perpetuate the genetic ties of blood kinship. In Karen Armstrong's words, "Like Jesus, Muhammad seemed to be turning father against son, brother against brother, and undermining the essential bonds, duties and hierarchy of family life . . . [It] soon became clear that Islam was beginning to split families right down the middle."[8] The subplot about Noah's son—"O Noah, he is not of your family"—then can be understood as providing a poignant illustration of the nature of the Muslim community, the *umma*. We might recall that it was Malcolm X's profound experience during his pilgrimage to Mecca, where he witnessed Muslims of all skin colors, cultures, and languages united in submission to God, that impelled him to leave the racially constructed Nation of Islam (Black Muslims) and to embrace orthodox Islam as a universal *umma*.

Surah 11:49
That is part of the tidings of the Unseen which We are revealing to you. Neither you, nor your people knew it before this. Forbear, then, the [good] outcome [that] belongs to the righteous.

The Qur'an here rehearses what I have already observed: this story of Noah's drowned son, who was foolish enough to seek safety outside the provisions of Allah, appears to be unique to the Qur'an. "Neither you, nor your people knew it before this." The Genesis story portrays Noah essentially as the new Adam, a new beginning for humanity, and is content to see this beginning in terms of Noah's extended family. The Qur'an, on the other hand, portrays Noah as one of the prophets, a figure who calls his people to obedience to God's will. Submission to that will provides the criterion for participation in—or exclusion from—the prophetic community. In the light of that criterion, even Noah must repent of his lamenting to God for the son he has lost to the raging waves. As a model Muslim, Noah does indeed repent.

Compared to the figure we meet in Genesis, the qur'anic Noah is noisy. Not only does he cry out to God, at least initially, over his son's drowning, but the Qur'an elsewhere also reports that he cried out to God before the flood. In that case the lament was over the rampant evil of his world, thereby implying that it was in answer to prayer that Noah "and his people" were "delivered . . . from the great calamity" (37:75–76). Meanwhile, Genesis offers no words of prayer at all, at any time, from Noah's lips. Indeed, the first and only time we read any actual words spoken by Noah, it is after the flood, in a curse upon his own son Ham for having caught his old dad in a state of drunken nakedness (Gen. 9:20–25). And for this Ham, and his descendants the Canaanites, are cursed by Noah! It goes without saying that the Qur'an does not include this decidedly shameful narrative development.

The rabbis, however, could not avoid it. Noah's somewhat questionable, if not downright lewd, behavior contributed to a distinct rabbinic tendency to damn him with faint praise. One rabbinic tradition, noting Genesis's opening observation that Noah was "blameless in his generation" (6:9), interpreted this to mean that Noah was only relatively blameless: it was only by comparison with everyone else "among the people of his time" that he came out looking righteous. Only because of all the sin, corruption, and violence that filled the world (Gen. 6:11–13) did Noah look good to God—righteous only when measured against the rest of the motley crew of human beings of his era. In this reading, Noah does not emerge as a particularly impressive figure.

Theologically, this may have been a way for the rabbis to underscore the notion that while God is attempting to "go back to the drawing board" with the flood and subsequent covenanting with all living things (including Noah and his family), even after this dramatic cleansing of the earth the Creator is left with less than sterling material with which to work. No wonder, the rabbis perhaps thought, the world continued (and continues) to be something of a mess. We recall Rabbi Levi's elaboration of Abraham's challenge to God: "If you want to have a world, there can be no justice; and if justice is what you want, there can be no world."[9] Here we have what is supposed to be the story of Noah as a new Adam, the human being who is called upon to represent God's fresh beginning with creation—and we as the readers of his story must close our eyes, embarrassed, and tiptoe quietly out of his presence (Gen. 9:23). In terms of the narrative sequencing of Genesis, in fact, it appears that the first act of this "man of the soil" (9:20) after disembarking from the ark is to plant a vineyard—and there seems to be little mystery as to why. Soon our new Adam plucks his grapes, makes some wine, and gets sauced.

Of course the text does not attempt to explain Noah's embarrassing drunkenness; it is simply reported as a matter of fact. There is a tradition of rabbinic criticism of Noah for planting a vineyard instead of "something valuable, such as a young fig-shoot or olive shoot."[10] Surely Noah had an idea about how he'd put those grapes to use. While the rabbis tended to agree that this was a shameful moment in the Noah narrative, it is noteworthy that the text of Genesis does not offer any condemning comment. The flood was a pretty traumatic event, one might surmise; what would it have been like to be among just a handful of human survivors? A bit lonely? Not enough people to talk to? Just too cataclysmic to process? And how about the memory of all those drowning, screaming people? Is this simply too insecure a situation, insofar as Noah might be wondering whether, notwithstanding promises to the contrary, this God might be a bit short on patience? What would it take for God to destroy even Noah and his fellow survivors? Would this be simply too threatening a situation in which to live, this post-deluge setting?

123

If one were to add to the mix the intriguing qur'anic twist that Noah lost a son in the flood—and, further, that God essentially denied Noah the fatherly privilege of mourning his drowned child—then Noah's drowning his anxieties and sorrows in fermented grape juice is perhaps rather to be expected. But of course, we really are not free to mix the stories in this way, since the Qur'an includes none of this distinctly unprophetlike drunken behavior of Noah's. *It simply does not fit the profile of the submissive Muslim prophet*—which is what Noah is in the Qur'an and, of course, in subsequent Islamic tradition.

To be sure, this kind of hagiographic overhaul of the biblical characters is typical of the Qur'an—and before the Qur'an, of Jewish and Christian interpretive traditions as well. James Kugel notes that particularly in the development of Israel's wisdom literature, a "polarization takes place in ancient exegesis: biblical heroes are altogether good, with any fault air-brushed away, whereas figures like Esau or Balaam are altogether demonized—as if their neither-good-nor-evil status in the Bible itself was somehow intolerable."[11] The Qur'an, then, continues an interpretive process already begun in Jewish and Christian readings of biblical characters.

By contrast, we return again to the fascinating fact that the figure of Noah is not all that compelling or attractive in the Genesis version of the story. While we do read in 6:9 that he "walked with God," even here the rabbinic tradition found cause for criticism.

> Rabbi Judah said: "This may be compared to a king who had two sons, one grown up and the other a child. To the child he said, 'Walk with me,' but to the adult, 'Walk before me.' Similarly, to Abraham, whose moral strength was great, 'Walk before Me' [Gen. 17:1]; of Noah, whose strength was feeble, 'Noah walked with God.'" (*Genesis Rabbah* 30:10)

In other words, at least some rabbinic interpreters read Noah as overly passive and acquiescent. Abraham "walked *before* God" as a responsible adult, daring even to challenge God regarding the justice of destroying all human lives in Sodom and Gomorrah; on the other hand, Noah "walked *with* God" like a dependent child, making not even the slightest peep over the fate of the entire world! Thus, whereas the Qur'an proclaims that God commanded Noah "not [to] plead with Me regarding the wrongdoers" (11:37), there was a strand of rabbinic tradition that found fault with Noah precisely for having made no plea at all. True, he did what he was told; but he offered no intercession for all the people and animals about to be destroyed. Rabbi Johanan ben Zakkai—founder of the influential first rabbinic school after the destruction of Jerusalem in 70 CE—went so far as to surmise that Noah "lacked faith; had not the water reached his ankles he would not have entered the ark" (*Genesis Rabbah* 32:6). In the summary statement of contemporary Israeli philosopher David Hartman, "Noah never achieves the stature of a responsible covenantal human. He responds; he never initiates."[12]

Perhaps, though, that is part of the point in the Genesis story. Noah is a "man of the soil," identified with the earth—even to the point of imbibing the wine that comes from the earth's luscious grapes and lying exposed on the ground from which he came, his naked body having been (like all human bodies) made from the dust or ground (*adamah*) of the earth. Noah embraces nature; he becomes absorbed by its soil; he becomes drunk with its juices. The rabbis noted that Genesis's description of Noah as a righteous man (6:9) is later eclipsed by the designation "man of the soil" (*'ish ha'adamah*, 9:20), as though to imply that, in the end, Noah had sunk to his true level of character.[13] This second *adam* of God's re-creation project for Earth is himself decidedly earthy! Perhaps his passivity in some ways embodies the quiet receptivity of the natural world to its Creator; after all, following the flood God makes *berit* or covenant with Noah and his descendants *and* "with every living creature that was with you . . . every living creature of all flesh," a covenant "established between [God] and all flesh that is on the earth" (9:10, 15, 17). Noah represents the human kind among all those kinds of creatures, but there is little to single him out from the rest of creation.

Reading Noah this way yields us a human who is deeply enmeshed in the natural world, whose drunken nakedness only further exemplifies his thoroughly natural and earthy status. Indeed, Hartman suggests that "Noah's presence [in the account of God's covenantal promises] appears to be relevant solely by virtue of his being a member of the class of 'living things on the earth.'"[14] For that matter, we should note that God's covenantal promise to sustain rather than to destroy creation comes immediately as a result of having "smelled the pleasing odor" of Noah's burnt offerings (8:21)—a decidedly earthy rendering of God as well.

So do we know Noah or not? When we tell his story, what do we say? Is Noah a forthright preacher of righteousness, as much of Jewish and Christian apocalyptic literature claims? Similarly, is he a faithful messenger of Allah, and so another prototype of Muhammad, as the Qur'an claims? Or is he perhaps a relatively passive and overly acquiescent creature of dust, as many talmudic rabbis thought? Perhaps the reply we offer will depend on the extent to which we are willing to live with ambiguity, to rest easily with something other than the black-and-white categories of air-brushed religious heroes and models, the telling of whose stories we cannot allow to betray even the slightest hint of doubt, wavering, or fear. Noah in the Qur'an feels like just one among a long line of stereotypes who say essentially the same thing and act essentially the same way. I submit that while the Noah of rabbinic interpretation is no stalwart spiritual giant, he is much more like most of us human beings—and thus far more interesting. *I think* I think that's the Noah I prefer to know.

8

THE SIGN OF SINAI

And We raised the Mount over them, in view of their covenant,
and We said to them: "Enter the door prostrate," and We also said:
"Do not transgress on the Sabbath," taking from them a solemn
pledge.

—Qur'an 4:154

Along with this chapter's epigraph, in three other passages of the Qur'an
we encounter language describing something that sounds like a surpassingly
odd event—one having something or other to do with a mountain. Beyond
that, context makes it clear that in each of these passages the mountain in
question is Sinai, where, according to the biblical book of Exodus, God
established a covenant with the people of Israel through the giving of the
Torah (e.g., Exod. 11:11). Here are the other three qur'anic passages, with
the surprising element in each one italicized:

Those who believe [in the Recitation given to Muhammad], and those who
are Jews, and Christians, and Sabaeans—whoever believes in Allah and the
last day and does what is right—surely their reward is with their Lord, and
no fear shall come upon them, nor shall they grieve. And *remember when We
made a covenant with you, and We raised above you the Mount*, saying, "Hold

firmly to what we have given you, and always remember what is therein so that you might become holy people." (2:62–63)

And when it is said to [the Jews], "Believe in what Allah has sent down," they reply, "We believe in what was sent down to us"—Yet they reject anything more, even if it be Truth that confirms what is with [i.e., what has been given to] them. Say: "Why then have you slain the prophets of Allah in times past, if you did indeed believe?" There came to you Moses with clear proofs; yet even after all that you worshipped the Calf, and you behaved wrongly. And remember that *when We made a covenant with you and raised above you the towering Mount*, saying, "Hold tightly to what We have given you, and give heed to Our Word"—they said, "We hear, and we disobey." (2:91–93)

When we shook the Mount over them, as though it were a canopy, and they thought it was going to fall on them: "Hold firmly to what We have given you, and bring ever to remembrance what is within it, so that you might fear Allah and obey Him." (7:171)

Later in this chapter I will offer a brief reading of each passage, seeking to highlight its unique accents. But first, let us consider the theme that these four passages bear in common: in each, God is portrayed as raising a mountain over the heads of the people of Israel as though to impress upon them the great importance of their holding firmly to the conditions of the covenant. Drawing upon the Qur'an's heavy usage of the concept of the "sign" (*ayah*), let us playfully assign a name to this scenario: the sign of Sinai. This sign, at least upon first reading, appears to be about some heavy-handed coercion on God's part to force the Israelites into compliance. Indeed, the ninth-century Muslim commentator Al-Tabari attributes the following expansion of the story to Ibn Zaid, one of Muhammad's early followers: "Then God sent His angels, and they shook the mountain over [the people of Israel], and it was said to them: 'Do you know what this is?' They said: 'Yes, this is the Mount.' They said: 'Take the scripture; otherwise we shall fling it down upon you.' ... Then they took it with the covenant."[1]

Mount Sinai hanging, suspended in midair, over the Israelites' heads? What is the meaning of this? Were it not for the privilege I enjoyed in 1988 of studying rabbinic literature under the tutelage of Israeli philosophers David Hartman and Tzvi Marx at the Shalom Hartman Institute in Jerusalem, I would not have recognized in these mountainous passages from the Qur'an yet another talmudic tale, another creative rabbinic reading of the biblical text. But I am convinced that this is what we encounter here. Behind these qur'anic passages lies a rabbinic yarn that in turn had evolved as a creative reading of the following passage in Exodus:

On the morning of the third day there was thunder and lightning, as well as a thick cloud on the mountain, and a blast of a trumpet so loud that all the people who were in the camp trembled. Moses brought the people out of the camp to meet God. *They took their stand at the foot of the mountain.* Now Mount Sinai was wrapped in smoke, because the LORD had descended upon it in fire; . . . the whole mountain shook violently. (Exod. 19:16–18)

Pertinent to our purposes is a particular strand of rabbinic interpretation of this passage that required taking the Hebrew term *tachat*, which in this context normally would be translated as "at the foot of," and interpreting it instead as "underneath." Thus, in this reading the people of Israel were not simply waiting at the foot of Mount Sinai to receive God's commandments issued through Moses; rather, they cowered *beneath* the mountain, which was uprooted and suspended over their heads by the Almighty! A classic instance of this surprising interpretation is found in *Avodah Zarah* (Heb. "idolatrous worship"), a rabbinic tractate that addresses the problem of idolatry and how to avoid Gentiles' harmful influences even while unavoidably living among them. In the relevant passage, the rabbis imagine the scene of the Final Judgment. In their eschatological scenario,

the nations will contend: "Lord of the Universe, have You given us the Torah; did we ever [have a chance to] decline it?" But how can they argue thus, seeing that it is written, *The Lord came from Sinai and rose from Seir unto them; He shined forth from Mount Paran* (Deut. 33:2). And it is also written, *God comes from Teman* (Hab. 3:3). What did God seek in Seir, and what did God seek in Mount Paran?—Rabbi Yohanan says: This teaches us that the Holy One, blessed be He, offered the Torah to every nation and every tongue, but none of them accepted it, until He came to Israel who received it. [How, then, will the nations be able to say that the Torah was not offered to them?] Their contention will be this: "Did we accept it and fail to observe it?"—[i.e., "At least we didn't say we'd accept it and then fail to do so!"]. But surely the obvious rejoinder to this their plea would be: "Then why did you not accept it?"—This, then, will be their contention: "Lord of the Universe, did You ever suspend the mountain over us like a vault [lit., 'cask' or 'tub'] as You have done unto Israel, such that we would still have declined to accept it?" For in commenting on the verse, *And they stood at the foot of the mountain*, Rabbi Dimi ben Hama said: This teaches us that the Holy One, blessed be He, suspended the mountain over Israel like a vault, and said unto them: "If you accept the Torah, it will be well with you; but if not, there will you find your grave." (*Avodah Zarah* I.2) [2]

What a marvelous story of the Age to Come! I have already reflected briefly in chapter 2—and will do so far more thoroughly in chapter 12—on the function of eschatology as a mode of theodicy, that is, of dealing with the pressing everyday problem of evil. We know the questions. Why is there so much hardship and suffering in God's good creation? More particularly, why do God's people, who are trying to live righteously, undergo such difficulties? Why do the Gentile nations have such power that they are able to enforce their will upon the Jewish communities? These are the plaints the rabbis and their people raised.

One perennial answer to such questions is essentially a function of the human imagination: we can dream, we can envision, we can hope for a radically different kind of world where the tables have been turned, where God's rule is made plain, where God's people enjoy obvious blessing and approval from God. Given that eschatological scenario, the people of Israel could imaginatively anticipate this great Day of Reckoning, a time of reward for all who had lived by the Torah's precepts. The greatness of the Gentile peoples whose power the Jews had known—nations like the Persians, the Babylonians, the Romans—would then be on the other side of the ledger.

But perhaps those powerhouse nations could plead ignorance of the Torah as their defense. "Lord of the Universe, have You given us the Torah; did we ever [have a chance to] decline it?" In this eschatological courtroom scene, the rabbis then cite several verses from the Tanakh to demonstrate that, in fact, God had gone out looking among the Gentiles for a people who would accept the joyous burden of the Torah. The rabbis imagine a decisive rejoinder to the plea of ignorance: "The Holy One, blessed be He, offered the Torah to every nation and every tongue, but none of them accepted it, until He came to Israel who received it."

But perhaps the nations would offer a counterargument. "Did we accept it and fail to observe it?" At least they had not agreed to accept Torah and then failed to live up to their promise! The rabbis imagine the heavenly retort: Why had these Gentile powerhouses rejected the offer in the first place? The nations, however, apparently will have a highly competent defense attorney, who will point out that it was not a level playing field. In this imagined final judgment, it will become clear to everyone that God, after having canvassed all the other nations, whittled down the possibilities just to this scraggly bunch of ragtag slaves, freshly liberated from Egypt. Given the extremity of the situation, one could imagine that God might feel it necessary to flex some muscle to coax some folks to agree to the covenant of Torah. "This, then, will be the nations' contention: 'Lord of the Universe, did You ever suspend the mountain over us like a vault as You have done unto Israel, such that we would still have declined to accept it?'"

In this fascinating if highly imaginative scenario, the rabbis envision the Gentile peoples protesting that Israel's concession to covenantal terms had, after all, been coerced. And the rabbis appear to admit that these contentious Gentiles will have a point. "For in commenting on the verse, *And they stood at the foot of the mountain*, Rabbi Dimi ben Hama said: This teaches us that the Holy One, blessed be He, suspended the mountain over Israel like a vault, and said unto them: 'If you accept the Torah, it will be well with you; but if not, there will you find your grave.'" Simply put, the people of Israel faced stark alternatives: it was the Torah or their lives.

The theological issues with which the rabbis wrestled in this case seem to have begun with the simple observation that the Israelites had been called by their God to be a distinct people, set apart from all the other peoples of the world for exclusive devotion to Adonai. But Adonai, their God, was God of all—Creator and Sustainer of all things. Why had they, of all peoples, been called to be the covenantal people of Torah? The rabbinic reply developed in this talmudic passage is that God truly is the God of all peoples and had sought covenantal partnership with them all.

But that raises a new question. If all other peoples had rejected God's offer of the Torah, why had Israel of all peoples said yes? Were the Jews inherently a superior people? More spiritually sensitive? Religious geniuses? Ontologically a cut above? No: the answer that developed in this particular strand of rabbinic reflection bears a note of realism about the people of Israel. In a stroke of healthy self-critique, the tradition attributes to Rabbi Dimi ben Hama of Haifa this wildly imaginative interpretation of Exodus 19:17: "This teaches us that the Holy One, blessed be He, suspended the mountain over Israel like a vault." Thus, in this slice of rabbinic narrative theology, we encounter several important themes: (1) God truly is Lord of all the earth, and of all its peoples; (2) God does not show extravagant favoritism toward Israel, for all peoples were offered the covenantal terms of Torah; and (3) even Israel's acceptance of Torah does not signify Jewish superiority over the other peoples of the world. The rabbis' eschatological scenario thus testifies not only to God's interest in covenantal relationship that invites and respects human responsibility but also to God's sovereign power to enact the divine will if necessary. When (God's) push comes to shove, an uprooted mountain hanging over human heads can be very persuasive.

It seems reasonable to presume that this highly creative reading of the Exodus story had reached Muhammad's ears in one way or another—and presumably in the form of an oral tradition among the Jews of his milieu. It seems reasonable, too, to suspect that Muhammad assumed that this scene of Mount Sinai hanging suspended over the children of Israel was the unvarnished biblical story. Once again it must be duly noted that the traditional Muslim understanding of the Qur'an, or of Muhammad's (non)role in its writing, does not readily allow for influence from Jewish tradition nor for

Muhammad's need to depend on anything but direct revelation for his Sinai account. Thus, while it is safe to stipulate that the traditionally dominant and most obvious reading of the Exodus passage is that the people of Israel stood at the foot of Mount Sinai while Moses ascended to receive the Torah, the Qur'an apparently validates the far more sensationalistic but relatively obscure rabbinic interpretation in which Israel quivers beneath the bulk of Sinai. As I read the evidence, it appears obvious that the Qur'an is drawing directly upon this Jewish elaboration of the Exodus story. The signs of Sinai are there for anyone to read.

Let us now return to the Qur'an's three substantive citations of the Sinai story. In 2:62–63, the primary point seems to be that for the peoples who have received divine revelation—"Jews, and Christians, and Sabaeans" are specifically named—all will be well in the Day of Judgment, provided that they remain faithful to what has been revealed to them. "Whoever believes in Allah and the last day and does what is right—surely their reward is with their Lord, and no fear shall come upon them, nor shall they grieve." Then comes the mention of the Mount hovering above the children of Israel—except that now, of course, it is an event recollected by Allah and described in divine first-person voice. "And remember when We made a covenant with you, and We raised above you the Mount, saying, 'Hold firmly to what we have given you, and always remember what is therein so that you might become holy people.'" Again, the point seems to be to underscore the radical importance of maintaining lives of faithful obedience to the covenant each people has received from God.

The second citing of the sign of Sinai, though in the same surah, occurs in a more contentious context (2:91–93). Here the Qur'an observes that the Jews are not responding in droves to Muhammad's proclamation. When challenged with the new revelations, the Jews were replying, "We believe in what was sent down to us"—even though, the Qur'an retorts, the new revelations actually confirm the Jews' Torah. Then the Qur'an instructs Muhammad to challenge them with a question reminiscent of Jesus's stinging indictment of his contemporaries in the gospel of Matthew (23:29–36): "Why then have you slain the prophets of Allah in times past, if you did indeed believe?" It is in this spirit of accusation against his Jewish critics that Muhammad now once again mentions the towering mountain, proclaiming that God had commanded the Israelites to "hold tightly to what We have given you, and give heed to Our Word." However, unlike the account of Exodus in which the people respond to Moses' covenantal legislation by chorusing, "Everything that the LORD has spoken we will do" (19:8), the Qur'an offers this biting alternative: "They said, 'We hear, and we disobey'!" Though perhaps somewhat unexpected, it is a twist to the Exodus text that fits the accusatory agenda of the passage.[3]

The third use of the story adds little to our reflections here, other than to ensure that we cannot easily read the qur'anic rendering of the story figuratively. "When we shook the Mount over them, as though it were a canopy, . . . they thought it was going to fall on them." Can there be any question that Muhammad assumed the historical factuality of the story of Sinai suspended overhead? "Hold firmly to what We have given you, and bring ever to remembrance what is within it," the Qur'an recalls as the divine instruction given during the momentous, mountainous event, "so that you might fear Allah and obey Him" (7:171). Keep in mind, too, that according to Q 2:93 the children of Israel responded, "We hear, and we disobey." One would have to wonder what kept that mountain afloat.

On the other hand—and supporting the Qur'an's emphasis upon Israel's disobeying—both the story in Exodus and later rabbinic interpretation bluntly narrate Israel's virtually immediate fall into idolatry before the golden calf fashioned by Aaron. Israel's vow of obedience, so tragically short-lived, undoubtedly contributed significantly to the story as Muhammad heard it. It does raise the stakes significantly to recall a story in which the Israelites, so recently threatened by the looming sign of Sinai, could nonetheless readily depart from their promised loyalty to God.

It is likely, then, that Muhammad used the story for shock value, to cajole his Jewish audience into taking his revelations more seriously. Though there was no mountain hanging over anyone's head, the intended rhetorical effect of recalling the sign of Sinai would be to reenact the drama, to re-create the threat of sheer divine power ever ready to bury the disobedient under a mountain of rock. To be sure, Muhammad did not invent the imagery, for it had a rabbinic life of its own. But Muhammad obviously put it to use, invoking the portrait of a transcendent deity fully able and willing to enforce his will.

This extrapolation on Exodus is not confined to *Avodah Zarah* and the Qur'an. Like all stories, this one truly does possess a life of its own; we find further rabbinic commentary on the sign of Sinai that radically reinterprets it. Presumably, Jewish interpreters could not rest content with this image of divine threat overhead. Later rabbis suggested that Mount Sinai, rather than looming like a sledgehammer over Moses's people, was instead suspended over them like a wedding canopy. According to this reading, writes Benjamin Blech, "God was enacting a scene readily recognizable to every Jew. The mountain served as the *hupah*, the divine canopy, which turned the Jews' commitment to accept God's law into an everlasting union of wedded bliss and harmony."[4] In this happier interpretation the scenario changes radically from "Do or die" to "Till death do us part." God weds Israel beneath the canopy of Sinai.

This nuptial metaphor has, in fact, become the dominant one in Judaism, revived annually during Shavuot, the Festival of Weeks. It is obviously a far happier, more positive framing of the Sinai narrative, for here the accent falls on covenantal love and long-suffering rather than on what can feel like heavy-handed threat. The Torah is no burden accepted under coercion but instead the marriage contract between God and Israel. Might this interpretation have arisen as a rabbinic response to the Qur'an's adoption of the more forcible depiction, possibly cited by Muslims in religious disputation with Jews? While this is an interesting scenario, the exact circumstances of the *hupah* interpretation appear to be historically inaccessible. What is historically certain is that the imagery of a marriage between God and Israel—with their anniversary celebrated annually during Shavuot, the Day of the Giving of the Torah—is developed in the *Zohar*, the mystical commentary on the Torah written by Moses de Leon, a late thirteenth-century Spanish Jew who certainly would have had contact with Muslim scholars. Roughly three centuries later, the Jewish mystic and poet Israel Najara wrote a Shavuot hymn, in the form of a marriage contract, for synagogue worship in Safed, Israel. In this hymn God pledges deep Torah-loyalty to Israel: "Many days wilt thou be Mine and I will be thy Redeemer. Be thou My mate according to the law of Moses and Israel, and I will honor, support and maintain thee, and be thy shelter and refuge in everlasting mercy."[5]

There seems initially to be a world of difference between these two images: God suspending Sinai over the people's heads and God vowing to be their "shelter and refuge in everlasting mercy." However, even in the Shavuot hymn God's promise of protection is not unconditional; it hinges upon the people's agreement to be God's bride "according to the law of Moses and Israel." Further, in the more ominous version of the story, God's use of force surely can be interpreted as a benevolent sign: God acts coercively out of great love for Israel, for their own good pushing them into a promise of obedience. So perhaps the differences are not so vast. Nonetheless, it is clear that such a story of divine threat will not sustain the life and hope of a religious community over generations. The deity portrayed in that story is precarious and arbitrary, too frightful to inspire love for the long haul. It becomes all the more distressing when a story such as this is no longer only an "inside story" among the community's members but has leaked out and become common lore among outsiders—indeed, among the members of a competing religious tradition. The story's canonization in the Qur'an provided Muhammad and the subsequent Muslim community with a rather uncomplimentary portrait of Israel: even with divine violence looming, the People of the Book made nothing but empty promises.

Thus it is no surprise that Jewish tradition found new, more affirming ways to read the story of the ancestors at Mount Sinai. Like all signs, the sign of Sinai yields many interpretations. The rabbis who bore the brunt of the burden of interpretation for their historical communities developed readings that helped to sustain the Jewish people over the generations in loyalty to their God. Obviously, Muslim imams and Christian ministers—not to mention spiritual teachers and guides from the host of other religious traditions in the world—have tried to fulfill the same task for their respective communities of interpretation. In considering these tangled, complex histories of interpretive communities, a compelling interpretation begins to suggest itself: the ambiguities of historical existence, of our religious traditions' texts, and of our interpretive differences all suggest the intriguing possibility that, somehow, all of this demanding labor of reading and rereading is divinely de-signed.

9

MARY, MOTHER OF JESUS

We made Mary's son and his mother a sign, and We sheltered them
on a lofty ground which had meadows and a spring.

—Qur'an 23:50

One of the most surprising facts about the Qur'an is that, for all of its 114
surahs and hundreds of pages of text, in the entire book only one woman is
mentioned by name. Further, that woman is named on many occasions, and she
even has a surah named after her. That surah or chapter is 19—"Maryam"—
and the woman in question, of course, is Jesus's mother.

Why does Mary receive so much attention in the Qur'an, while no other
woman does? Granted, other women are alluded to, including biblical figures
such as Eve and Sarah, but never by name. Surely part of the answer lies
in the likelihood that the Qur'an reflects the growing reverence for Jesus's
mother among Christians during the centuries prior to Muhammad's era.
Christian folklore regarding the child Jesus and his mother had spread rap-
idly among Christians, imaginative storytellers having worked to fill in the
considerable gaps left by the canonical gospels. This process of developing
a Mother-and-Baby-Jesus folklore included romanticizing Mary as the
paragon of purity, innocence, and chastity, a victim of unjust and unkind
accusations who is eventually vindicated by God. This is the gist of her
portrayal in the Qur'an.

It may also help to consider that relatively few men are mentioned by name either, and most who do receive such attention are prophets. While Mary is not a prophet—and as a woman, according to Islam if not the Qur'an itself, she cannot be one—there is a moment in the Qur'an when she functions in a prophetic role. Significantly, in that moment Mary is literally speechless.

We will come to that moment later in the chapter, but let us proceed by considering one of the more remarkable parallels between the Bible and the Qur'an: the angel's announcement to Mary of her impending role as the mother of Jesus the Messiah. The careful reader will keep in mind that there are two nativity accounts among the New Testament's four gospels— Matthew and Luke. Matthew tells the story of Jesus's birth and infancy entirely from the perspective of Joseph; Luke, on the other hand, focuses on Mary. The structural similarities between the Lukan and qur'anic accounts are striking, including the story of Zechariah and Elizabeth, the parents of John the Baptist. But in the following parallels, we pick up the story at the angelic announcement to Mary of her impending motherhood:

The Bible	The Qur'an
Luke 1:26–30	*Surah 3:42–43*
In the sixth month the angel Gabriel was sent by God to a town in Galilee called Nazareth, to a virgin engaged to a man whose name was Joseph, of the house of David. The virgin's name was Mary.	
And he came to her and said,	And when the angels said:
"Greetings, favored one!	"O Mary, Allah has chosen you and
The Lord is with you."	purified you, preferring you to all womankind. O Mary, be obedient to your Lord, prostrate yourself and bow down with those who bow down."
But she was much perplexed by his words and pondered what sort of greeting this might be. The angel said to her, "Do not be afraid, Mary, for you have found favor with God."	

While acknowledging the similarity between the accounts in their introduction of Mary as God's chosen vessel, we may note significant differences too. The language of prostration is distinctively Muslim in its connotation; similarly, the command to "bow down with those who bow down" implies the Islamic discipline of communal ritual prayer. So this initial angelic greeting conforms well to qur'anic contours. Luke, on the other hand, characterizes Mary's reaction as somewhat uncertain, perhaps even mildly ambivalent.

Surah 3:44
This is part of the tidings of the Unseen which We reveal to you. You were not in their midst when they cast their [lots] to see who will take charge of Mary, and you were not in their midst when they were disputing.

This brief aside in the qur'anic text—obviously a departure from the flow of the interchange between the angel and Mary—in all likelihood reflects a story from the so-called *Infancy Gospel of James*. Most scholars believe it was written around the middle of the second century and agree on its importance for understanding the development of early Marian lore.[1] In this noncanonical gospel, Mary's parents, Joachim and Anna, dedicate their little girl, conceived in their advanced years in answer to their prayers, to a life of service to God and temple. From age three to twelve, Mary "lived in the temple of the Lord. She was fed there like a dove, receiving her food from the hand of a heavenly messenger" (8:2)—the narrative thereby ensuring the purity of her (lack of) contact with the temple priests. But as she nears puberty, the priests get antsy, fearing that her menstrual blood will pollute the temple (cf. Lev. 15:19–24). The high priest then receives instructions from God to "assemble all the widowers of the people and have them each bring a staff. She will become the wife of the one to whom the Lord God shows a sign" (8:7–8). Joseph, an elderly widower who is part of the gathering, becomes the reluctant beneficiary of God's blessing: "a dove came out of his staff and perched on Joseph's head" (9:6). In a detail undoubtedly intended to assure its hearers that Mary remained sexually chaste, Joseph protests the apparent meaning of the sign: "I already have sons and I'm an old man; she's only a young woman. I'm afraid that I'll become the butt of jokes among the people of Israel" (9:8). The high priest insists, reminding Joseph of the fates of earlier Israelites who resisted the divine will. Old Joseph relents.

It is not difficult to hear strong hints of this story in the Qur'an's allusion to the casting of lots "to see who would take charge of Mary," and even to the "disputing" that occurred. Further, the insistent use of the phrase "you were not in their midst" (with the "you" a singular masculine form) when these things were supposed to have happened strongly suggests that Muhammad, while having heard of this story of Mary, had harbored doubts about its veracity. In this case, then, Muhammad receives revelatory assurance of the story's reliability.

Luke 1:31–33	Surah 3:45–46
	When the angels said:
"And now, you will conceive in your womb	"O Mary, Allah bids you rejoice in a

Luke 1:31–33	Surah 3:45–46
and bear a son, and you will name him Jesus.	word from Him, whose name is the Messiah, Jesus, son of Mary.
He will be great, and will be called the Son of the Most High, and the Lord God will give to him the throne of his ancestor David. He will reign over the house of Jacob forever, and of his kingdom there will be no end."	He shall be prominent in this world and in the next and shall be near to God. He shall speak to people from the cradle and while an old man and will be one of the righteous."

Again, while the angelic response is far from identical in the two narratives, the structural similarity between them is readily apparent. In both, the angel's response not only reassures Mary but predicts the greatness of her promised child. This is, incidentally, one of several passages in the Qur'an in which Jesus is described as the Messiah. Its usage here immediately raises the question of what that term may have meant for Muhammad and early Muslim reciters of the Qur'an.[2] This would be a difficult question to answer. Perhaps it would be enough to say, with the qur'anic angels, that "Messiah" means that Jesus "shall be prominent in this world and in the next and shall be near to God."[3] Note too that the Qur'an here calls Jesus "a word from [Allah]," suggesting that he will not simply speak forth divine communication as a prophet but will in some sense embody this communication. This is a remarkable possibility, and while it certainly cannot simply be equated with the Johannine notion of Jesus as God's Word become flesh (John 1:14), it does suggest a singular greatness of Jesus's prophetic role.[4]

Luke 1:34	Surah 3:47a
Mary said to the angel,	She said:
"How can this be, since I am a virgin?"	"Lord, how can I have a child when I have not been touched by any man?"

Obviously, the striking structural similarity between these passages continues. Both the Qur'an and the gospel of Luke present Mary as asking the obvious question for a virgin to ask. The angelic announcement regarding the child's impending greatness in the divine economy moves the conversation to a point of both tension and expectation: "How can this be?"

Interestingly, the aforementioned *Infancy Gospel of James* portrays the young virgin as asking a different question of the angel: "If I actually conceive by the Lord, the living God, will I also give birth the way women usually do?" (11:6). Here the question is not about the manner of her conceiving but of her birthing this child. Whereas both Luke's gospel and the Qur'an assume that in fact the actual birthing of Jesus was in "the way women usually do," in this noncanonical infancy gospel the angel replies, "No, Mary, because the power of God will overshadow you. Therefore, the child to be born will be called holy, son of the Most High" (11:7).[5] In other words, while the angelic reply in the *Infancy Gospel of James* echoes Luke's account immediately below, it is put to a different purpose, proclaiming that even the manner of the child's birth will be unique because of his miraculous conception. On the other hand, we will find later that the Qur'an not only assumes that the normal process of childbirth was Mary's lot but even emphasizes the strain of her labor in a way that most (if not all) Christian literature of the first millennium appears to have avoided.

Luke 1:35	Surah 3:47b–48
The angel said to her,	Allah said:
"The Holy Spirit will come upon you,	"Thus Allah creates whatever He
and the power of the Most High will	pleases. When He decrees a matter, He
overshadow you; therefore the child to	simply says to it: 'Be,' and it comes to
be born will be holy; he will be called	be."
Son of God."	And [Allah] will teach [Jesus] the Book, the Wisdom, the Torah and the Gospel."

It may be surprising to learn that the Qur'an teaches that Mary was a virgin when she conceived Jesus. But even in this matter there are important differences between the Bible and the Qur'an. While Christian tradition has often interpreted the virginal conception as a sign of Jesus's divinity, Mary's condition carries no such connotations for Muslims. This is partly due, it seems, to the divergent ways in which the conception of the child in Mary's womb is described in these accounts. In Luke the description of the Holy Spirit coming upon Mary, and especially of the Spirit's "overshadowing" her, is reminiscent of Genesis 1:2, where God's *ruach* (spirit or breath) blows across "the face of the deep," sweeping over and stirring "the face of the waters." It is language that in the Jewish tradition came to be associated with a mother dove's brooding over her nest of eggs—warming, nurturing, giving life. Thus this Spirit came to be identified, at least roughly, with the *Shekhinah* (from *shakhan*, the Hebrew word for "dwelling"), God's (in)dwelling Presence among the people of Israel and throughout all creation.

The Qur'an offers differing imagery. Rather than the overshadowing of a life-nurturing Spirit, we find the omnipotent fiat of sheer transcendence. The child does not emerge from an ineffably mysterious union of the female

141

womb and the indwelling Spirit of life but from God's creative command "Be!" Thus the virginal conception, as far as the Qur'an is concerned, testifies only to God's transcendent power to accomplish what God wills. This is no sign of God's incarnation in the world, no testimony to God's dwelling among us as one of us, one with us. It is, rather, a sign of God's sheer power to call anything into being, including a boy child in the womb of a virgin.[6] This is explicit a little later in the same surah: "Jesus in Allah's Sight is like Adam; He created him from dust, then He said to him: 'Be,' and there he was" (3:59).

In Surah 19 ("Maryam") we find the story of mother Mary and her newborn recited with additional details. It is fascinating that Luke identifies Mary's angelic visitor as Gabriel (1:26) while the Qur'an does not, given the fact that Gabriel otherwise is a highly visible figure in the Qur'an. However, in "Maryam" we find the provocative claim "We [Allah] sent to her Our Spirit and it appeared to her in the form of a well-shaped human being" (19:17), a saying that may have contributed to Islam's eventual identification of the Qur'an's references to a "holy spirit" with the angel Gabriel. In any case, in this version of the story when Mary asks how she could become pregnant "when no man has touched me and I have not been an unchaste woman" (19:20), the angel replies, "Thus [it will be], your Lord has said: 'This is an easy matter for Me; that We may make him a sign unto mankind and a Mercy from Us.' And thus it was decreed" (19:21).

Once again, such language should not be overlooked or downplayed. The Qur'an accords Jesus a remarkable role; he is a "sign" and even a "mercy" from God to all humanity. It is as though the Qur'an could borrow Jesus's estimation of John the Baptist—"A prophet? Yes, I tell you, and more than a prophet" (Matt. 11:9)—and apply it to Jesus himself. Qur'anic texts such as 19:21, in Rizwi Faizer's words, "proclaim . . . a very distinct position regarding the nature of Christ which is no longer emphasized by Muslims today," leading her even to suggest that this particularly high regard for Jesus "was originally . . . as much a part of [early Islam's] creed as was the belief in one God and His prophet, Muhammad."[7] Given this possibility, it is not surprising that the Qur'an reflects as well the honor accorded by Christians to Jesus's mother.

We have already seen the likely role that *The Infancy Gospel of James* played as a backdrop to the Mary story in Surah 3. Now, with our resumption of the narrative as it is recited in Surah 19, it appears that material from another noncanonical gospel, *The Infancy Gospel of Pseudo-Matthew*,[8] looms in the background. Given the difficulty of dating this material precisely, not to mention the fluid nature of all oral (to say nothing of written) traditions, it is probably safest simply to assume that stories of Mary's conception and

Jesus's birth circulated in many variant forms in the centuries before and after Muhammad. Given that such stories were popular especially among rank-and-file Christians (the "people in the pew"), though routinely discouraged by the more theologically informed church leaders, it is not terribly surprising that Muhammad would have heard, and have been influenced by, this lore. Note the parallels:

The Qur'an

Surah 19:22–23	Pseudo-Matthew
So, she conceived him and she withdrew with him to a distant place. Then labour pangs drove her toward the trunk of a palm tree. She said: "I wish I had died before this and had become completely forgotten."	It so happened that, on the third day after their departure [from Bethlehem], Mary was fatigued by the excessive heat of the sun of the desert and, seeing a palm tree, said to Joseph, "I want to rest a bit under its shadow."

While the circumstances in the two stories are not identical, the similarities to ensue will leave no doubt as to the integral relationship between them. The most obvious difference, though, is that the Qur'an describes, even if briefly, the extremity of Mary's birthing labors. In her influential work *Qur'an and Woman*, Amina Wadud comments on this qur'anic passage:

> Despite the centrality of Jesus to Christianity, no similar affirmation of the unique experience of childbirth is given such detailed consideration in any Christian theological work—not even in the Bible. That special function is elevated to the status worthy of detailed mention to attest to its significance in the Qur'anic worldview. We are not left to just take it for granted.[9]

To Wadud we must reply yes—and no. On the one hand she is generally correct that no Christian literature gives such attention to the harsh reality of Mary's labor, though we must note that early Christian thinkers and leaders certainly assumed that her labor was typical. It was in second-century Gnostic texts that the struggle, pain, and humanness of Mary's labor and Jesus's birth would have been downplayed if not denied altogether. For example, second-century theologian Irenaeus's *Against Heresies* opposes as heretical a teaching that "Jesus . . . had passed through Mary like water through a tube"[10]—presumably meaning smoothly, freely, and painlessly. Regrettably, such docetic renderings of Jesus have a certain appeal for the popular imagination; we have already encountered a typical example in *The Infancy Gospel of James*, in which the birth of Jesus is mostly a matter of an exceedingly bright light filling the cave where Mary, reclining alone, has no need of a midwife. The baby just—appears. Certainly in this regard the Qur'an offers a vast improvement.

On the other hand, it must at least be acknowledged that the story itself, at least in terms of its overall structure, is not unique to the Qur'an. Granted, the form of the story as it comes to us in *The Infancy Gospel of Pseudo-Matthew* does not narrate Mary's birthing labors but the strain of subsequent travel to Bethlehem. But in either case we encounter the real humanity of this young mother. And in both stories, a palm tree figures as a source of solace.

Pseudo-Matthew

Joseph quickly led her to the palm and let her get down from the animal. While Mary sat, she looked at the top of the palm and saw it full of fruit. She said to Joseph, "I wish, if it is possible, that I have some fruit from this palm." Joseph said to her, "I am astonished that you say this, when you see how high this palm is, that you think to eat from the fruit of the palm. I think more of the lack of water, which already fails us in the water bags; we now have nothing by which we can refresh ourselves and the animals."

A brief comment will suffice: in the popular Christian version of the story, Joseph shares in Mary's extreme situation. Indeed, he insists that Mary is missing the point of their real need, and he helps to establish their hopelessness as far as getting to the tree's fruit. Perhaps the story even vaguely mirrors—or, more important, reverses—the Genesis story of Eve, Adam, and a certain tree's beguiling fruit.

Surah 19:24–26a	Pseudo-Matthew
	Then the infant Jesus, who was resting with
Whereupon [a voice] called her from	smiling face at his mother's bosom, said to
beneath her: "Do not grieve. Your Lord has	the palm,
created below you a stream.	
Shake the trunk of the palm tree towards	"Bend down, tree, and refresh my mother
you and it will drop upon you fresh ripe	with your fruit." And immediately, at his
dates.	voice, the palm bent down its head to the feet of Mary, and they gathered fruit from it by
Eat,	which all were refreshed. After they had gathered all its fruit, it remained bent down, waiting so that it should raise up at the command of him who had commanded it to bend. Then Jesus said to it, "Raise up, palm, and be strong, and be a companion of my

Surah 19:24–26a	Pseudo-Matthew
[Your Lord has created below you a stream.]	trees which are in my Father's Paradise. Open a water course beneath your roots which is hidden in the earth, and from it let flow waters to satisfy us." And the palm raised itself at once, and fountains of water, very clear and cold and sweet, began to pour out
drink,	through the roots. When they saw the
and rejoice."	fountains of water they rejoiced with great rejoicing, and they and the beasts of burden were all satisfied, and they gave thanks to God."

The Qur'an is unclear as to the source of the voice that instructs Mary from "beneath her." But if we do assume a common story at work in these two documents, then the logical assumption is that it was the unborn child Jesus, speaking to Mary from "beneath her" in the womb, who uttered these words. In *Pseudo-Matthew*, baby Jesus speaks—to the palm tree, no less—early demonstrating both miraculous power and theological acumen, to say nothing of simply being able to speak at all. From the perspective of Christian orthodoxy, this fanciful story of Jesus's infancy is particularly problematic because it posits Jesus as a fully developed adult human (or even divine) consciousness in early childhood. Such a view of Jesus, while popular and attractive for many Christians throughout the centuries and even today, was justly condemned as a heresy in the fourth century for not taking seriously Jesus's human nature. It is associated most notoriously with the Alexandrian theologian Apollinaris, who taught that Jesus had a human body but lacked a human mind, having no need for one because the Logos, the Divine Mind, indwelt and dictated the body's every move. This interpretation of Jesus would have given the church a less-than-human Jesus, his mental life not truly human at all. It would take a Christology of this heretical sort to have a wonder-working, walking talking baby Jesus—except when it comes to the Qur'an! For, assuredly, the Qur'an does not assume or teach an Apollinarian Christology.

But does the Qur'an teach that the infant Jesus spoke in complete sentences? It is difficult to avoid such a conclusion. The qur'anic story obviously is not nearly so miraculous as that of *Pseudo-Matthew*, with its palm tree bending down to Mary's fruit-picking reach at the very command of the infant; nonetheless, the structural similarity between the two is sufficiently compelling to suggest that in the Qur'an, it is the unborn child who is speaking from "below" Mary. That is miracle enough! Indeed, it is miracle too much. We will further explore this question momentarily; for the moment, I note that in the Qur'an the mysterious voice continues with important instructions for Mary:

145

Surah 19:26b
Then if you see any human say: "I have vowed to the Compassionate to fast, and so I shall not talk today to any human being."

If nothing else, these instructions regarding a vow of silence on Mary's part help to set up a dramatic denouement in this qur'anic nativity story. Her vow of silence means she will not speak up in her own defense. For the Qur'an repeatedly insists that unjust and degrading accusations were hurled at the pure and chaste mother of Jesus—accusations that the Qur'an invariably associates with the Jewish people. Again, we find structural similarity between the Qur'an and the *Infancy Gospel of James*. In the latter's telling of the story Mary is forced to face her accusers during her pregnancy rather than after Jesus's birth; nonetheless, the common theme is immediately recognizable:

Surah 19:27–28	The Infancy Gospel of James 15:9–12
	The temple assistants went and found
Then she brought him to her people, carrying	her . . . and then they brought her, along
him. They said: "O Mary, you have surely	with Joseph, to the court. "Mary, why have
committed a strange thing. Sister of Aaron,[11]	you done this?" the high priest asked her.
your father was not an evil man and your	Have you forgotten the Lord your God, you
mother was not unchaste."	who were raised in the Holy of Holies and were fed by heavenly messengers? You of all people, who heard their hymns and danced for them— why have you done this?"

We should recognize in both versions of Mary's story a distinct sense of indignation, on the part of both narrators, about the insinuations being made of this chaste virgin. Both the reciter and the hearer of the story want to leap to her defense, to set the record straight. Additionally, in both narratives Mary's sexual purity is being defended and also romanticized, while her Jewish accusers suspect her of loose living.

Surah 19:29a	The Infancy Gospel of James 15:13–18
Whereupon she pointed to him.	And she wept bitterly: "As the Lord God lives, I stand innocent before him. Believe me, I've not had sex with any man." And the high priest said, "Joseph, why have you done this?" And Joseph said, "As the Lord lives, I am innocent where she is concerned." And the high priest said, "Don't perjure yourself, but tell the truth . . ." But Joseph was silent.

It is interesting that in both stories a parent is reduced to silence. However, Mary's silence in the Qur'an is far more significant and is itself ultimately a prophetic act. In *The Infancy Gospel of James* both Mary and Joseph eventually are vindicated by submitting to, and passing, a test of their honesty and sexual purity that appears to be based loosely on a Torah passage (Num. 5:11–31). But in the Qur'an, Mary stands alone, vulnerable and silent, with only a babe in arms. She stands accused, and it appears that none is able to speak in her defense.

"Whereupon she pointed to him." She is not a prophet, but this is Mary's proto-prophetic deed. She does not speak but merely points to her baby, the little one who has excited the accusations of her people against her.

Surah 19:29b–33

They said: "How will we talk to one who is still an infant in the cradle?" He [Jesus] said, "Indeed, I am the servant of Allah, Who gave me the Book and made me a Prophet. And He made me blessed wherever I am, and has commanded me to pray and to give the alms, so long as I live; and be devoted to my mother; and He did not make me arrogant and mischievous. Peace be upon me the day I was born, the day I die and the day I rise from the dead."

The remarkable nature of this holy child continues to blossom for the reader of the Qur'an. This child was conceived by a virgin, spoke like a little prophet in his mother's arms, and—if we so interpret the earlier story of the palm tree—even gave sage advice to his mother while yet in the womb. This presents a serious exegetical issue for readers of the Qur'an. As already mentioned, Christians who told stories like these about Jesus, far beyond the limits of the canonical gospels, fell prey to the heresy of denying Jesus's true humanity. Babies do not preach, not if they're human babies. Again, to assume such mental and spiritual abilities of Jesus is essentially to be guilty of Apollinarianism. This has been a particularly difficult heresy for Christian believers to shake; as the Roman Catholic theologian Karl Rahner (1904–84) observed, the ghost of Apollinaris still haunts the church.[12] For Christian believers haunted by this heresy, the baby Jesus could do these things because he was God, after all. Obviously, however, such is not the case in the Qur'an. Thus we must ask: on what basis would the Qur'an be able to proffer the notion that the infant Jesus was a little baby prophet?

I suggest that the answer lies in the model of divine-human interaction that we have repeatedly encountered already in the Qur'an. For Muslim tradition, the claim that Muhammad was illiterate serves to underscore the divine origin and nature of the Qur'an; Muhammad's own mind and linguistic capabilities would only be a hindrance to divine communication.

Similarly, we have seen that God taught Adam the names of everything, because human beings (and angels, for that matter) are only passive recipients of divine knowledge. Further, God need only say "Be!" and it is. Thus, it would be no difficulty for God to manipulate the vocal cords, tongue, and lips of the baby in Mary's arms such that the baby mouthed Allah's words. In the Christian heresy of Apollinarianism, Jesus's human infancy is denied in favor of the scenario of God masquerading as a baby; in the Qur'an, Jesus's human infancy is simply rendered null by the almighty power of Allah to accomplish divine purpose.

The Christian doctrine of the incarnation of the Logos properly avoids both of these interpretations of Jesus. The doctrine of the incarnation affirms the full and true humanity of Jesus, taking seriously Luke's claim that the boy Jesus "increased in wisdom and in years, and in divine and human favor" (2:52). The doctrine of the incarnation insists that Jesus underwent normal physical, emotional, mental, and spiritual development as a first-century Jewish boy. It also insists that God, in utter mystery, was and is fully present and labors faithfully in, with, and through that real human being of Galilee. Jesus's truly human existence is not short-circuited or compromised by the divine fullness indwelling him.

Such considerations as these move us toward the two chapters to follow.

10

JESUS, SON OF MARY

Bless your envoy [Muhammad] and your servant Jesus son of Mary,
and peace be upon him on the day of his birth and the day of his
death and on the day he is raised up again. Such is Jesus, son of Mary;
it is the truth which they dispute. It is not fitting for Allah to have
a son. Glory be to Him; when He decrees a thing, He simply says:
"Be," and it comes to be. Allah is truly your Lord and my Lord; so
worship him. That is a straight path.

> —Part of the inscription around the inner face of the
> Dome of the Rock, Jerusalem (*derived from Q 19:33–36*)

It can be an unsettling experience for Christians to hear Muslims speak
with deep respect and even reverence for Jesus as a great prophet, invariably
pronouncing the benediction "Peace be upon him" with every mention of his
name. This is a common practice among Muslims when invoking any of the
prophets' names, but that fact does not do much to alleviate the strangeness
of the phrase "Jesus—peace be upon him" to Christian ears.

We should note that in the case of this chapter's epigraph, the pro-
nouncement "Peace be upon him," directed to "Jesus son of Mary," is a
direct adaptation of the infant Jesus's words spoken from his mother's
arms, according to the qur'anic passage with which the previous chapter
concluded: "Peace be upon me the day I was born, the day I die and the

day I rise from the dead." So the ritual blessing of Jesus's name by faithful Muslims follows Jesus's own precedent as found in the Qur'an. Nonetheless, we will find later in this chapter that these words attributed to baby Jesus present a considerable exegetical challenge to Muslim scholarly tradition.

Perhaps part of the oddity for Christian faith of a blessing pronounced upon Jesus is that, instead of receiving the benediction of peace from us, Jesus is himself the bestower of peace. "Peace I leave with you; my peace I give to you," Jesus says to his disciples in his last discourse in the gospel of John (14:27); later in the same gospel, the resurrected Jesus appears among his frightened and confused followers and greets them with "Peace be with you" (20:19, 26). The letter to the Ephesians proclaims that Jesus *is* our peace (Eph. 2:14), the very embodiment of divine peacemaking in this world, who breaks down the dividing walls between Jews and Gentiles, and in principle between all estranged peoples (Eph. 2:17; cf. Acts 10:34–36). So even in as simple an act as bestowing a benediction, we might rightly suspect that differences begin to emerge between the Muslim and the Christian interpretations of the figure of Jesus.

My intent in what follows is not to magnify or to sensationalize those differences; there may, after all, be more common ground to share beneath the feet of Jesus, as it were, than what is typically anticipated. On the other hand, we cannot minimize the differences or, in the interest of peaceability with Islam, jettison the church's historical testimony and traditional confessions regarding Jesus as the Messiah, God's uniquely and supremely Anointed One, "the Son of the living God" (Matt. 16:16).

Surely there is no doubt that it is precisely at the point of Jesus's identity—his ministry, mission, and meaning—that the divide is deepest between Christianity and Islam. These are critical questions to be considered carefully. Indeed, the Qur'an itself calls upon Christians to engage these questions: "After [the earlier prophets] We sent Jesus, son of Mary, confirming what he had before him of the Torah, and We gave him the Gospel, wherein is guidance and light, confirming what he had before him of the Torah and a guidance and admonition to the God-fearing. *And let the People of the Gospel judge in accordance with what Allah has revealed in it.* He who does not judge according to what Allah has revealed, those are the transgressors" (Q 5:46–47). In this chapter I will attempt to navigate these Christological issues, to "judge in accordance with what God has revealed in the gospel"—even while acknowledging that for Islam the church has misunderstood and misconstrued that very gospel—under three rubrics: Jesus's identity and mission; the end of Jesus's earthly ministry; and Jesus and the age to come.

Jesus's Identity and Mission

The first thing to say about Jesus, so far as Islamic teaching is concerned, is that he was a great prophet whose greatness does not change the fact that his teaching was essentially identical to that of all other prophets: the oneness of God, demanding singleness of devotion and obedience. "Such was Jesus, son of Mary," insists the Qur'an in Surah 19, as we pick up the passage at verse 33, precisely where we left off at the conclusion of this book's previous chapter. In Muslim tradition, the Qur'an's frequent designation of Jesus as "son of Mary" is naturally taken to underscore Jesus's true humanity: he is Mary's son and not God's. This, in turn, "is the truth which they"—Christians, presumably—"dispute" (Q 19:34). It is not difficult to discern Muhammad's awareness of Christian disagreements and debates regarding Jesus's identity and nature. The Qur'an's judgment is that "it is not fitting for Allah to have a son" (19:35) and that the only mode of relation properly obtaining between God and Jesus is that of Creator and creature. What the Qur'an says so often in regard to creation in general—"when He decrees a thing, He simply says 'Be,' and it comes to be" (19:35)—is here directly applied to the person of Jesus. While in one important sense this is a fundamental Christian affirmation, too, about Jesus—that as a truly human being he shares fully in creaturely existence—the Qur'an leaves the matter there. Christian faith could not and does not leave the matter there, of course, for from the very beginnings of Christianity Jesus has been worshiped as the Son of God. Indeed, often the greater challenge for many Christians has been to acknowledge that Jesus was a real human being. In the context of these Christological issues, the Qur'an comes down solidly on the judgments that Jesus was a human creature and a great prophet and attempts thus to bring correction to the confusion among Christians: for "the sects among them differed" (19:37).

Yet on the other hand, the Qur'an includes stories of Jesus that would have been more at home among Gnostic Christians who tended to downplay Jesus's authentic humanity. In the previous chapter we considered qur'anic passages that portray the infant Jesus, in his mother Mary's arms, proclaiming Allah's greatness. None of the church's canonical gospels presents Jesus in this way or even hints that Jesus as a child could have done such a thing. Another example of this sort of popular Christology, discouraged by most church leaders and theologians (then and hopefully now) is the well-known story of the boy Jesus's talents with clay. (See table, p. 152.)

Simply stated, the story of how Jesus as a boy created living birds from mud is not canonically authoritative for Christians; it is for Muslims. This fact is, at the very least, surprising. However, it must again be understood that two very different Christologies underlie this story as it is told in the *Infancy Gospel* and in the Qur'an. Among the second-century Christians who would have found the story attractive, Jesus the child does these things because he is already fully conscious of his divine identity and power. He is a little boy who is God and knows it, and who is not beyond throwing his power around! In the Qur'an's retelling of the story, Jesus the child does these things because, strictly speaking, he does not do them at all: they are all God's doing.

	The Qur'an
The Infancy Gospel of Thomas 2:1–6	*Surah 3:49*
When this boy, Jesus, was five years old, he . . . made soft clay [from a pool of water] and shaped it into twelve sparrows . . . on the sabbath day . . .	[God will send Jesus forth as a] Messenger to the Children of Israel [saying]: "I bring you a sign from your Lord. I will create for you out of clay the likeness of a bird;
[When accused of breaking the sabbath,] Jesus simply clapped his hands and shouted to the sparrows, "Be off, fly away . . ."	then I will breathe into it and it will become a bird, by Allah's Leave.
The Jews watched with amazement . . .	
	And I will heal the blind and the leper and will raise the dead, by Allah's Leave. And I will inform you concerning what you eat and what you hoard in your homes. In all this there is surely a sign for you, if you are believers!"

The other deeds in Q 3:49 attributed to Jesus—or, more properly, to God, since they are all accomplished "by Allah's Leave" or permission—are consistent with the canonical portraits of Jesus. The frequent qualifier "by Allah's Leave" undoubtedly is intended to stress that Jesus is but a faithful servant who carries out God's will. The Qur'an, then, clearly stresses divine sovereignty over Jesus's life and ministry—a notion not unfamiliar to careful gospel readers. Especially in John's gospel we find Jesus making claims such as "I can do nothing on my own . . . I seek to do not my own will but the will of him who sent me" (5:30); "my teaching is not mine but his who sent me" (7:16); and "I speak these things as the Father instructed me" (8:28). Similarly, the Qur'an's insistence upon Jesus's status as a prophet may help to remind Christians that Jesus apparently did not shy away from so designating himself (Luke 13:33–35). Further, an early prayer of the apostles, quoted in Acts 4, bears considerable consonance with the qur'anic sensibilities about Jesus: the prayer addresses the "Sovereign Lord, who made the heaven and the earth, the sea, and everything in them" (4:24), refers later to "your holy servant Jesus, whom you anointed" (4:27), and concludes with an appeal that God might "stretch out your hand to heal, and signs and wonders [be] performed through the name of your holy servant Jesus" (4:30). Only a little earlier in the same New Testament document, the apostle Peter preaches that "Jesus of Nazareth [was] a man attested to you by God with deeds of power, wonders, and signs that God did through him among you" (2:22). While such texts are often conveniently overlooked in popular Christian piety, their careful consideration might help to create a more sympathetic appreciation for the Qur'an's depiction of Jesus.

This does not at all mean, however, that there is perfect agreement between the witness of the New Testament and that of the Qur'an regarding Jesus. In the Qur'an, as we have seen, Jesus is understood to be only a human creature and nothing more:

> Unbelievers are those who say: "Allah is the Messiah, son of Mary." Say:
> "Who could prevent Allah, if He wished, from destroying the Messiah, son of Mary, and his mother too, together with all those on the face of the earth?"
> To Allah belongs the kingdom of the heavens and the earth and what lies between them. He creates whatever He pleases, and Allah has power over everything! (Q 5:17)

Once more, Christians ought to hear the important grain of truth in this qur'anic protest: properly speaking, Christian faith does not teach, simply, that "God is the Messiah." God is not *simply* or *merely* Jesus Christ, though we do believe and confess that Jesus Christ, God's Son, is truly and fully God, participating thoroughly in the divine nature. Jesus does not simply *equal* God, pure and simple, without remainder. This is why we have that difficult doctrine of the Trinity, to be considered more fully in the following chapter.

Nonetheless, from a Christian perspective the Qur'an overstates the distinction, the "wholly otherness," between God and Jesus the Messiah. While it is only a theoretical possibility for the Qur'an, we still read that "if He wished," God could destroy Jesus Christ along with everything else—for "Allah has power over everything!" Islamic commentator Sayyid Mawdudi suggests that this shift in Q 5:17 away from "the Messiah, the son of Mary" and toward God's creative and destructive powers is meant to imply that Jesus was only one sign among many others in creation, and not even particularly the most noteworthy; thus, "had their [i.e., Christian unbelievers'] perception been wider they would have been able to see that there are even more inspiring examples of [God's] creation and infinite power."[1]

In stark contrast, several centuries before Muhammad's time the Christian thinker Gregory of Nyssa wrote: "God's transcendent power is not so much displayed in the vastness of the heavens, or the luster of the stars, or the orderly arrangement of the universe or his perpetual oversight of it, as in his condescension to our weak nature. . . . We marvel at the way the Godhead was entwined in human nature and, while becoming man, did not cease to be God."[2] We should add that it is not only God's "condescension to our weak nature" but also what God *did* during the time of "condescension to our weak nature" that matters profoundly. This is especially the case for the gospel of John, whose prologue states that while "no one has ever seen God," the good news is that "the only Son" (or "God the only Son") has made God known (1:18) through his works and words. Thus, for Christian faith Jesus is not simply one "sign" among many others in creation; Jesus is *the* Sign, *God's* Sign par excellence. In that light, the following texts from John and from the Qur'an, while strictly speaking not parallel passages, may be read fruitfully side by side:

The Bible	The Qur'an
John 13:3	*Surah 5:17*
Jesus, knowing that the Father had given all things into his hands, and that he had come from God and was going to God . . .	Unbelievers are those who say: "Allah is the Messiah, son of Mary."

The Qur'an's warning is not without merit. Orthodox Christian teaching in fact does not encourage the idea that God is Jesus, the Messiah, period. Even the term *messiah*, meaning "anointed one," immediately implies an anointing provided by another; in New Testament terms, God is the Anointer, not the Anointed (Luke 9:20; Acts 10:38). So there is an important sense in which the Qur'an is certainly correct to deny that "Allah is the Messiah, son of Mary." Indeed, in the passage above from John, we read that Jesus was aware that "he had come from God and was going to God"—implying a real distinction between himself and God, as well as a close relation or kinship of some kind.

John 13:4–5	*Surah 5:17*
. . . [Jesus] got up from the table, took off his outer robe, and tied a towel around himself. Then he poured water into a basin and began to wash the disciples' feet and to wipe them with the towel that was tied around him.	. . . He creates whatever He pleases, and Allah has power over everything!

It is not difficult to comprehend the logic of divine power as presented in the Qur'an. This is the God of sheer omnipotence, the God worshiped not only by Muslims but also by many Jews and Christians—and a great many others, for that matter. It is, however, more difficult to comprehend the logic of divine power in John's gospel. This God is indeed the Creator of all things, and in an important sense does indeed exercise "power over everything"—and yet this God has "given all things into [Jesus's] hands." This is a common strand in the New Testament writings: in Matthew Jesus says that "all things have been handed over to me by my Father" (11:27) and, later, that "all authority in heaven and on earth has been given to me" (28:18). Paul in his letter to the Philippians writes that "God . . . highly exalted [Jesus] and gave him the name that is above every name" (2:9), and Hebrews states that Jesus has been "appointed heir of all things," having inherited a name far greater than the angels' (1:2, 4).

While much of this language may seem foreign, we surely can recognize a common pattern: God who (by divine right) has all power and authority, being Creator and Lord of all things—Jesus himself in a prayer addresses God as "Lord of heaven and earth" (Matt. 11:25)—has freely given over this power to Jesus the Son. There is a distinction maintained between God and Jesus, and yet there is a mysterious outpouring from the Father toward, and into, the Son. These two are not identical, but they are inseparable. God, in the New Testament proclamation, is not self-enclosed, self-protecting, or self-aggrandizing. God does not hoard power; God outpours and freely shares "all authority in heaven and on earth." It may even be that this outpouring of God, this free sharing of divine power and even identity, is at least part of what that mysterious phrase "the Holy Spirit" signifies.

Surely, then, it is crucial that "Jesus, knowing that the Father had given all things into his hands" (John 13:3), becomes in the next moment a living parable—a Sign, to employ the Islamic term—of the nature of divine authority. God has given "all things into his hands," and the next things in those very hands are the dirty feet of his disciples! If God outpours power and authority into Jesus, Jesus in turn outpours this power and authority in a strangely unexpected way. Undertaking the lowliest servant's role, he washes feet. This is the nature of God's power, according to the gospel of John. Indeed, this is the nature of God; *this is God*, for Jesus is God's Sign.

John 13:12–14	Surah 5:17
After he had washed their feet, . . . he said to them, "Do you know what I have done to you? You call me Teacher and Lord—and	Say: "Who could prevent Allah, if He wished, from destroying the Messiah, son of Mary, and his mother too, together with all those on the

155

John 13:12–14	Surah 5:17
you are right, for that is what I am. So if I,	face of the earth?"
your Lord and Teacher, have washed your feet, you also ought to wash one another's feet."	

The gist of the question before us is not really whether God is omnipotent. It is the nature of that all-potency that we are interrogating. Even though the Qur'an's question is rhetorical, it is posed in terms of God's ability to destroy: Jesus, Mary, everything else, *if God wished*. For Christian faith—at least as it is instructed and informed by the gospel of John—divine power is humble servanthood, on its knees, washing the feet even of a traitor. It is also the empowering of human creatures likewise to serve one another in love (Gal. 5:13), "to wash one another's feet." We simply are not used to thinking of power in this way. Such a God as revealed in Jesus could not possibly wish to destroy. If that is true, it seems likely that many of our ideas of divine power as wrathful destruction are projections of our own sinful distortions of God's loving empowerment and empowering love. According to John, later that evening, only a little while after washing his friends' feet, Jesus made a most revolutionary statement. I set it beside one more sentence from Q 5:17:

John 14:7	Surah 5:17
If you know me, you will know my Father also. From now on you do know him and have seen him.	To Allah belongs the kingdom of the heavens and the earth and what lies between them.

Again, it is not at all that the Bible would deny that "the kingdom of the heavens and the earth and what lies between them" belongs to God; instead, what we must appreciate is that the God revealed in Jesus does not hoard "all things" (John 13:3). God gives all things into Jesus's hands, and Jesus immediately is washing feet. And in washing feet, Jesus is revealing God; as the above Johannine passage states, to perceive Jesus in action is to perceive the One Jesus calls Father. Power insisted upon, power hoarded, is a fragile power indeed. It is a power all too human. Christians understand Jesus to be the unveiling, the revelation, of a radically different vision of God the Creator of all things. We recall that John 1:18 states that "no one has ever seen God," but Jesus Christ, God's Word become flesh (1:14), "has made [God] known." Combine that remarkable pair of propositions with John 14:7; directly after washing his disciples' feet Jesus makes the remarkable claim, *"From now on you do know [the Father] and have seen him."* Is it possible that for John,

Jesus's act of foot washing is precisely the event in which God has become "seen," visible? That God is made known precisely here, in this act of radical humility? If this challenges much of what Muslims believe about God, it does much the same for many others, including not a few Christians.[3]

The End of Jesus's Earthly Ministry

Undoubtedly the most controversial passage in the Qur'an regarding Jesus, and one of the most difficult to interpret, is concerned with whether Jesus actually was executed. Indeed, the vast majority of Muslims, both now and throughout Islam's history, have taken the Qur'an to teach that Jesus has not died at all—not yet. Here is the passage:

> The People of the Book . . . neither killed nor crucified him; but it was made to appear so unto them. Indeed, those who differ about him are in doubt about it. Their knowledge does not go beyond conjecture, and they did not kill him for certain; rather, Allah raised [Jesus] unto Him. Allah is Mighty and Wise. (4:157–58)

The context of these verses is a condemnation of "the People of the Book" (4:153), against whom a litany of unfaithfulness is pronounced. In light of his Jewish critics' challenge to Muhammad "to bring down a book from heaven for them," the Qur'an retaliates with a recitation of their ancestors' demand to Moses to "show us God face to face. Thereupon the thunderbolt struck them for their wickedness." Even so, after such "clear proofs, . . . they worshipped the calf" (v. 153; cf. Exod. 32). In the course of this extended diatribe against Muhammad's detractors we encounter one of the passages alluding to the sign of Sinai, the mountain suspended over the Israelites' heads (v. 154), explored in chapter 8. Even under that threat, the Qur'an continues, "they broke their covenant, disbelieved in Allah's Revelations, killed the Prophets unjustly, . . . imput[ed] to Mary a great falsehood," and obstinately declared, "We have killed the Messiah, Jesus, son of Mary and the Messenger of Allah" (vv. 155–57). But in fact "they neither killed nor crucified him" (v. 157).

Why would the Qur'an deny Jesus's violent death? Even granting his qur'anic status as a great prophet and servant of Allah, what would be gained by this denial? The traditional Muslim reply, of course, would be that the Qur'an says this about Jesus because it is the truth. This would be taken as a correction of the gospel accounts of Jesus's crucifixion. The closest the Qur'an comes to a theological rationale for Jesus's eluding execution is found in another passage (3:54): "And they contrived and Allah contrived; Allah is the Best of the contrivers." From this one might surmise, as Muslim inter-preters often have, that God would not allow such a righteous prophet and faithful servant as Jesus to suffer and die so shamefully. There is no power, no glory, no vindication in being crucified. Anglican theologian Kenneth Cragg, longtime leader in Muslim-Christian dialogue, comments on this Islamic reading of Jesus: "God will not, cannot, allow faithful servants to suffer ignominy, or allow their detractors a final triumph. So Jesus did not suffer. It was more appropriate to the nature of things, divine and prophetic, that Judas should have taken his place—a proper end for him, a manifest outwitting of the Jews and a fitting climax for Jesus. How far indeed from the sense of the Gospels and 'the cup that my Father has given me.'"[4]

While the Qur'an makes no claim that Judas died in Jesus's place, this has been a leading traditional supposition among many Muslim interpreters. And of course, if Jesus did not suffer or die, then it is obvious that he could not have suffered or died "for our sins" as Paul wrote (1 Cor. 15:3), or that he offered "a sacrifice of atonement for the sins of the people" (Heb. 2:17), or that he "suffered for sins once for all, the righteous for the unrighteous, in order to bring you to God" (1 Peter 3:18). Notwithstanding the serious challenges awaiting anyone attempting atonement theorizing, it is clear that the New Testament writers interpret Jesus's suffering and death as real, and as redemptive in their effects. In denying Jesus's death, then, the Qur'an also undercuts Christian theories of redemption.

But it is not at all clear or obvious that Muhammad had all of this in mind. Why would he have denied Jesus's death? Since the Qur'an is so insistent upon the mere humanity of Jesus the "son of Mary," who exists (like everyone and everything else) only because God says "Be," then why insist that he was never killed? Again, for the Qur'an this demonstrates that God is a better "contriver" than those Jews who opposed Jesus; those who ridiculed Jesus's mother as a slut and sought to destroy her popular son were themselves undone by God's superior planning. But there is more than this rationale at work in the qur'anic passage; I side with those who suspect that Muham-mad was swayed by interpretations of Jesus's death popular among Gnostic Christian sects. While Muhammad would not have been sympathetic to the generally docetic Christologies (i.e., teachings denying that Jesus was truly a human being) of these sects and their writings, it seems likely that he felt the influence of their crucifixion scenarios. Alongside the Qur'an let us set a passage from *The Second Treatise of the Great Seth*, a Gnostic meditation claiming to be a revelation given by Christ, probably dating from sometime in the late second century of the Christian era:

Gnostic Christology

The Second Treatise of the Great Seth

. . . I exist with all the greatness of the Spirit, . . . [and] I visited a bodily dwelling. I cast out the one who was in it first, and I went in.

The Christology in *Seth* is typical of Gnostic treatments of Jesus: it assumes a strong soul-body dualism in which the Christ-spirit displaces the human soul. Indeed, in this case the Christ-spirit actually enters a body previously inhabited by a different soul altogether; in New Age literature, advanced souls who enter bodies, usually with some form of agreement of the departing, replaced soul, are called "walk-ins." It hardly need be said that the Qur'an presents no such notion about Jesus. So if indeed Muhammad felt the influence of Gnostic Christians' docetic Christology, it was not at the point of their radically dualistic anthropology in which Christ is a divine spirit who "went in" to a human body like the proverbial ghost in the machine. For Muhammad, Jesus was a human creature who, like all other creatures, relies entirely and always upon God's continuing command "Be!"

The Second Treatise of the Great Seth	Surah 3:54, 4:157b
And the whole multitude of the Archons became troubled . . . And the plan which	
they devised about me . . .—I did not	And they contrived
succumb to them as they had planned. But	and Allah contrived . . .
I was not afflicted at all. Those who were	
there punished me. And I did not die in	They neither killed nor crucified him;
reality but in appearance, lest I be put to	but it was made to appear so unto them.
shame by them because these are my	
kinsfolk . . . For my death which they think	Their knowledge does not go beyond
happened, happened to them in their error	conjecture—
and blindness, since they nailed their man	
unto their death . . . But in doing these	[Allah has sealed them on account of
things, they condemn themselves. Yes,	their disbelief]—
they saw me; they punished me. It was another, their father, who drank the gall and the vinegar; it was not I. They struck me with the reed; it was another, Simon, who	
bore the cross on his shoulder. It was	and they did not kill him for certain . . .
another upon whom they placed the crown of thorns . . . And I was laughing at their ignorance.[5]	

As we have seen in other passages of the Qur'an, the judgment that "those who differ about him are in doubt about it" may well reflect the controversies that still raged among orthodox and Gnostic streams of Christianity. At the very least, of course, it reflects disputations about Jesus between the Jewish and Christian communities of Muhammad's milieu. In any case, while the Qur'an's characteristic portrayal of Jesus as prophet is far removed from the docetism of Gnostic Christians, it appears that the docetic denial of Jesus's death may have influenced Muhammad. Perhaps he could not imagine a great prophet like Jesus coming to such an ignoble end; it seems likely too that he relished the notion that God had outwitted the ancestors of his Jewish gainsayers. "Allah is the Best of the contrivers."

Not all Islamic scholars agree with this interpretation of Q 4:157–58; some think that the Qur'an is only insisting that though Jesus's enemies thought they had rid themselves of his prophetic significance by crucifying him, they were wrong: nothing can destroy Jesus's importance, so his "spirit" (i.e., example and influence) lives on. Others believe the passage is fundamentally about God's ultimate authority, such that those who boast of having crucified Christ do not realize that "in fact, men could not kill the Messiah; only God could do that in his mysterious purposes"[6]—and that God did so by decreeing Jesus's crucifixion. However, the great majority of Muslims, scholarly or otherwise, over the centuries have insisted that Jesus did not die on the cross or by any other means.[7] Instead, God rescued Jesus before he was executed, whisking him up to heavenly safety and leaving behind, in his place, a look-alike. Sayyid Abul A'la Mawdudi's comments on the passage reflect this traditionally dominant interpretation; for him, the Qur'an "categorically states that Jesus was raised on high before he could be crucified, and that the belief of both the Jews and the Christians that Jesus died on the cross is based on a misconception. . . . The person the Jews subsequently crucified was someone else who, for one reason or another, was mistaken for the person of Jesus. This, however, does not lessen the guilt of 'those Jews.'"[8]

Lest it be assumed that such an important idea about Jesus is found in only one qur'anic passage, let us look briefly at a comparable portrayal in 3:52–60:

> When Jesus sensed their disbelief, he said: "Who are my supporters in Allah's Way?" The disciples said: "We are Allah's supporters; we believe in Allah, so bear witness that we submit." [Then they prayed:] "Lord, we believe in what You have revealed, and we have followed the Messenger; write us down with those who bear witness."
>
> And they [the unbelievers] contrived and Allah contrived; Allah is the Best of the contrivers. When Allah said: "O Jesus, I will take you [*alternative translation*: I will cause you to die], will lift you up to Me, purify you from

those who have disbelieved and place those who followed you above those who have disbelieved [*or* blasphemed], till the Day of Resurrection. Then unto Me is your [*plural*] return, so that I may judge between you regarding what you were disputing. But as for those who disbelieved, I will sternly punish them in this world and the Hereafter, and they shall have no supporters." . . . Jesus in Allah's Sight is like Adam; He created him from dust, then He said to him: "Be," and there he was. [This is] the truth from your Lord; so do not be one of the doubters.

Because "Allah is the Best of the contrivers," all the best-laid plans of Jesus's opponents cannot undo God's triumph. It is possible, in fact, to suspect a kind of hierarchy at work in the passage: God clears Jesus of the charges of those who blaspheme, most likely referring to Jews who reject Jesus altogether; in the next grade up, those who follow Jesus are deemed to be superior over ("placed above") those who do not; then in the final day of resurrection the believers in Jesus will themselves experience the gradation of Allah's judgment "regarding what you were disputing." But before all of this, we hear Allah's words of assurance: "O Jesus! I will take you and raise you to Myself." While the translation I have utilized throughout this book states "I will cause you to die, will lift you up to Me," this has not been the historically mainstream or popular translation, not at least without some fairly tortured interpretation. Mawdudi's comments again are reflective of the historically dominant Islamic approach to this passage. He notes that the verb in "I will take you" is *mutawaffika*, the root meaning of which is "to take and receive." Hence, God has "taken and received" Jesus. Mawdudi deduces:

> Had the traditions cherished by the Christians regarding Jesus' ascension into heaven been without foundation, they would have been told that he whom they regarded as either God or the son of God had died long ago and become part of the earth, and that if they wanted to satisfy themselves on that score they could go and witness for themselves his grave at a certain place. But not only does the Qur'an not make any categorical statement that Jesus died, it employs an expression which, to say the least, contains the possibility of being interpreted as meaning that he had been raised into heaven alive. Further, the Qur'an tells the Christians that Jesus, contrary to their belief, was not crucified. This means that the man who cried out at the end of his life: . . . "My God, my God, why hast thou forsaken me?" (Matthew 27:46), and the one whose image was seen on the cross was not Christ; God had already raised Christ into heaven.
>
> As for those who try to interpret these Qur'anic verses as indicating the death of Jesus, they actually prove only that God is incapable of expressing His ideas in clear, lucid terms.[9]

Make no mistake about Mawdudi's last line: for him, God certainly is entirely capable of "expressing His ideas in clear, lucid terms," so it is only those (Islamic scholars!) who think that Jesus died—on the cross, or indeed at all—who are ignoring the obvious meanings of the qur'anic passages. No cross—and obviously, then, no resurrection. In mainstream traditional Islam there is only Jesus the great prophet, "peace be upon him," who was delivered from an awful and humiliating death by the superior planning and power of God.

But this leaves at least two questions dangling: (1) Will Jesus have anything to do in the eschatological future of planet Earth? (2) What did the infant Jesus mean when he pronounced from his mother's cradling arms, "Peace be upon me the day I was born, the day I die and the day I rise from the dead"?

Jesus and the Age to Come

For Muslims who hold to the traditional interpretation of Q 4:157–58—that Jesus was not killed by his opponents but taken up into God's presence, where he is even now alive—the door of eschatological expectation is open for Jesus's return from heaven as the sign of the end of the present age. It is surprising for many Christians to learn this, but for most Muslims Jesus is expected to return to earth from heaven as the vanguard of the eschaton. While the Qur'an does not explicitly teach any of this, the traditional expectation is that Jesus will make his appearance in Damascus to engage in battle with an Antichrist figure, restore the world to righteousness, bring judgment upon Christians for their idolatry toward him—breaking all the crosses on church steeples in the process—and lead all repentant people into Islam.[10]

For the dominant trend in traditional Muslim eschatological expectation, then, Jesus has yet to die and thus, of course, has yet to be raised from death. What, then, of his words as a little child from his mother's arms, "Peace be upon me the day I was born, the day I die and the day I rise from the dead"(Q 19:33)? These words must refer to events yet to occur. Thus, it is generally (though not universally) believed among Muslims that after his eschatological appearance Jesus will subsequently die, likely of old age, be buried alongside Muhammad and at some subsequent time be raised along with everyone else in a general resurrection. As in traditional Jewish and Christian belief, Muslims expect that following this general resurrection God will render the final judgment upon all human beings who have ever lived.

Probably the most dramatic passage in the Qur'an dealing with Jesus and eschatology is in Surah 5, called "The Table" because of its intriguing description of a heavenly table of luscious food that Jesus is believed to have called down from heaven. (Indeed, the passage is sufficiently rich that we will return to "The Table" for another taste in subsequent chapters.) Most scholars see in this passage the qur'anic version of the only miracle of Jesus's earthly ministry described in all four of the canonical gospels: the feeding of the multitudes with a few loaves and fishes. For the gospel writers, the eschatological significance of this miracle is obvious: Jesus's meals (or "table fellowship") are foretastes of the world to come. These meals signify God's future for creation in which, in the words of the Hebrew prophet Isaiah, "the LORD of hosts will make for all peoples a feast of rich food, a feast of well-aged wines, . . . [and] will destroy on this mountain the shroud that is cast over all peoples, the sheet that is spread over all nations; he will swallow up death forever" (25:6–8; cf. Rev. 21:24). Similarly, in Luke's gospel Jesus says to his disciples during their last meal together that "from now on I will not drink of the fruit of the vine until the kingdom of God comes" (22:18). So it is not difficult to interpret Jesus's sharing of meals, whether with his immediate disciples or with the larger crowds who would gather around him, as signs and foretastes of God's coming reign. Further, in the following qur'anic passage the story of "the Table" is set explicitly within an eschatological context:

The Bible	The Qur'an
Romans 2:16	Surah 5:109
. . . on the day when, according to my gospel,	The day [comes] when Allah shall assemble the Messengers, then say: "What response were you given?" They shall say: "We have no
God, through Jesus Christ, will judge the secret thoughts of all.	knowledge; You are indeed the Knower of the Unseen."

This eschatological scenario in the Qur'an opens with a vision of God gathering all of the divine messengers on the day of judgment. These prophets confess ignorance as to the true response of their hearers; only Allah can judge that. Similarly, Paul writes that God will judge the unseen, unknown secrets of all people in that day. The only difference—the decisive difference—is that for Paul God shall exercise this judgment "through Jesus Christ." In Paul's, and thus the Christian, eschatological expectation, Jesus will not be simply one among many "messengers" or prophets, but the One in whom, and through whom, God shall judge.

Acts 10:38	Surah 5:110a
	When Allah will say: "O Jesus, son of Mary, remember My grace upon you and upon your
God anointed Jesus of Nazareth with	mother, how I strengthened you with
the Holy Spirit and with power.	the Holy Spirit . . ."

On the face of it, it appears that both of the above texts espouse what is called a "Spirit-Christology," a doctrine of Christ that begins its reflections on the gospels' descriptions of Jesus as a human being uniquely anointed and empowered by the Spirit of God. That, of course, begs the question of who or what this "Holy Spirit" is. I have already noted the relative reticence of the Qur'an to offer any definitive reply to that question, though in subsequent Islamic tradition the most prominent interpretation is that this Spirit is none other than the angel Gabriel. Similarly, it must be admitted that the language of the New Testament regarding the Spirit is far from obvious; it would take several centuries' worth of discussion and debate among theologians, bishops, and priests to establish the doctrine of the Spirit's deity within the development of a trinitarian vision of God (to be explored in the following chapter). For now, the point to be appreciated is that the Qur'an offers a Christology in passages like the above that is similar, though not identical, to that found in the New Testament, especially in Luke-Acts (a two-volume work, generally believed to be by the same author). It is undoubtedly significant, too, that the above quotation from Acts 10, from a sermon of Peter, includes the proclamation that the risen Jesus "is the one ordained by God as judge of the living and the dead" (Acts 10:42)—a fortuitous connection to what we have already encountered regarding divine judgment through Christ as envisioned by Paul in Romans 2:16.

Surah 5:110b
. . . So that you could speak to people in the cradle and as an old man; how I taught you the Book, the Wisdom, the Torah and the Gospel; and how, by My Leave, you created out of clay the likeness of a bird, and breathed into it, and then, by My Leave, it turned into a bird. And you could heal the blind and the leper by My Leave and you could raise the dead by My Leave. And [remember] how I restrained the Children of Israel from hurting you, when you brought them the clear signs; whereupon the unbelievers among them said: "That indeed is nothing but manifest sorcery."

Having already engaged, earlier in this chapter, a similar listing in Surah 3 of Jesus's miraculous deeds accomplished by God's "Leave" or permission, I shall not rehearse that material. Three observations will suffice. First, we should appreciate that in both of these qur'anic passages (Q 3:49 and Q 5:110) all of Jesus's mighty works are performed by Allah's "Leave," emphasizing that sovereignty of the divine will and power as operating supremely in Jesus's deeds. Second, in the above passage the reminder that God "restrained the Children of Israel from hurting" Jesus tends strongly to support the interpretation of the Qur'an offered in this chapter's previous section on the crucifixion: that Jesus did not suffer and die on the cross because God outwitted Jesus's enemies and received him into heavenly glory before they could apprehend him. Third, it is interesting that one of the more common designations of Jesus within the Talmud is that he was "a sorcerer who led Israel astray"—not unlike the judgment upon Jesus rendered, according to the Qur'an, by "the unbelievers" among the Jewish people, "the Children of Israel": "That indeed is nothing but manifest sorcery."

John 14:1	Surah 5:111
[Jesus said to his disciples,] "Believe in God, believe also in me."	And when I revealed to the disciples: "Believe in Me and My Messenger," they replied: "We believe, and You bear witness that we submit."

This is a surprisingly strong statement in the Qur'an: God calling upon Jesus's disciples to believe both "in Me" and in "My Messenger"! It assuredly is not Christian faith per se to which the disciples are called in the qur'anic passage above, but it is strikingly elevated language. It is not the same as Jesus's invitation to his disciples in John 14:1, but we should not exaggerate the difference too quickly either.

Now we come to the actual narrating of the story of Jesus's heavenly feast:

Matthew 14:15–17	Surah 5:112–13
The disciples came to him and said,	When the disciples said: "Jesus, son of Mary, is
". . . Send the crowds away so that they	your Lord able to bring down for us a table
may go . . . and buy food for themselves."	[spread with food] from heaven?";
Jesus said to them,	he said:
". . . You give them something to eat."	"Fear Allah, if you are true believers."
They replied, "We have nothing here but	They said: "We would like to eat from it so that
five loaves and two fish."	our hearts may be reassured and know that you have told us the truth and be witnesses thereof."

The similarity between these stories is primarily structural, though of course what initially invites the side-by-side reading is that these conversations between Jesus and the disciples involve food, and the need for a lot of it. The disciples in the gospel story want to send away the crowds so that everyone can go buy food; in the Qur'an the disciples directly request of Jesus a heavenly feast, with no pressing crowd as a backdrop to force the issue. Jesus's responses in the two stories, of course, are widely divergent; in Matthew, Jesus apparently emphasizes the disciples' role, while in the Qur'an emphasis of attention is placed entirely upon Allah. However, it could perhaps be argued that Jesus's response in the gospel story—"You give them something to eat"—has a similar intention: the disciples' very inability to produce the requisite feast for the multitude would push them to seek God's help.

Further, in both the Bible and the Qur'an the disciples' reply to Jesus betrays insufficient faith. In the gospel story, the disciples are realistically frank in their assessment of culinary resources to deal with such an overwhelming crowd of dinner guests. In the Qur'an, the disciples acknowledge that their request for a heavenly table arises from a need for dramatic validation of Jesus's prophetic teaching.

Matthew 14:19	Surah 5:114–15
Taking the five loaves and the two fish, he looked up into heaven, and blessed and broke the loaves, and gave them to the disciples, and the disciples gave them to the crowds.	Jesus, son of Mary, then said: "O Allah, our Lord, send down to us a table spread with food from heaven that it may be a festival for the first and last of us and a sign from You; and provide for us, for You are the Best Provider." Allah said: "I will send it down to you, so that whosoever of you disbelieves thereafter I will inflict on him a punishment I do not inflict on any other being."

The gospel writers' penchant for describing this miracle in Eucharistic terms becomes most obvious when they tell us that Jesus "looked up into heaven, and blessed and broke the loaves" to distribute them to the crowds. And insofar as the feeding is framed in Eucharistic metaphor, so it is also eschatological: we are witnessing a dramatic foretaste of the great messianic banquet. In that regard the Qur'an is perfectly appropriate in describing the meal as "a table spread with food from heaven."

While the great eighth-century Muslim commentator Ibn Kathir reported disagreement among his fellow Muslim scholars as to whether a heavenly table actually did descend, he was among those who affirmed the miracle. Indeed, Ibn Kathir insisted that the table descended with seven fishes and seven loaves—this detail lends support to the decision to read

"The Table" alongside the gospel story—along with vinegar, pomegranates, and other fruits. "It had a very strong aroma," wrote Ibn Kathir, offering then this distinctly Qur'an-like comment: "God said 'Be,' and it existed."[11]

Ibn Kathir's extra details are not in the Qur'an but are part of oral traditions of interpretation called *hadith* that were traceable, allegedly, back to Muhammad himself; however, it is difficult if not impossible, in most cases, to establish with certainty such lineage for these midrashic embellishments. Nonetheless, they are fascinating examples of a community's interpretive processes over time. For example, Ibn Kathir reports that Jesus ordered his disciples to eat, but they insisted that they would not eat from the heavenly table until Jesus did; is this perhaps an echo of Jesus's vow in the synoptic gospels not to eat again of the Last Supper fare, nor to drink of the fruit of the vine, until he eats and drinks with his disciples in the great messianic feast in the fulfilled eschatological reign of God? The hadith material continues with Jesus insisting to his disciples, "But you're the ones who asked for the heavenly table"—and yet they persist in their refusal. "So Jesus ordered the poor, needy, sick and lame to eat from it. There were close to 1800 there eating from it. All who were sick, lame, infirm or ill were healed from eating it."[12] It certainly does begin to sound like the great messianic feast of Isaiah, when "the Lord GOD will wipe away the tears from all faces" (25:8).

Isaiah's promise of the fulfillment of God's reign helps to usher us, finally, back to the qur'anic Last Day as imagined in "The Table":

Surah 5:116

And when Allah said: "O Jesus, son of Mary, did you say to the people: 'Take me and my mother as gods, apart from Allah'"? He said: "Glory be to You. It is not given me to say what is untrue. If I said it, You would have known it; You know what is in my soul, but I do not know what is in Thine. You are indeed the Knower of the Unseen."

The setting appears now to have shifted back to God's interrogation of Jesus on the day of final judgment. God proceeds, in this vision of final things, to question Jesus regarding what he had actually taught during his prophetic ministry. Note that Allah's question is framed in terms of the divinization of Jesus and Mary. Indeed, there are passages in the Qur'an that appear to assume that the Christian doctrine of the Trinity includes Mary as the third Person. But Jesus categorically denies having ever encouraged his followers to adopt such practices of *shirk*. The passage also reaffirms a recurring theme in the Qur'an: only God knows anything truly. Even Jesus is made to say to God, "You know what is in my soul, but I do not know what is in Yours."

Surah 5:117–20

"I told them only what You commanded me: 'Worship Allah, your Lord and mine,' and I was watcher over them while I was among them, but when You took me to Yourself, You became the Watcher over them; for You are the Witness of everything. Should You punish them, they are surely Your servants; but should You forgive them, You are truly the Mighty, the Wise." Allah said: "This is a Day in which their truthfulness shall profit the truthful; they will have Gardens beneath which rivers flow, dwelling therein forever; Allah is pleased with them and they are pleased with Him. That is the great triumph." To Allah belongs the dominion of the heavens and the earth and all there is in them, and He has power over everything.

In this scenario of the judgment day, Jesus insists that he said nothing to encourage the beliefs and behaviors of Christians that are inconsistent with Muslim teaching. "I told them only what You commanded me: 'Worship Allah, your Lord and mine.'" Thus Jesus is examined and found to be a faithful prophet, submitted to God—and Christianity, on the other hand, is judged to be an idolatrous aberration. When we read that Jesus described God to his disciples as "your Lord and mine," it is tempting to recall the words of the resurrected Jesus to Mary Magdalene, according to the gospel of John: "But go to my brothers and say to them, 'I am ascending to my Father and your Father, to my God and your God'" (20:17). Muslim readers would gravitate toward the language of "my God and your God," while Christians have tended to shy away from this relation and have stressed the language of "my Father and your Father." Undoubtedly, both phrases are necessary to an adequate Christian estimation of Jesus Christ in relation to God.

It may be noteworthy, as this chapter draws to a close, that the qur'anic passage seems to hint even at a kind of intercessory role for Jesus before God, in behalf of his confused Christian followers, on that final judgment day. This is unusual precisely because it is far more typical to find the Qur'an denying that anyone or anything will be able to plead one's case, or to intercede in any way, in the hour of judgment. While the role envisioned for Jesus on that day is relatively mild, there is no mistaking its intercessory nature: "Should You punish them, they are surely Your servants; but should You forgive them, You are truly the Mighty, the Wise" (Q 5:118). We may grant that this is somewhat less robust than Paul's triumphant proclamation that "it is Christ Jesus who died, yes, who was raised, who is at the right hand of God, who indeed intercedes for us" (Rom. 8:34). It is remarkable, nonetheless, that the Qur'an can provide its readers' (and hearers') imaginations with an eschatological scenario in which Jesus exercises any intercessory effect whatsoever.

Of course, the Qur'an ultimately leaves the final fate of Christian believers to God, and Jesus can only acknowledge that whatever fate God decides for them, it is justly only God's business. For God "has power over everything" (Q 5:120). This leads us to the question I have already begun to probe in this chapter: might the Christian doctrine of God as triune call to us to think about divine power differently?

11

ADONAI, ALLAH,
AND THE TRIUNE GOD

Say: "He is Allah, the only One, Allah the Everlasting. He did not beget and is not begotten, and none is His equal."

> —Part of the inscription around the outer face of the Dome of the Rock, Jerusalem (*quoted from Q 112*)

In Islam, a specific public act marks the moment of conversion to the Muslim way. This act is the *shahada*, a confession of the most fundamental tenets of Islam in the hearing of other Muslims. The first half of this confession is the beautifully alliterative phrase *La ilaha illallah*—meaning that "there is no god but the one true God"; the second half, and closely related, is that Muhammad is God's final prophet, the "seal" or culmination of a long historical line of prophets who have proclaimed the reality, sovereignty, and authority of this one true God.

This confession of God as truly and thoroughly *One*—solitary in divine majesty, utterly unique and thus having no "partners" or "associates," as the Qur'an often recites—is the root of Islam's doctrine of *tawhid*, or the sheer unity of God's being and nature. As mentioned in chapter 3, any compromising of this profound insistence on the divine unity is called *shirk*, which can be roughly translated as idolatry.

Small wonder, then, that the Muslim teaching on *tawhid* has from the very beginnings of Islam rendered Christianity's trinitarian faith suspicious to Muslim eyes. By the time of Muhammad, the church already for several centuries had been laboring to articulate, delineate, and defend its doctrine of God's triunity: one God existing *somehow* as Father, Son, and Spirit. To Muhammad then, and to Muslims now, that *somehow* sounds a lot like *shirk*.

In this regard, Muhammad apparently understood Christianity to be duplicating an error that was widespread among his pagan Arab neighbors. As Muslims traditionally have interpreted this era, prior to Muhammad's revelations was a "time of ignorance," *jahiliyah*, on the Arabian Peninsula and, for that matter, everywhere else. Despite the revelations and covenants granted to the Children of Israel and the Christian community, superstition and warped religious ideas and practices dominated the landscape. There was, however, a small minority of believers in the one true God—the Qur'an calls them the *hunafa* (sing. *hanif*)—who held steadfastly to what the Qur'an testifies to be the true primordial religion of Adam, Noah, Abraham, Jesus, and the rest of the prophets. These *hunafa* prayed and submitted to "Allah," a title that (it is highly likely) originates from the Arabic phrase *al-ilah*, "the God."[1] Such a designation distinguished the supreme God from other lesser deities to whom most people gave most of their attention. These gods were usually associated with natural phenomena, special sites, or heroic ancestors and undoubtedly were perceived as more readily reachable, and thus more relevant, in the religious sensibilities of the great majority of people during this era of ignorance.

Thus, when Muhammad began to proclaim submission to Allah alone, he was calling his fellow Arabs away from their devotion to lesser, localized deities and instead to the one Supreme, All-Encompassing, and Omnipotent God—*the* God. In this regard Muhammad's message is comparable to the *Sh'ma* of the ancient Hebrew scriptures: "Hear, O Israel: The LORD is our God, the LORD alone. You shall love the LORD your God with all your heart, and with all your soul, and with all your might" (Deut. 6:4–5). In both the *Sh'ma* and the *Shahada*, the oneness of the divine being calls for a corresponding singleness of heart, an undivided love and devotion unmixed with idolatry.

This appears to have been one of the teachings that distinguished Muhammad's prophetic ministry during his lifetime. Most of Muhammad's Arab contemporaries would have acknowledged the existence of the supreme God who, as Creator of all things, ruled over creation. But they would also have associated their more localized gods with Allah, likely very often understanding these underling deities to be their intercessors before Allah. A prominent manifestation of this was a shrine, or perhaps several shrines, near Mecca devoted to goddess figures identified as the "daughters of Allah." Given this context, it is not difficult to understand Muhammad's criticizing Christianity as simply another example of *shirk*, associating lesser powers (such as Jesus or even Mary) with the One Supreme God. In contrast, the Qur'an instructs the true Muslim convert to recite that "we shall never associate anyone with our Lord; and that He, may our Lord's Majesty be exalted, has not taken a consort or a son; and that our fools used to speak impertinently of Allah; and that . . . [we] only call upon [our] Lord, and do not associate with Him anyone else" (Q 72:2–4, 20).

If the Muslim doctrine of God allows for no "associations" with Allah, its warning against what it understands to be the trinitarian faith of Christians cannot be terribly surprising:

> O People of the Book, do not exceed the bounds of your religion, nor say [anything] about Allah except the truth. The Messiah, Jesus, son of Mary, is only Allah's Messenger and His Word, which He imparted to Mary, and is a spirit from Him! So believe in Allah and His Messengers and do not say "three." Refrain; it is better for you. Allah is truly One God. How—glory be to Him—could He have a son? To Him belongs what is in the heavens and on earth. Allah suffices as a Guardian! The Messiah does not disdain to be a servant of Allah, nor do the angels nearest to Him. (Q 4:171–72)[2]

The earliest sustained written response to the Qur'an's critique of trinitarian doctrine (at least as popularly understood) comes from the great John of Damascus (675–749), who like his father before him, served as a court official in the Muslim government of his home city. The Damascene is most often remembered as a champion of the use of icons in Christian worship and instruction, arguing that the immortal, invisible God had set the precedent for iconography by providing the supreme Icon to humanity in the incarnation of the Logos in Jesus Christ. Regarding trinitarian faith he wrote,

> I worship one God, one Godhead, but I adore three persons: God the Father, God the Son made flesh, and God the Holy Spirit, one God. I do not adore the creation rather than the Creator, but I adore the one who became a creature, who was formed as I was, who clothed Himself in creation without weakening or departing from His divinity, that He might raise our nature in glory and make us partakers of His divine nature . . . [and] who worked out [our] salvation through matter.[3]

On the basis of the Christian confession of the incarnation, then, John resisted not only Christian iconoclasts but also Islam's judgment against Christian faith as tritheistic idolatry. His argument ran like this: both the Bible and the Qur'an testify that God sends forth the divine word and spirit into the world. While the Qur'an denies that either God's word or God's spirit actually shares in the divine nature, the Bible and Christian tradition insist that the word and spirit of God are thoroughly inseparable from God. The Word that God speaks and the Spirit that God breathes share fully in God's very being. Thus, the Damascene argued, Christians are not guilty of *shirk*; rather, Muslims are guilty of mutilating God by severing the Word and Spirit from God's essence.[4]

We might think of it in this way. In the language of scripture and theology, *word* and *spirit* are what theologians sometimes call "bridge terms," words/concepts that refer to the activity of God in reaching out to bridge the gap between the realms of the transcendent and the mundane. We might take another step and suggest that *word* implies God's bridging of this gap by communicating with us, "speaking to" us, imparting a set of meanings to us by means of human language and interpretation. The term *spirit*, on the other hand, immediately derived as it is from "breath" or "wind," is not so much about communicating ideas or meanings as it is about imparting life, vitality, energy. Logos is structure, rationality, message, *yang*; Spirit is breath, renewal, ecstasy, *yin*. These two "bridge terms," then, denote distinctive yet inseparable modes of outreaching from God toward creation. The difference between Islam and Christianity (and, perhaps to a less dramatic extent, between Judaism and Christianity) has to do with whether or not these terms *word* and *spirit* actually signify the very reality of *God moving savingly and revealingly into the world*.

The answer of Christian faith to this question, as John of Damascus indicated long ago, is a resounding yes. Both the Word that God utters and the Spirit that God breathes toward creation share fully in God's own being. Any student of Christian tradition knows that this answer did not arise easily or quickly; it was several centuries in the making and was formulated with soteriology (the doctrine of salvation) always foremost in mind. For example, at the Council of Nicaea in 325, Athanasius led the opposition against Arius's teaching that the Logos was a creature of God—the highest and best and first of God's creatures, but a creature nonetheless. Arian Christology was rejected on the basis of the Athanasian argument that only the Power that created all things could also redeem all things by participating fully in the realm of creation through the act of incarnation. If that which became incarnate in Jesus is anything less or other than God, then no true or lasting healing has entered the human stream. Similarly, later in the fourth century Basil of Caesarea argued that Scripture instructs us that the healing of human lives entails their sanctification, that is, their growing increasingly in the likeness of the One who created them (Col. 3:10). If the Holy Spirit is given to believers to empower them in this transformation toward Godlikeness, insisted Basil, then the Spirit must likewise be nothing other, and certainly nothing less, than God. Only God can re-create the human creature toward becoming godly, or like God. The Christian logic of salvation essentially demanded that the healing and redeeming of creaturely existence could be effected only by the true and immediate Presence of God who created all things.

It barely need be said that the Muslim understanding of the Creator-creature relation neither follows nor requires this logic. In the Qur'an, Jesus the Messiah is a great prophet but nothing more; even though he is described also as "God's word" or "a word from God," Muslim tradition has insisted on a clean break between the divine nature and the divine word that Jesus embodied. Indeed, we have seen earlier that there is an interpretive tradition in Islam that reads this divine word embodied in Jesus to be no more than the command "Be!"—implying, essentially, that Jesus's existence instantiates little else than God's sovereign authority to speak all things (including, of course, Jesus himself) into existence.[5]

Similarly, the Qur'an does mention a "holy spirit" in numerous passages, but the Islamic tradition has opted largely to interpret these references as signifying the angel Gabriel. A particular *hadith*, or story from Muhammad's life, is especially important for providing support for identifying this holy spirit as Gabriel. "A group of Jews asked the Messenger of God, may God bless him and grant him peace, saying: 'Tell us about the Spirit.' He said: 'I adjure you by God and by His days with the Children of Israel, do you know that it is Gabriel, and that it is he who comes to me?' They said: 'Yes.'"[6] Interestingly, in this traditional story Muhammad is portrayed as offering to his Jewish interlocutors an interpretation of the holy spirit with which they readily agree—a somewhat unusual circumstance! It would, in any event, put Jews and Muslims on the same page in differing from the Christian teaching about God's triunity. Since Gabriel, like all angels, is a creature of God, obviously for Muslims this holy spirit cannot possibly participate in Allah's unique and utterly solitary being.

Thus, in neither the term *messiah* nor the phrase *holy spirit* do Muslims assume anything like God's actual, immediate presence in creation. Allah, the One Supreme God, remains entirely transcendent to the world.[7] Meanwhile, the doctrine of the Trinity is the church's testimony to the one God who moves dynamically into creation in a fully participatory way. Several centuries before Muhammad's era, the Christian thinker Gregory of Nyssa (330–95) wrestled with this issue in his classic essay "That We Should Not Think of Saying There Are Three Gods." After insisting that Christians are called to uphold the *Sh'ma* as faithfully as Jews, Gregory suggests an intriguing hermeneutical device for reading biblical texts testifying to God's saving activities. Given the biblical calling to love with all of our heart and mind the one God of Israel, Gregory argues, the New Testament language concerning Father, Son, and Spirit cannot be read polytheistically. Furthermore, biblical language cannot be read in a straightforwardly literal way, because this language does not and cannot signify God's nature, infinitely beyond human thought and expression. This implies that no matter how subtle our trinitarian models or ingenuous our doctrinal formulations, we are not thereby granted access into the mystery of God's rich being. Instead, writes Gregory, scriptural language invariably signifies God's *operations* or activities within creation. Holy Scripture always testifies of these activities as having been effected by the one God; thus, references to the labors of the Son or the Spirit can never be read as independent or individual actions of distinct identities within the divine nature. "Rather," writes Gregory, "does every operation which extends from God to creation and is designated according to our differing conceptions of it have its origin in the Father, proceed through the Son, and reach its completion by the Holy Spirit."[8] The salient points here are, first, Gregory's notion that trinitarian language signifies "every operation [of God] which extends from God to creation," and, second, that each of these operations or movements of God toward creation "is designated according to our differing conceptions of it." Gregory's rhetoric bespeaks a profound humility regarding the human capacity for putting into words God's mysterious but redemptive labors in the world. The church's doctrine of the Trinity is just such an attempt.

No doubt a considered Muslim evaluation of this attempt would come down in the negative, and forcefully so. But the point here is not to develop a Christian rhetoric regarding God that Muslims would approve; it is, though, to suggest an avenue of interpretation of triune doctrine that might more aggressively protect the shared Jewish, Christian, and Muslim conviction that there is "no God but one . . . from whom are all things and for whom we exist" (1 Cor. 8:4, 6). For Muslims, this one God who is Creator of all things by the power of the word "Be!" remains entirely transcendent to creation; for Christians, "it is the God who said, 'Let light shine out of darkness,' who has shone in our hearts to give the light of the knowledge of the glory of God in the face of Jesus Christ" (2 Cor. 4:6).

Christian theologian Michael Nazir-Ali probes the heart of this matter when he writes, "The fundamental issue at stake is the nature of religious experience."[9] When Paul writes that God "has shone in our hearts to give the light of the knowledge of the glory of God in the face of Jesus Christ," Christian interpretive tradition takes that to mean that it is truly God who "shines" in human hearts as "uncreated light" (to employ a phrase from the Greek Orthodox tradition) by the very presence of God's own Spirit, and that this "shining" of God is given contour and depth by Jesus Christ, the Incarnate Word in whose "face," that is, bodily life among us, God is truly seen, heard, and encountered. This immediately implies a "religious experience" that is *experience of God*. By contrast, the Muslim conviction is that Muhammad was not encountered directly by Allah but indirectly through the angel Gabriel. Neither Jesus nor any spirit nor any angel can legitimately lay claim to deity or be associated with "the God," Allah. But if such is the standard *Muslim* interpretation of Muhammad's experience as God's prophet—that Muhammad's intimate interactions with the so-called holy spirit do not denote direct communion in God's presence but rather the reception of revelation as recitation from the angel Gabriel—might there be an alternative avenue of interpretation available for a *Christian* reading of Muhammad's experiences?

We may humbly begin to answer this question by considering a somewhat surprising *ayah* in the Qur'an, probably its strongest declaration regarding God's immanence or nearness to the creaturely realm: "We have indeed created man, and We know what his soul insinuates to him. We are to him closer than the jugular vein" (50:16). Of course the text is not surprising for its claim for God as the Creator of human beings, nor for its affirmation of divine omniscience regarding the human heart or soul. But to stipulate that Allah is "closer than the jugular vein," nearer to each human being than her or his vital life-blood, is unexpected if not remarkable. Indeed, a consideration of this verse in its context within Surah 16 virtually begs for a side-by-side reading with Acts 17, which narrates Paul's sermon to the pagan poets and philosophers who gathered to hear his apologetic in the arena of the Areopagus in Athens:

The Bible	The Qur'an
Acts 17:18–20	*Surah 50:2*
Epicurean and Stoic philosophers . . .	They marvel that a warner has come to them . . .
took [Paul] and brought him to the	from among them, and so the unbelievers say:
the Areopagus and asked him, "May we know what this new teaching is that you are presenting?	
It sounds rather strange to us . . ."	"This is a strange thing!"

Interestingly, as these scenes of proclamation are set up in the Bible and the Qur'an, in both cases the specific point of instigation is the message of resurrection from the dead. Paul attracts attention in the Athens marketplace "because he was telling the good news about Jesus and the resurrection"

(17:18), while the Qur'an describes Muhammad's critics as being incredulous about a remarkably similar message: "What, when we are dead and have become dust—that is a far-off return!" (Q 50:3). Both audiences find this preaching about the resurrection of the body to be strange. We will return to this point in chapter 12.

Acts 17:22–28	Surah 50:6–7, 16
Then Paul stood . . . and said, . . . "The God who made the world and everything	
in it, he who is Lord of heaven	Have they not beheld the heaven above them
and earth, does not live in shrines	. . . ? And the earth We have spread out and set
made by human hands, as if he needed anything,	in it immovable mountains;
since he himself gives to all mortals life and	and We cause to grow in it every delightful
and breath and all things.	variety . . .
From one ancestor he made all nations . . .	We have indeed created man,
so that they would search for God and	
perhaps grope for him and find him	and We know what his soul insinuates to him.
—though indeed he is not far from each one of	
us. For 'In him we live and move and have	We are to him closer than the jugular vein . . .
our being' . . ."	

Both the Bible and the Qur'an affirm that the God of resurrection power is also the Creator of all things. In fact, in the Qur'an the divine acts of creation and resurrection are regularly and tightly bound together. The Qur'an explicitly argues that those who scoff at the preaching of the resurrection as God's re-creative act in the age to come have not given sufficient attention to the miracle of life in the present age. "Were We wearied by the first creation? No, [and yet] they are in doubt regarding a new creation" (Q 50:15).

More important for our present purposes, both texts proceed to surprise the reader, probably, with strong statements regarding the intimacy of God's presence with every human being, everywhere and at all times. These are categorical propositions regarding God's radical nearness. Paul, speaking not to fellow Christians or Jews but to pagan philosophers, insists that God "is not far from each one of us," and drives the point home with a quotation from Epimenides' "Ode to Zeus," "In Thee we live and move and have our being"![10] Similarly, the Qur'an affirms God's intimate nearness, "closer than the jugular vein," to every human being.

178

The question at hand is this: If God truly is this near, this immanent—the One who is present with and within us all and the very Presence in whom we exist—might this Presence be actually, even if only fleetingly, discernible? On the basis of the Acts 17 sermon under consideration, I believe we can say that Paul—and thus at least some segment of early Christianity—seems to have believed so. Presumably a large part of the reason that people "search for God and perhaps grope for God and find God," to use the language of Acts, is precisely because God "is not far from each one of us." Perhaps the Paul of Acts 17 felt free to quote pagan religious poetry not only for apologetic purposes but because of a confidence that such poetry, even when addressed to Zeus, arises from an awareness of the mysterious divine Presence closer to us than our own jugular vein.

If this suggestion carries any validity, then perhaps the Christian is forced to ask about what Muhammad may have been responding to as he sought to discern what he took to be recitations from an angel named Gabriel. Was he attempting to respond to the felt Presence of the One in whom we live and move and have our being?

Acts 17:30–32	Surah 5:20–21, 26, 43–45
While God has overlooked the times of	
human ignorance, now he commands all	The Trumpet will be blown:
people everywhere to repent, because	"That is the Day of Warning."
he has fixed a day on which he will have	Every soul will come forward . . .
the world judged in righteousness	(Allah will say) . . .
by a man whom he has appointed,	"Who has set up another god beside Allah[?]" . . .
and of this he has given assurance to all	It is We Who give life and cause to die and
by raising him from the dead."	unto Us is the ultimate return;
When they heard of the resurrection	The Day that the earth shall be rent asunder
of the dead,	around them, as they hasten forth.
some scoffed;	That, indeed, is an easy mustering for Us.
but others said,	We know better what they say
"We will hear you again about this."	and you are not a tyrant terrorizing them.
	So, remind, by the Qur'an, him who fears My Warning."

Both proclamations conclude with the eschatological expectation of a final day of judgment closely associated with the resurrection. As noted in the previous chapter, however, in the New Testament message the promised resurrection has already been enacted initially in the raising of "a man whom [God] has appointed," Jesus of Nazareth. Further, God "will have the world judged in righteousness" by means of this same man. Let us acknowledge that in a chapter exploring the Christian doctrine of the Trinity, the Acts 17 sermon is not an obvious scriptural candidate. It features a "low" Christology, or "Christology from below," describing Jesus as "a man whom God has appointed" to serve as humanity's judge, validated as such by God's "raising him from the dead." It is, nonetheless, the fairly typical approach to Christology throughout the Luke-Acts corpus.

Even so, it is important to recognize that the New Testament repeatedly testifies that God has acted redemptively in and through this Jesus; indeed, God will continue to do so in the future judgment, according to the present text and many others. Earlier in the same book of Acts we read of Peter's preaching at Pentecost about "Jesus of Nazareth, a man attested to you by God with deeds of power, wonders, and signs that God did through him among you," concluding that "God has made him both Lord and Messiah, this Jesus whom you crucified" (2:22, 36). The point is that *Jesus is the Activity of God.* According to the proclamation of Acts, God performed signs through Jesus, anointed him "with the Holy Spirit and with power" (10:38), and "raised him on the third day and allowed him to appear, not to all the people but to [those] who were chosen by God as witnesses" (10:40–41). God is the actor. Jesus is the one through whom God acts. The immediacy and vitality of the divine presence and activity through Jesus is the Spirit. We recall Gregory of Nyssa's classic formula: every operation that extends from God to creation, and is designated according to our differing conceptions of that operation, has its origin in the Father, proceeds through the Son, and reaches its completion by the Holy Spirit.[11]

Meanwhile, in the qur'anic text an eschatological scenario is imagined in which God will ask of every human being, "Who has set up another god beside Allah?" Not only does God exist alone, and absolutely so, but the standard of judgment executed on that final day is none other than *shirk.*

> Those who say that Allah is the Messiah, son of Mary, are unbelievers. The Messiah said, "O Children of Israel, worship Allah, my Lord and your Lord. Surely, he who associates other gods with Allah, Allah forbids him access to Paradise and his dwelling is Hell. The evildoers have no supporters!" Unbelievers too are those who have said that Allah is the third of three. For there is no god except the One God; and if they will not refrain from what they say, those of them who have disbelieved will be severely punished. . . . The Messiah, son of Mary, was only a Messenger before whom other Messengers had gone; and his mother was a godly woman. They both ate [earthly] food. Look how We make clear Our Revelations to them; then look how they are perverted! (Q 5:72–73, 75)

For the Qur'an and for Islam, then, Christians are guilty of having commit-ted *shirk* in their beliefs about Jesus, setting him up as another god alongside God. The Christian solution, however, is not simply to equate Jesus with God, period, such that there would be no "alongside God," as it were. Instead, there is an important sense in which Jesus does indeed stand alongside God. But for the New Testament writers and Christian faith, Jesus stands alongside God precisely because the human person and work of Jesus owe themselves entirely to God's initiative in entering into creation to heal creation. God is, we believe and confess, pleased to dwell and to labor in creation in this very way (Col. 1:19–20; 2:9).

The Qur'an is decisive in its rejection of this incarnational logic. As I have already suggested, however, it may yet be possible to affirm, even if only guard-edly, that Muhammad's recitations were his attempts to put into his Arabic tongue a sense of the Spirit. To utilize the language of the Acts 17 sermon to the Athenians, perhaps the Qur'an textualizes Muhammad's searching for God, perhaps groping for God and even finding God, because "indeed God is not far from each one of us"—including, to be sure, Muhammad.

One may find a kind of theological precedent for this interpretation in the writings of the eighteenth-century Anglican missionary and founder of Methodism, John Wesley (1703–91).[12] Undoubtedly the most dramatic example occurs in his reading of Micah 6:6–8—

> With what shall I come before the LORD,
>   and bow myself before God on high?
> Shall I come before him with burnt offerings,
>   with calves a year old?
> Will the LORD be pleased with thousands of rams,
>   with ten thousands of rivers of oil?
> Shall I give my firstborn for my transgression,
>   the fruit of my body for the sin of my soul?
> He has told you, O mortal, what is good;
>   and what does the LORD require of you
> but to do justice, and to love kindness,
>   and to walk humbly with your God?

Noting that in the verse immediately preceding this famous passage the Moabite king Balak and his oracle-prophet Balaam[13] are mentioned (Mic. 6:5), Wesley assumed that the passage in question represented a conversa-tion between this pair of non-Israelites. Thus, wrote Wesley, this "beautiful passage" is given "a peculiar force" when we "consider by whom and on what occasion the words were uttered." King Balak asked the series of questions about what sacrifices might please Adonai, the God of Israel; the prophet

Balaam replied with the immortal words "He has told you, O mortal [*adam* in the Hebrew], what is good." Importantly for our purposes, Wesley assumed the active presence of God's Spirit, or prevenient grace, as prompting this interchange. Accordingly, for him the prophet Balaam was "then under divine impressions"; indeed, "probably Balak too, at that time, experienced something of the same influence. This occasioned his consulting with, or asking counsel of, Balaam—his proposing the question to which Balaam gives so full an answer."[14] Significantly, Wesley assumed this classic biblical passage that calls its hearers to "do justice, and to love kindness, and to walk humbly with your God" to have originally been the inspired words of a pagan prophet to his king's tortured query, "With what shall I come before the Lord?" Essentially, Wesley read this passage as a textual fragment of prevenient grace in action, an ancient testimony to God's faithful, loving Presence laboring among Moabite people outside of—and, for that matter, inimical toward—the people and practices of Israel.

If Wesley could interpret this classic prophetic text of Micah to be a quotation from a pair of pagans conversing under the influence of the Holy Spirit, perhaps we are not so far off in wondering about the same influence working upon and within Muhammad. Like us all, Muhammad existed within the limitations of time, place, language, and education—what the Acts 17 sermon poetically calls "the boundaries of our habitation" (v. 26 KJV). He, like us all, could see only as "in a glass, darkly" (1 Cor. 13:12 KJV). Islamic tradition certainly remembers him as a man of religious sensitivity, seeking wholeheartedly for answers to his troubling theological questions. Surely in this regard Muhammad was a prime candidate for receiving a significant measure of light from God. For Wesley the Micah passage was crucial not only as representing the conversation between a pagan king and a pagan prophet but also for the specific content of the prophetic oracle. He stressed that the one addressed by Balaam is called "O mortal," or "O human"—and that the One who shows the human (i.e., every human being) "what is good" is none but God. "So that we may say to every human creature, 'He,' not nature, 'hath showed thee, O man, what is good.'"[15] Wesley, then, rejected the Enlightenment notion of a simply "natural" conscience and argued instead for the immediately active Presence of the living God toward and within every human being. Again, this would obviously include Muhammad—and one is left to wonder whether considering Muhammad to be a prophet is any more difficult than making the same assumption of the earlier pagan oracle, Balaam. If the apostle Paul could write that "we know only in part, and we prophesy only in part" (1 Cor. 13:9), perhaps we could say something of the sort of Muhammad. Granted, this is less—far less!—than what Muslims would want to say about Muhammad; it is also more—perhaps far more—

than what most Christians would want to say. It may nonetheless provide something of a middle way.

The doctrine of prevenient grace, I am suggesting, may provide the beginning point for a Christian theology of Muhammad's religious significance. For Wesley prevenient grace is God's active presence at work in every human to evoke "a divine conviction of God, and the things of God [that] . . . enables every one that possesses it to 'fear God and work righteousness.' And whosoever, in every nation, believes thus far, the Apostle declares, is 'accepted of [God].' He actually is, at that very moment, in a state of acceptance."[16] This grace, for Wesley, was a divine gift, indeed a divine self-giving, not only to some predetermined company of "elect" people but to all people everywhere at all times. "Every man has a greater or less measure of this, which waiteth not for the call of man," Wesley preached. "Every one has some measure of that light, some faint glimmering ray, which, sooner or later, more or less, enlightens every man that cometh into the world."[17] In this construal of the relation between God and human beings, indeed all creation, one might interpret Muhammad as a particularly striking case, undoubtedly unique in many ways and unquestionably a profoundly gifted seeker after God "in whom we live and move and have our being," the One who is "closer than the jugular vein" to us all.

This would not necessitate Muhammad's being infallible, of course, any more than Peter who, by virtue of divine revelation, confessed that Jesus is the Messiah but still had many preconceptions about messiahship that required correction (Matt. 16:13–23). Likewise, with Wesley's reading of Micah 6:6–8, King Balak asked about acceptable sacrifices to Israel's God while "under the divine influence," but his presuppositions were themselves questioned and corrected by Balaam, who also operated "under divine influence" of the Spirit of God. Divine influence, we might suggest, does not ensure correctness or certitude regarding one's ideas or practices. Prevenient grace names God quietly and subtly—and thus not infallibly—laboring within us and with us as we are, situated within the "boundaries of our habitation."

As I have already acknowledged, this is likely to be an unacceptable interpretation of Muhammad for Muslims—and probably for most Christians as well, though of course for very different reasons. But it is nonetheless an attempt to interpret Muhammad from a Christian perspective without demonizing him or simply dismissing him as a charlatan or fool. Among Muslim writers, probably the one who interpreted Muhammad's revelatory experiences in a way most conducive to the possibility being explored here was Fazlur Rahman (1919–88). In his *Major Themes of the Qur'an* Rahman offered a stimulating discussion of the "agent" or source of revelation, writing that "the Qur'an describes the agent of Revelation, at least to Muhammad, never as an angel but always as Spirit or spiritual Messenger."[18] Rahman's observation moved against the dominant stream of Islamic tradition, which has insisted that it was in fact the angel Gabriel who recited the heavenly Qur'an to Muhammad. Rahman cited Q 40:15, "Exalted in rank, Owner of the Throne, He casts the spirit by His command upon whomever of his servants He wishes, to warn of the Day of the Encounter," pairing it with Q 16:2, "He sends down the angels with the Spirit by His Command upon whom He pleases of His servants [saying]: 'Warn that there is no god but I; so fear Me.'"[19] In both cases, of course, God's transcendent authority is underscored: it is by divine command that either angels or the spirit is sent by God to the prophetic servants of God.

It is difficult to know with certainty how to parse the difference(s) between this spirit and the angels, particularly when the angel in question is Gabriel. Granting that difficulty, it is nonetheless fascinating that Rahman connected the qur'anic language of the Spirit impregnating Mary (Q 19:17; 21:91; 66:12) with that of God inbreathing Adam (Q 15:29; 32:9; 38:72). He continued, "Believers, too, 'on whose hearts Faith is firmly inscribed,' are supported by God's Spirit (58:22). Jesus, however, was supported with the 'Holy Spirit' (*ruh al-qudus*) (2:87, 253; 5:110), which is also the agent of the Qur'anic Revelation (16:102). Jesus himself is described as 'the Prophet of God, His Word that He cast into Mary and a Spirit from Him' (4:171)—presumably because his mother was impregnated by the Spirit."[20]

If *ruh al-qudus* is not simply equated with the angel Gabriel—or, approached otherwise, if Gabriel is not considered to be simply an angel but something more—then one may edge toward an understanding of Allah not entirely removed from the Christian doctrine of the triune God. That doctrine itself, of course, did not come ready-made from the Bible but required centuries of reading, reflection, and dispute within the Christian community. Pentecostal theologian Amos Yong rightly encourages us "to contrast the historical factors leading to the Christian trinitarian understanding with the historical factors sustaining Islamic monotheism and anti-trinitarianism." The point is, perhaps it is time for Christians to offer greater grace toward Muhammad and his attempts to come to grips, theologically and spiritually, with the biblical testimony regarding the God of Israel. In that light Yong asks, "In what ways does the Qur'anic understanding of *ruh* reflect a pre-Nicene viewpoint perhaps prevalent in the Arabian peninsula of the sixth century?"[21] This is an especially pertinent question given the conflicts Muhammad witnessed among Jews and Christians in their numerous arguments over this God's identity, purpose, and mode of working in the world.

In the final analysis, however, Christian theology must employ an important canonical test for adjudicating human claims to divine inspiration or insight. It is a criterion arising particularly from the "Johannine circle" in early Christianity: "Beloved, do not believe every spirit, but test the spirits to see whether they are from God; for many false prophets have gone out into the world" (1 John 4:1). Too often Christian citation of this passage places all the emphasis upon "testing the spirits" with little attention given to how one would go about this testing. But the epistle immediately follows with the criterion: "By this you know the Spirit of God; every spirit that confesses that Jesus Christ has come in the flesh is from God, and every spirit that does not confess Jesus is not from God" (4:2). This standard of judgment, presumably offered to the churches of Asia Minor somewhere around the turn of the first century CE, was apparently directed originally against proto-Gnostic Christians who denied the true, physical humanity of Jesus but claimed to speak under divine revelation. The criterion of judgment, then, had to do with the actual material body of Jesus the first-century Jew, living as the Word incarnate among us; as the same letter opens, "We declare to you what was from the beginning, what we have heard, what we have seen with our eyes, what we have looked at and touched with our hands, concerning the word of life" (1 John 1:1). The fundamental criterion for discerning the presence, activity, and guidance of the Spirit is the historical figure of Jesus as witnessed to in the church's gospels. This criterion "suggested that a discarnate spiritualism would undermine the community's distinctive construction, fore-figured in the flesh of Jesus, of a new holiness of *embodiment*," Catherine Keller has written. "Spirit, as the immanence of the holy in the material world, must be expected to con-spire with the radically immanent project of the incarnation."[22] This incarnate Word, in turn, provides the fundamental criterion for a Christian understanding of God's character and ways in the world. This is an inescapably trinitarian mode of reflection.

It is obvious that Muhammad did not deny the flesh-and-blood body of Jesus—indeed, he insisted robustly on it. Further, as we have seen, the Qur'an could also call Jesus a "word" of God (Q 3:45; 4:171). But we must also acknowledge that Muhammad clearly did not understand the Word that became flesh and dwelled among us to have been, in any sense whatsoever, truly God. Indeed, in one influential interpretive tradition within Islam that "word" is identified as God's command "Be!" addressed to the potential existence of the human being Jesus of Nazareth.[23] Based on this canonical Christian criterion for adjudicating religious experiences or theological claims, we must finally judge Muhammad's proclamation to be found wanting. This, in turn, will bear considerable consequences for any attempt to offer a thoroughly Christian interpretation and evaluation of the qur'anic proclamation. Presumably such consequences will make themselves felt also in the matters of eschatology to which we now finally turn.

12

APOCALYPSE WHEN?

If He wishes, he will annihilate you and bring forth a new creation.
That for Allah is not a grave matter.

—Qur'an 35:16

For Muhammad, it surely was "the end of the world as we know it." A dramatic apocalyptic ending of the present world is a recurring and powerful theme in the Qur'an, especially in what are thought to be some of the earliest surahs. Muhammad, however, was not exactly feeling fine about it.

What he did feel, apparently, was the weight of the world gone wrong. Like the writer of the book of Revelation in the New Testament, who wrote long ago about "what must soon take place" (Rev. 1:1), it appears that Muhammad felt the immediacy of the world to come pressing in upon the present, already shattering it. The new creation was about to break through. The sounding of the trumpet, the resurrection of the dead, and the final judgment of all people were just on the horizon, and many extensive passages describe in colorful (and sometimes lurid) detail what was to be expected in the event of this universal denouement.[1]

At the heart of qur'anic eschatology is the conviction that human beings are called to account by God who created them. This accounting is ever just around the corner, always already demanding responsibility before our Creator. What frustrated Muhammad, like the prophets before him, was that so many people refused to live in the light of this eschatological dawning—which meant they were living in denial. There are many passages in the Qur'an that sound this theme; perhaps the most compelling is Surah 36, often regarded by Muslims to be "the heart of the Qur'an."[2] This surah's name is "Ya Sin"; this is the English rendering of two Arabic letters, making for a somewhat mysterious title. Islamic tradition, from early on, has favored the idea that the letters are an abbreviation for "O Human!" Thus the surah's title evokes the sense of a divine address calling all human beings to answer for themselves.

Interestingly, "Ya Sin" has come to be one of Muhammad's nicknames in Muslim parlance. Interesting, but not surprising: he functions as the model Muslim, the ideal human being. Likewise, there is certainly good reason for honoring this surah as the heart of the Qur'an, for it summarizes in a series of jabbing lines the fundamental thrusts of the book: God, the almighty Maker of all things, calls all people to acknowledge their Creator, to submit entirely to the divine will, and to know that they must render an account of their lives before God. The words of the prophet Micah—or are they the words of Balaam, the pagan oracle?—again come to mind: "God has told you, O mortal, what is good" (Mic. 6:8).[3]

Here are the concluding *ayat* of "O Human!"

> Does not man see that We created him from a sperm;
>   and behold, he is a manifest trouble-maker?
> And he produced an equal for Us, forgetting Our creating him.
> He said: "Who brings the bones back to life, once they are withered?"
> Say: "He Who originated them the first time
>   will bring them back to life and He has knowledge of every
>   creation."
> It is He Who produces fire from green trees for you;
>   and behold, you are kindling flames from it.
> Is not He Who created the heavens and the earth able, then,
>   to create the like of them?
> Yes, indeed, and He is the All-Knowing Creator.
> His Command is indeed such that if He wills a thing,
> He says to it: "Be," and it comes to be.
> Glory, then, to Him in Whose Hands is the dominion of everything
>   and unto Whom you will be returned.

(Q 33:77–83)

There are so many classic qur'anic themes in this passage. First, the Qur'an often contrasts the humble beginnings of human beings—made almost from scratch in their mothers' wombs—with their prideful rebellion, as they grow up, against God. How could something so insignificant in its origin become so troublesome, so stubborn, in its maturity? How *could* we? How could human beings, created to be *muslims* (submitters), stray so far from our divinely-ordained purpose? telos? Given our radical insignificance, so clearly evident especially in the earliest stages of human development, how dare we question either the existence or the power of God? For the Qur'an, one of the most common manifestations of our rebellion is our "produc[ing] an equal for [God]," or *shirk*, idolatry. Similarly, Paul the apostle wrote that "though [all people] knew God" through the signs of creation, "they did not honor him as God or give thanks" but instead "by their wickedness suppress[ed] the truth" (Rom. 1:21, 18).

The Qur'an frequently also speaks of a recurring tendency among Muhammad's hearers to dismiss his proclamation of the resurrection of the body. This doubt arises from the same human pride that the Qur'an finds so ironic, given our eminently humble beginnings as drops of liquid. It is only in forgetting this that we have the nerve to ask, "Who brings bones back to life, once they are withered?"[4] Muhammad is instructed to recite, "He Who originated them the first time will bring them back to life and He has knowledge of every creation." The point is that if God can create complex human bodies from a mere "clot" of fluid, then surely God can easily re-create bodies in the time of resurrection. In this anticipated divine act of re-creation, nothing stands in God's way: "The unbelievers say: 'Shall we show you a man who will tell you that, once you have been torn to pieces, you shall become again a new creation?'" (Q 34:7). The man in question, of course, is Muhammad, and the Qur'an proceeds to assure its hearers that he is no madman or liar (Q 34:8). The God who says "Be!" to create worlds surely faces no difficulty in the promised act of re-creation. "[If you] should you wonder, the [real] wonder is [in] their saying: 'What? If we turn into dust, will we be created anew?' Those are the ones who disbelieve in their Lord, and those are the ones around whose necks are chains, and those are the people of the Fire, abiding therein forever" (Q 13:5).

It should be clear, then, that qur'anic eschatology is tightly connected with creation. God shall re-create human bodies; likewise, the Creator of all things is fully capable of bringing all bodies, human and otherwise, to their proper fulfillment. "Say: 'Travel in the land and see how Allah originated the creation; then [know that] Allah produces the other generation [i.e., the age to come].' Allah truly has power over everything" (Q 29:20). Islam, like the traditions of Zoroastrianism, Judaism, and Christianity that preceded it, insists upon an eschatology in which material creation is embraced, redeemed, and gathered up into the compassionate purposes of the One who called it into being. This is the One, testifies the Qur'an, "in Whose Hands is the dominion of everything and unto Whom you will be returned" (Q 36:83).

Inspiringly hopeful as it is, an eschatology that affirms the goodness of creation's materiality and anticipates its redemption also creates profound challenges for religious faith and thought. It is far less problematic to postulate a spiritual realm, quite transcendent to this material world, to which redeemed souls shall float to enjoy eternal bliss. In such a scenario, this world of struggle, pain, and death shall be entirely "left behind." The goal in that case is not the healing of the present world but escaping from it, longing to leave here for God's true realm, a spiritual world utterly unlike this one. This world becomes at best a testing ground, a temporary state whose highest function is to purge souls. This spiritualized eschatology has, admittedly, been a recurring temptation especially for Christianity. We may find it far easier to live with its claims, for no experience in the present world can count against it as evidence. But of course this eschatological dream inevitably fuels an otherworldliness that undermines the doctrine of creation's goodness. For that reason alone, none of the religious traditions that have occupied our attention in this book can finally rest content simply with the eschatological hope of a transcendent, spiritual realm to which saved souls ascend.

By contrast, then, if God is not only the Creator of all things but also their final End, not only Maker but also Redeemer, then the expectation of a renewal of all things—supremely typified, perhaps, in the hope of the resurrection of the body—is a coherent hope. Thus, the dominant qur'anic conviction that "Allah truly has power over everything" provides grounding for the apocalyptic expectations of Muhammad and Muslims after him— expectations not unlike those of Jews, Christians, and, considerably earlier than any of these, Zoroastrians. But a problem persists. To put it simply: God is praised as the Creative Power ruling over everything, but everything is a mess. *Why?* Why so much suffering, whether at the hands of violent enemies or illness? Why hunger? Why sorrow, heartache, broken dreams and promises? Why sexual, physical, emotional abuse, especially of children, so vulnerable? Why slavery, oppression, hatred, and apathy? What is going on here? Why is so much of life filled with struggle, anxiety, and disappointment? Why is life so *hard?* What is God waiting for? In the psalmists' words of lament, "How long, O Lord?"

Whatever reply a religious tradition might offer to questions like these, the ultimate answer postulates a definitive and dramatic ending to the world as we know it. For the world as we know it is too hard, too painful, too disappointing. Most of our religious traditions teach us to anticipate that the sovereign God will re-create all things, right all wrongs, and rid the world of evil, suffering, and disobedience to the divine will—though we know not when. Muslims expect this end, as do many Jews. Christians learn to recite in the Apostles' Creed that Christ will return from "the right hand of the Father, . . . to judge the living and the dead." For that matter, we have seen that most Muslims also are expecting Jesus to return as the herald of the age to come—but that the first thing he will do is to bring judgment upon the worldwide Christian community for having perverted his gospel into idolatry.

Eschatological hope, though, is not limited to Jews, Christians, Muslims, and Zoroastrians. Millions of Buddhists (though far from all Buddhists) have expected, and are expecting, the dramatic incursion of a messianic Buddha named Maitreya to deliver the world from evil and restore righteousness. Similarly, countless Hindus anticipate the coming of another avatar, the deity Vishnu descending into the world to set it straight yet again. New Age spiritualities, ostensibly relying on ancient Mayan astrological speculation, are counting down to 2012 in a wide variety of eschatological scenarios. It would seem that the world as we know it is always, everywhere, ripe for a dramatic, universal transformation possible only for a supreme power.

The recurring religious reply to the questions raised by the problem of evil, then, is to propose to the dashed human spirit the promise of a divinely fashioned world to come. Never mind that this world is such a painful disappointment; God will do a much better job of it next time around. Eschatology is, most fundamentally, theodicy. It is a longingly speculative answer to our most pressing questions about the entire world's—and our own—suffering and evil.

> When the sun shall be coiled up; and when the stars shall be scattered about; and when the mountains shall be set in motion; and when the pregnant camels shall be discarded; and when the beasts shall be corralled; and when the seas shall rise mightily; and when souls shall be paired off; and when the buried infant shall be asked: "For what sin was she killed?" And when the scrolls shall be unrolled; and when heaven shall be scraped off; and when Hell shall be stoked; and when Paradise shall be brought near; then each soul shall know what it had brought forth. (Q 81:1–14)

The faithful will be gloriously rewarded in a realm the Qur'an often describes in imagery reminiscent of a luscious oasis in the Arabian desert: "Surely, those who believe and do the good, their Lord shall guide them for their belief; beneath them rivers will flow in the Gardens of Bliss. Their prayer therein shall be: 'Glory be to You, O Allah'; and their greeting in it shall be: 'Peace!' and they conclude their prayer by saying: 'Praise belongs to Allah, the Lord of the Worlds'" (Q 10:9–10). But for the disobedient, especially those who have spurned Muhammad's preaching, "sufficient is the scourge of Hell. Those who have disbelieved Our Signs, We shall surely cast them into the Fire; every time their skins are burnt, We will replace them by other skins, so that they might taste the punishment. Allah indeed is Mighty and wise!" (Q 4:55–56).

Stark scenarios like these are familiar in evangelical Christian preaching, even if dwelling upon them in sermonic rhetoric has fallen somewhat out of fashion. The point is that the "turn or burn" theme is hardly unique to the Qur'an or to Islam. While there are far more than enough warnings in the Qur'an to scare the hell out of anyone, there are more interesting (and hopefully more important) eschatological issues awaiting consideration. The specific question before us, given the rough similarity between traditional Islam and traditional Christianity regarding heaven and hell, is whether or not we can discover and probe eschatological divergences between the two traditions. Perhaps the difference will not be so dramatic as that between heaven and hell, but I suspect that exploring it will be its own reward.

Though in chapter 10 I have already offered a side-by-side reading of Surah 5, its eschatological offerings are sufficiently rich as to justify a second helping at "The Table." My hope is that by reading from that surah again, this time side by side with a passage from Paul, we may be able to probe possible differences between these documents—and at least potentially between Christian and Islamic traditions—regarding the nature of eschatological hope.

The Bible	The Qur'an
Philippians 2:1, 5	*Surah 5:109*
If then there is . . .	The day when Allah shall assemble the
any sharing in the Spirit, . . .	Messengers, then say: "What response were you given?"
Let the same mind be in you that	They shall say: "We have no knowledge; You
was in Christ Jesus,	are indeed the Knower of the Unseen."

I should first acknowledge that the rhetorical settings for these two passages are not readily comparable. The qur'anic passage anticipates the final day of judgment, while Paul writes a letter of appeal to an early Christian congregation. Nonetheless, this difference can be effaced somewhat. Paul certainly did assume that this congregation, like all his churches, was an eschatological community. Indeed, his hope that the Philippian believers "share in the Spirit" was a straightforwardly eschatological conviction, since the outpoured Spirit was understood to be a foretaste and glimpse of God's future for creation. What Paul hopes will happen in that congregation is a kind of "local eschaton"—a socially constructed embodiment of the rule of God—not in some future transcendent realm but in the midst of the present world.

In the qur'anic anticipation of the eschaton, it will be for the great messengers or prophets just as it had been for the angels in the time of creation: no one but God knows anything truly. God alone knows, and knows all. The issue is knowledge, and the assurance is that God alone possesses it. Meanwhile, though in his letter to the Philippians Paul writes of the *"mind . . . that was in Christ Jesus,"* it is evident that knowledge per se is not the driving issue. Sharing in the Spirit, which entails allowing the "mind" of Christ Jesus to rule in the fellowship of the church, will have as its end, it seems, something more like divine wisdom. Further, in the Qur'an it is repeatedly the case that only Allah knows, accentuating the absolute otherness and distance of God from all creaturely reality; for Paul, on the other hand, in the sharing of the Spirit Christians participate in none other than God's own richly outpoured "self." In the Spirit, God's own being is given to grace the human creature. To be sure, God remains God and creature remains creature; there is no denying transcendence. Yet it is precisely in divine transcendence, and as the transcendent Triunity, that God gifts the Christian community with the divine Spirit in and through the incarnate Word Jesus Christ.

Philippians 2:6–8	Surah 5:110
. . . Who, [being] in the form of God,	When Allah will say: "O Jesus, son of Mary,
did not regard equality with God	remember My Grace upon you and upon your
as something to be exploited,	mother, how I strengthened you with the Holy
but emptied himself, taking the form	Spirit, so that you could speak to people
of a slave, being born in human likeness.	in the cradle and as an old man; how I taught
	you the Book, the Wisdom, the Torah and the
And being found in human form,	Gospel; and how, by My Leave, you created out
he humbled himself	of clay the likeness of a bird, and breathed into it, and then, by My leave, it turned into a bird. And you could heal the blind and the leper by My Leave and you could raise the dead by
and became obedient to the point of	My Leave. And [remember] how I restrained
death—even death on a cross.	the Children of Israel from harming you, when you brought them the clear signs; whereupon the unbelievers among them said: 'That indeed is nothing but manifest sorcery.'"

The two construals of Jesus's relationship to God represented in these passages differ dramatically. In the Qur'an, Allah addresses Jesus from the position of supreme authority and sovereignty. In Philippians, Paul quotes an early Christian hymn that begins with the idea that Christ shared in the very "form" (*morphe*) or nature of God. More importantly, while many English translations imply a contrast between Christ's "being in the form of God" and Christ's self-emptying, the Greek text itself carries no such implication. That is, many English translations state that Christ, *although* he was in very nature God, emptied himself and became a servant, but Paul's Greek—admittedly, again, likely reflecting the language of a hymn of the early church—suggests no such contrast. Instead, we read that Christ, *being in the form of God*, did not grasp at power or insist upon divine authority. Perhaps we are closer to Paul's point to say that Christ, precisely because he shared in the very nature of God, "emptied himself, taking the form of a slave." Here the implication would be that God is like that—self-emptying Servant of all—and Jesus is the supreme revelation of this divine character.

Again, this would destabilize the hierarchy the Qur'an assumes to hold between Allah and Jesus. Rather than a portrayal of God who, from a position of supreme authority, calls Jesus to account on the last day, we find in Philippians 2 an image of God as One who becomes outpoured into creation "in human form" (*morphe* again), in the very nature of the human creature. And not just any human: rather, in concert with this divine outpouring, this self-emptying, Jesus is humble, "obedient to the point of . . . death on a cross." This kenotic movement is not contrary to God but revealing of God. Even though both the qur'anic and biblical passages acknowledge Jesus's obedience and submission—the Qur'an expresses this by emphasizing that, as we have seen in previous chapters, Jesus's wondrous works were performed by God's "leave" or permission—the critical difference is that in the Pauline passage this humility of Jesus is the embodiment of divine humility.

Philippians 2:9	Surah 5:116
Therefore also God highly exalted him,	And when Allah said: "O Jesus, son of Mary,
and gave him the name that is above	did you say to the people: 'Take me and my
every name,	mother as gods, apart from Allah'?" He said: "Glory be to You. It is not given me to say what is untrue. If I said it, You would have known it; You know what is in my soul, but I do not know what is in Thine. You are indeed the Knower of the Unseen."

The marked contrast continues. In the Qur'an's anticipation of the final Day, God puts the question to Jesus: did you ever even once encourage *shirk* among your disciples? Of course God already knows the answer to this question before asking, but in this way the text affords us an opportunity to hear once more Jesus's own strictly *muslim* commitments. The "wholly other" contrast and difference between God and Jesus, Creator and creature, is held tightly.

According to Paul, on the other hand, it is because of Jesus's thorough humility and obedience all the way to death on a Roman cross that God "highly exalted him and gave him" the name or title of highest honor. "Gave" here is a rather pale English translation of *echarisato*, better translated "graciously and lavishly bestowed." What God has so lavishly bestowed on Jesus—the humble, obedient, shamefully crucified Jesus—is the "name that is above every name." It is highly likely that the "name" Paul has in mind in this case is the title "Lord"—*kyrios* in the Greek, and the term used in the Septuagint to represent the holy name of God, *YHWH* or (as I have most often put it in this book) Adonai. Thus, Christ who is in very nature God—and precisely because he is in very nature God—does not grasp at or insist upon his "divine right," we could say, of being God. *Perhaps it is not God's nature to insist upon "being God" but instead always to be self-giving, self-emptying, Spirit-outpouring.*

It may be helpful to recall that Paul's very point in this complex Christological description is to offer to the Philippian congregation a model for how to live together with one another: "Let each of you look not to your own interests, but to the interests of others" (2:4). The relation between Jesus and Israel's God provides that model. Hence, while Jesus does not at all insist upon divine right or honor or even recognition, he is not left in the dust. He need not exalt himself, because he has been "highly exalted" by God, who graciously bestows the title of sovereign deity upon him: "the name that is above every name."

Philippians 2:10	Surah 5:117
	"I only told them what You commanded me:
So that at the name of Jesus every knee	'Worship Allah, your Lord and mine,' and I was
should bend . . .	watcher over them while I was among them, but when You took me to Yourself, You became the Watcher over them; for You are the Witness of everything. Should You punish them, they are surely Your servants; but should You forgive them, You are the Mighty, the Wise."

For Paul, God has exalted this humble servant Jesus with the divine name and authority—this very Jesus who died so shamefully, crucified on a Roman cross. God has done this so that "every knee should bend," that all people might be moved to bow before Jesus, to become *muslims* (submitters) to the Submissive One. Is it possible that Paul would actually consider this to be an open question, whether or not "every knee" *shall* bend? No doubt the popular Christian interpretation of this text would not allow such an open-ended eschatology. Generally speaking, the articulated Christian hope is that the Day will come when all shall bend the knee, willingly or not. But would such an end be coherent with the portrait of the humble, self-emptying God we encounter in this text? If Christ, *being in very nature God*, emptied himself instead of insisting upon establishing divine power and authority, then presumably God is like that. In that case, Jesus's humble servanthood is not a temporary ruse but the definitive revelation of God's character and God's way of being in the world.

To be sure, much popular eschatology today thrives on a portrayal of God that celebrates absolute power, that hopes for an ultimate demonstration of brute divine strength fully capable of overcoming all opposition and thus in some way ensuring ultimate compliance. No question, the Qur'an (and very often the Bible) espouses just such an eschaton. It fits the theme of a final submission, an ultimate validation of Muhammad's prophethood and vindication of Islam. Clearly, every knee will bend before Allah. In the qur'anic passage above that very scenario is being imagined. Jesus insists that he consistently shirked *shirk*, that he faithfully preached worship of Allah alone. On this final Day, Jesus can only commit his followers to the wise mercies of God: "Should You punish them, they are surely Your servants; but should You forgive them, You are truly the Mighty, the Wise" (Q 5:118).

The fundamental point before us: In the Qur'an, God alone is "the Exalted in power." In Paul's gospel, God has "highly exalted" the humble and humiliated Crucified One. God exalts Jesus, who is our representative. God, accordingly, is unveiled as the One who shares glory with the Other(s).

Philippians 2:10–11	Surah 5:119–20
	Allah said: "This is a Day in which their
. . . In heaven and on earth and under the	truthfulness shall profit the truthful; they will
earth,	have Gardens beneath which rivers flow, dwelling therein forever; Allah is pleased with
and every tongue should confess	them and they are pleased with Him. That is the great triumph."
that Jesus Christ is Lord,	To Allah belongs the dominion of the heavens and the earth and all there is in them, and He has
to the glory of God the Father.	power over everything.

The eminent Christian theologian Paul van Buren (1924–98) insisted that Paul in this passage provided the church with a critical rule: "Every proper

Christological statement, however 'high,' will make clear that it gives the glory to God the Father."[5] In this regard Paul's vision of eschatological glory offered to God veers near the qur'anic benediction, "To Allah belongs the dominion of the heavens and the earth and all there is in them." Equally important, however, is the recognition that for Paul the glory ultimately accorded to God the Father is a glory that the Father did not grasp, exploit, or hoard. Rather, it is a glory God outpoured upon Jesus. It is the glory of "the name that is above every name," a glory freely shared with the humble, crucified Son.

It becomes clear, then, what this "name above every name" is. It is "Lord," *kyrios*. It is of course no coincidence that *kyrios* was the Greek term used in the Septuagint to translate the divine name *YHWH*. God, Paul writes, has "highly exalted" the lowly Jesus and graciously bestowed upon him the name, or title, of the Holy One, Adonai. It is crucial to Paul's vision and argument to appreciate that it is the Holy One, Adonai, who has done this. Jesus did not exalt himself; Jesus was and is exalted, in order that all people might confess him as Lord. Christ, being "in very nature God" (2:6), did not clutch greedily at deity or divine authority; it was graciously lavished upon him (2:9). A strong implication of the text is that God has humbled God's own self as well, gifting Jesus with the divine name and authority that he would not take by force (or by right). So also Jesus in turn is confessed as Lord by those who believe, but this confession does not end with Jesus; he is not the end in himself. As van Buren carefully noted, the confession of Jesus as Lord is offered by us "to the glory of God the Father"—the very One who exalted Jesus. Paul writes of a mutually enriching, upbuilding, giving-and-receiving relation between the Father and the Son that we believe to be the dynamic of life and love divine. That dynamic is then poured out into creation through the incarnate life of the Son, Jesus Christ. The church is called and formed into existence by this outpouring of the Spirit, the Breath of God, the blowing of the Father and the Son. "If then there is . . . any sharing in the Spirit, . . . do nothing from selfish ambition or conceit, but in humility regard others as better than yourselves" (Phil. 2:1, 3).

The only situation, finally, in which Paul's instructions to the Philippian believers are coherent is one in which it is believed that *God is like this*. At the risk of overstating the difference—for indeed my argument is no doubt unacceptable to many if not most Christians—such a God is not the Qur'an's Allah, "who has power over all things."

A God "who has power over all things" can be expected, perhaps even soon, to exercise that power in a dramatic and unambiguous expression of authority. Such is eschatological hope, far more often than not. But I am wondering about the viability of an alternative eschatology, a humbler, more localized hope. I am wondering about the possibility that God entertains a hope that, even yet, the exaltation of the Crucified Lord will attract more and more people toward Jesus and his community of disciples, the church. But that hope goes hand in hand with a church that actually does practice the sort of eschatological life Paul describes in Philippians 2:1–11. "Let each of you look not to your own interests, but to the interests of others. Let the same mind be in you that was in Christ Jesus . . ." (2:4–5). There is no evidence that God is interested in coercing Christians into such a life together; why should we expect that at some point God will resort to coercion, a kind of divine violence, in order to usher in a world of righteous love?

Granted, this is not a terribly robust eschatology. We may want more. Generally speaking, Christians historically have expected a far greater display of divine authority to occur at some point, and usually "soon." Islam surely does share in this expectation. My argument is that this expectation probably fits better within an Islamic interpretation of God and world than it does in a Christian one.

There are of course reasons that Christianity early and often described its eschatological hopes in terms of a dramatic, world-transforming apocalypse. Paul's language in Philippians 2 about bending knees and confessing tongues is not his own; he draws here on the language of the Hebrew prophets. That kind of language also found its way to Muhammad and the Qur'an. Perhaps the contrast I desire to draw shall be clarified by reading Paul and Isaiah side by side:

Isaiah 45:20–22	Philippians 2:9–10
Assemble yourselves and come together; draw near, you survivors of the nations! They have no knowledge—those who carry about their wooden idols, and keep on praying to a god that cannot save. Declare and present your case; let them take counsel together!	
Who told this long ago?	Therefore God also highly exalted him
Who declared it of old?	
Was it not I, the LORD?	and gave him the name that is above every
There is no other god besides me,	name, so that at the name of Jesus . . .
a righteous God and a Savior; there is no one besides me. Turn to me and be saved, all the ends of the earth! For I am God, and there is no other.	

198

It is striking, actually, how similar the prophet Isaiah sounds to the themes and even the sound of the Qur'an. Perhaps, again, we might ask whether Muhammad was and is, in some sense, a prophet. "There is no other god besides Me," proclaims Isaiah, "for I am God, and there is no other." Christians do not, indeed must not, reject or dismiss such preaching. *And yet*—in the very proclamation of the gospel of God in Jesus Christ, we do encounter One who is "other" than God. Or, more precisely, we encounter One who is God's "Other" in such a unique relation that in a sense we do not believe that God says, simply, "There is no one besides me." We cannot avoid the implication of Christian confession that there is One who is "beside" God, one who "sits at the right hand of God the Father Almighty" (Apostles' Creed). When Paul wrote that "God also highly exalted him," he did not mean that God "highly exalted" himself. God exalts this Other-than-the-Father and graciously bestows God's own holy name of *kyrios* upon Jesus. In so doing, God exalts humility and servanthood; God honors self-emptying love that gives itself in deep and shameful suffering for "all the ends of the earth."

Isaiah 45:23	Philippians 2:10–11
By myself I have sworn, from my mouth has gone forth in righteousness a word that shall not return:	
"To me every knee shall bow,	every knee should bend,
	in heaven and on earth and under the earth,
every tongue shall swear."	and every tongue should confess that Jesus Christ is Lord, to the glory of God the Father.

Does the humility of Jesus Christ make a difference in our reading of God? That is, ultimately, the question. Does Christ's own self-emptying, undertaken precisely because "he was in the form [*or* very nature] of God," communicate anything about the nature of divine power? The process of mutual giving-and-receiving in Philippians 2:1–11 which we have explored in this chapter—offered by Paul as the model for corporate existence together as the Christian community—does indeed suggest a very different rendering of divine power, and by extension a very different interpretation of Christian eschatology. The church is that gathered community, the eschatological community, which together makes this confession about the power of humble Love Divine.

Presumably, God continues to hope for the Day in which the church will live together in the light of this confession. Perhaps other religious traditions, most notably Islam, can justifiably await a dramatically divine denouement to the world as we know it. The church, on the other hand, apparently is called to embody, in the midst of the world as we know it, a radically different social reality. Perhaps the church is called to *be* the age to come. It is an age, we confess and hope, that looks a great deal like Jesus.

Reopening

Conversation Continues

Allah, there is no God but He, the Living, the Everlasting. He has
revealed the Book to you in truth, confirming what came before it;
and He has revealed the Torah and the Gospel . . . It is He Who has
revealed to you the Book, with verses which are precise in meaning and which are the Mother of the Book—and others which are
ambiguous.

—Qur'an 3:3, 7

It might seem that any book featuring an Opening ought also to have a
Closing. Closure is admittedly inviting, perhaps even desirable. But in a
book whose chapter on eschatology closes so open-endedly, it is difficult,
perhaps impossible, to provide any definitive closing. In the absence of such
a closing—of the book, of history's possibilities, of the world as we try to
know it, of our struggles to interpret all of these—perhaps a reopening is
all we can anticipate. For in the words of a well-worn rabbinic dictum, "The
world pursues its normal course." As long as it does so, we find ourselves
once more returning to our respective tradition's texts of holy writ, bearing
the happy burden of interpretation in behalf of, and in company with, our
respective communities. Every opening of these texts is, of course, always
already a reopening. We approach, we read, these texts with a history. And
we open, we read and interpret and live, these texts in the midst of a history
far larger than we are, and we do so within traditions that have struggled
long before us to understand and embody these texts. Every opening is a

reopening—perhaps more humble than grand—and beckons to us once again to become readers of our scriptures.

I have attempted, in the chapters between this book's Opening and Reopening, to offer a Christian engagement with the Qur'an alongside the Bible and, from time to time, other Jewish writings. I have come to realize ever more surely that no objectivity would have been possible, let alone desirable, in this undertaking. Even so, I can only hope and pray that I have labored amid these texts with at least some measure of integrity and compassion. From such a position, perhaps we may ask about where this journey of reading the Bible and the Qur'an side by side has taken us. I would like to suggest a few fundamental themes, all of which ultimately can be grounded in the specific difference between Christianity and Islam (and, for that matter, Judaism) that emerges from the Christian confession regarding the incarnation of God in Jesus Christ. It is a difference, I fear, too often underappreciated or overlooked by Christians themselves.

The difference makes itself felt quickly in the doctrine of God. The qur'anic depiction of God is indisputably one entailing great might, authority, and transcendence. In short, "Allah ... has power over everything" (Q 5:120). To be sure, the Bible often makes comparable claims for God. But as we have explored in the previous two chapters, divine "power over all things" begins to be interpreted differently in light of the Word that became flesh and lived among us (John 1:14). It seems less like "power over" and more like "empowering." Such a God is a colaborer, a collaborator—the Creator of all things who, in full consistency with the divine nature and indeed as the ultimate revelation of that nature (self-giving, other-receiving love)—enters intimately and truly into the realm of creaturely existence as a human being in order to accomplish the divine purpose of healing all creation. It might be argued that a deity of this nature is anticipated in stories of Genesis, like God bringing the animals to the human to see what he would name them, or God sitting down to dine with Abraham. Perhaps these stories, examined in early chapters of this volume, are early intimations of a theological trajectory that would culminate in the proclamation of the incarnation of the divine Word. This logic of the incarnation, it hardly need be said by now, is forcefully and repeatedly repudiated by the Qur'an.

Accordingly, divine revelation is interpreted in radically divergent manners by these traditions. The Islamic doctrine of God necessitates, apparently, a pristine and perfect recitation of divine words unsullied by human mind or tongue. Christianity, in principle at least, is far more open to recognizing, affirming, and even celebrating the human element in its rendering of revelation. While the Islamic tradition historically has insisted that the Qur'an is purely divine recitation, with Muhammad's role reduced to little if anything more than being an illiterate conduit, Christians have opened and reopened a very different book when they have read the Bible. Indeed, it is more like a library than a book, replete with documents written and edited in many different eras and places and by virtually countless people. Further, its human element is presented on the page. The examples of this are virtually countless, but a particularly revealing one, for our present purposes, comes from Paul as he addressed the Christian community in Corinth.

Frustrated by the divisions in the Corinthian church, Paul wrote, "I thank God that I baptized none of you except Crispus and Gaius, so that no one can say that you were baptized in my name. I did baptize also the household of Stephanas; beyond that, I do not know whether I baptized anyone else" (1 Cor. 1:14–16). Paul frankly acknowledged his uncertainties regarding his own memory, and this has become enshrined in Christian Holy Writ. But this in fact helps to underscore the important point: Paul's letter is not an end in itself, for Paul's purpose in writing it was to establish more firmly this congregation (and, by extension, all Christian congregations) upon the divine foundation "that has been laid; that foundation is Jesus Christ" (1 Cor. 3:11). It is the coming into the world of the Christ, "the power of God and the wisdom of God" (1 Cor. 1:24), and the community forming around him, that captivated Paul. It is no coincidence that this "power of God" and "wisdom of God" is made known in "Christ crucified" (1:23). Paul's letter is not the revelation, and thus by logical extension neither is the Bible per se. For Christian faith, Jesus the Crucified Servant / Exalted Messiah is the revelation. Obviously, this revelation does not spurn the human but *is in reality a human*—a human who, like all other humans at least in principle, "increased in wisdom and in years, and in divine and human favor" (Luke 2:52). In Christian confession, this human "offered up prayers and supplications, with loud cries and tears, to the one who was able to save him from death, and he was heard because of his reverent submission . . . [and] learned obedience through what he suffered; and . . . [thus] became the source of eternal salvation for all who obey him" (Heb. 5:7–9).[1]

As became evident particularly in chapters 2 and 3 of this volume, for traditional Muslims the Qur'an (in Arabic, of course) is the textual embodiment of *Umm al Kitab*, the "Mother of the Book" that resides in the divine realm. Within a few centuries after Muhammad, Muslim scholars were engaged in disputations regarding whether this heavenly book was "created" or "uncreated"—intriguingly similar to the arguments among Christian thinkers about the nature of God's Logos that climaxed in the Council of Nicaea in 325. In that council the Alexandrian priest Arius was condemned as a heretic for teaching that the Logos that became human and lived among us was not God but in fact the highest and greatest of God's creatures. Athanasius championed the winning side of the argument at Nicaea, insisting against Arius that the Logos or Son participated thoroughly in the divine nature and thus was truly and fully God.

The fallout of these debates is instructive for us. Perhaps most significantly, in both Christianity and Islam those who argued for the "uncreated" side of the debate were eventually the winning side. However, further careful probing begins to reveal significant differences.

The Mu'tazilites, the Islamic theological school that emphasized the role of human reason and agency and thrived for several centuries before virtually dying out in the eleventh century of the Christian era, argued against the notion of an uncreated Qur'an because they believed it threatened the fundamental Islamic conviction of *tawhid*, the absolute unity of God. For them, Allah *and* the Qur'an sounded suspiciously like *shirk*. (Similarly, one of Arius's motives was to protect the doctrine of God's unity.) They argued that because the Qur'an's ontological status rested in the realm of created things, it participated in the realities of historical situatedness and linguistic ambiguity. This in turn demanded a far more explicit recognition, if not celebration, of the role of reason in the act of interpreting the qur'anic text. Remarkably unusual in the history of Muslim thought, the Mu'tazilites did not shy away from the creaturely nature of the Qur'an, and the necessarily human element of interpreting the Qur'an, even as they affirmed its status as divine revelation. If one extends the comparison to the fourth-century Christological debates, the Mu'tazilites championed something like an "Arian" view of the Qur'an.

The problem is that with the eventual eclipsing of Mu'tazilite teaching, the Qur'an came to be viewed in Muslim tradition simply as the perfect, utterly infallible, inerrant Word of God. The most vocal proponents of creaturely status for the Qur'an were effectively silenced—a development comparable to the rejection of Arius's Christology at Nicaea. Unlike Nicaea, however, no "fully God, fully human" paradox would be deemed necessary in traditional Islam. In this understanding of the Qur'an, the human element is effectively, even if not entirely, effaced. Revelation is unilateral; the human is passive recipient. I believe that this understanding of divine revelation creates ripple effects throughout the entire body of Muslim doctrine regarding God in relation to the world, and to human beings in particular. For instance, it implies a dismissal of any real or potential contribution of human reason—of interpretation—to knowledge of God or of the world. As I suggested in chapter 5, such an approach surely undercuts the scientific endeavor to understand and "name" our world. Further, as I argued in chapter 12, on the question of eschatological hope the Muslim approach tends to assign to

God the role of Sole Actor, determining all things. Creaturely agency goes largely, if not entirely, unacknowledged.

In the Christological controversy of the fourth century, by contrast, the church's endeavor on the whole was to find a way to affirm that in the person of Jesus Christ the truly divine nature and the truly human nature unite without compromising the integrity essential to each. The divine does not overwhelm or negate the human; the human does not eclipse or compromise the divine. Thus, while the Council of Nicaea rejected Arius's teaching that the preexistent Son was a high and mighty creature of God—insisting instead that the Son was *homoousias* or "one nature" with the Father—it also sought to uphold the incarnate Son's authentic humanity. This became evident when, after the victory of the Athanasian party at Nicaea, Athanasius's own friend and theological heir Apollinaris pushed harder and more explicitly than had his mentor to offer a solution to the divine-human paradox. I have had occasion several times already to mention Apollinaris's Christology because its official rejection at the Council of Constantinople in 381 is crucial to this book's argument. Apollinaris seems not to have differed significantly from Athanasius; it is possible that his first mistake lay simply in being more explicit in his Christological formulations. He postulated that while Christ did truly have a human body (a strike against Gnostic, docetic Christology), in the place of Jesus's "rational soul" or human mind there dwelled the eternal, uncreated Logos. Analogically, this would imply that just as the Logos moved and controlled the shell that was Jesus's human body, so also God moves and controls what otherwise looks like creaturely agency in the world.

It is truly good news that the church recognized this for the dangerous heresy it was (and is). The great Cappadocian theologian Gregory of Nazianzus responded to Apollinaris's Christology: "If anyone has put his trust in [Christ] as a man without a human mind, that person is himself really lacking a mind, and quite unworthy of salvation. For that which [the Logos] has not assumed he has not healed."[2] If the incarnate Logos did not have a human mind and consciousness, then no human mind can possibly be redeemed. The Christian doctrine of salvation—the full-orbed healing of the whole human and indeed of all creation—depends upon the Logos's full identification with, and thorough participation in, creaturely reality. Happily, the church followed Gregory's argument against Apollinaris, and did it again in the seventh century's monothelite controversy. In that debate the church affirmed the truly human will of Jesus, opposing the popular notion that Jesus always very simply, automatically, and without exertion of moral effort performed the will of God precisely because only the divine will was operative in him. If we remember too that Christian leaders had decisively opposed early Gnostic interpretations of Jesus as a spiritual being who only appeared to have a physical body, we find a consistent Christological thread running through the history of the church's official theological reflection: at every turn, the church has affirmed that the preexistent Logos, which "was with God, and indeed was God" (John 1:1), truly "became flesh and lived among us" (1:14). Thus, the being of God is such that this One could, and did, become a genuine human being who participated fully in the creaturely constraints of space, time, body, culture, language, and history.

The crucial point, then, is that a Christian interpretation of God and God's activity in creation—whether we refer to the act of creating itself, or to revelation, or to salvation or eschatological expectation—should be unafraid and unashamed to acknowledge the role of human beings, or "the human element." A robust Christian humanism is rooted in the doctrines of creation and, even more deeply, the incarnation. This is not to deny or belittle the historical reality of an Islamic humanism[3] but to encourage its present flourishing even while soberly recognizing that Islam repudiates the incarnational logic that is endemic to a Christian affirmation of God's profound investment in divine-human collaboration.

A full appreciation of this theological vision of colaboring moves us, I believe, to resist the recurring temptation to demand closure, to formulate easy answers, to seek deliverance from ambiguity and the happy burden of interpretation which is our lot. It appears that we—Jews, Christians, Muslims, and many others from virtually countless religious traditions—shall continue to open, which means to reopen, the texts of Holy Writ and of the world in which we find ourselves. May we become faithful readers in the spirit of humble prayer.

Precisely in that spirit, I offer one more reading of the Bible and the Qur'an side by side. The closing biblical passage is the prayer that Jesus taught his disciples to pray. By its side there is a qur'anic prayer often described as the Muslim equivalent of the Lord's Prayer. It figures significantly in the five prayer sessions prescribed daily for faithful Muslims and also is recited in many other everyday blessings. Indeed, the Qur'an is opened to this prayer, for it is Surah 1; hence the appropriateness of its traditional title, *Al-Fatihah*, "The Opening." It is perhaps also noteworthy that the Arabic Qur'an—which is to say the true and only Qur'an—is read from right to left and thus, from the perspective of speakers and readers of Indo-European languages, from the "back" to the "front" of the book. So at least in terms of the material layout of the actual pages of the Qur'an, we have *Al-Fatihah* in the right place here. We close this book—or, again, we reopen it—with Islam's "Opening" prayer. In this opening that is a closing that is more truly a reopening, I shall dispense with theological commentary. May we simply pray:

The Bible	The Qur'an
The Lord's Prayer	*The Opening*
Our Father in heaven, hallowed be your name.	In the Name of Allah, the Compassionate, the Merciful:
Your kingdom come. Your will be done,	Praise be to Allah, the Lord of the Worlds,
	the Compassionate, the Merciful,
on earth as it is in heaven.	Master of the Day of Judgment.
Give us this day our daily bread.	Only You do we worship, and only You do we
	implore for help.
And forgive us our debts, as we also have	
forgiven our debtors.	Lead us to the right path,
And do not bring us to the time of trial,	the path of those You have favoured,
but rescue us from the evil one.	not those who have incurred Your wrath
	or have gone astray.
Amen.	

NOTES

Opening: Arguing over Abraham

1. While this notion of the Qur'an as a "corrective" revelation is a traditional, and probably the most commonly held, view among Muslims of the Qur'an's relation to the Bible, this need not imply that the Qur'an actually presents itself in precisely that way. Obviously the qur'anic material engages biblical characters and narratives often, but there is rarely a sense in the text that the Qur'an is correcting fuzzy or misleading biblical details. I owe this important clarification to friend and colleague Denny Clark.

2. Unless otherwise noted, all qur'anic quotations are from *An Interpretation of the Qur'an: English Translation of the Meanings, A Bilingual Edition*, trans. Majid Fakhry (Washington Square: New York University Press, 2000). All biblical quotations are from the New Revised Standard Version.

3. See Arthur Waskow, *Godwrestling* (New York: Schocken Books, 1978).

4. For a helpful exploration of the "performative" function of the Qur'an, see Frederick M. Denny, *Islam and the Muslim Community* (San Francisco: HarperSanFrancisco, 1987; repr., Long Grove, IL: Waveland Press, 1998), 62, 78–88. For further development of these ideas with scholarly detail, see William A. Graham, "Qur'an as Spoken Word: An Islamic Contribution to the Understanding of Scripture," in *Approaches to Islam in Religious Studies*, ed. Richard C. Martin (Tucson: University of Arizona Press, 1985), 23–40; and Neal Robinson, *Discovering the Qur'an: A Contemporary Approach to a Veiled Text*, 2nd ed. (Washington, DC: Georgetown University Press, 2003), 9–24.

5. Michael Sells's *Approaching the Qur'an: The Early Revelations* (Ashland, OR: White Cloud, 1999) is a moving introduction to the early surahs of Muhammad; Sells describes them as "characterized by a hymnic quality, condensed and powerful imagery, and a sweeping lyricism" (4).

6. See James Kugel, *The Bible as It Was* (Cambridge, MA: Harvard University Press, 1997).

7. For a probing and sensitive examination of these and other issues arising from a comparative literary approach to the Bible and the Qur'an, see Marilyn Robinson Waldman, "New Approaches to 'Biblical' Materials in the Qur'an," *Muslim World* 75, no. 1 (January 1985): 1–13. This excellent article can be found also in *Studies in Islamic and Judaic Traditions*, ed. William M. Brinner and Stephen D. Ricks (Atlanta: Scholars Press, 1986), 47–64.

Chapter 1 Arguing over Abraham Arguing with God

1. This story of Abraham is found also in Q 15:51–60 and 51:24–37. *Surah* (or *sura*) is the Arabic term used by Muslims for a particular "chapter" or section of the Qur'an. There are 114 surahs in the Qur'an, of widely varying length. While in this book I will usually identify a surah with a numeral (e.g., Surah 2), in Islam it is far more common to use the particular nickname that has become associated with a surah. For example, Surah 11, which provides the passage for this chapter's study, is called "Hud"—after the name of one of several prophets mentioned in the Qur'an who are not in the Bible. This surah is a recitation, then, of the preaching and deeds of an extensive list of prophets, including Abraham. It immediately becomes clear that the story has a different function in Surah 11 from its function in Genesis 18.

2. Cited by Brannon M. Wheeler, *Prophets in the Quran: An Introduction to the Quran and Muslim Exegesis* (New York: Continuum, 2002), 96.

3. James L. Kugel, *The Bible as It Was* (Cambridge, MA: Harvard University Press, 1997).

4. H. Freedman and Maurice Simon, eds., *The Midrash Rabbah*, vol. 1 (London: Soncino, 1977).

5. While rabbis were perfecting the use of *Shechinah* as a circumlocution for the present-yet-omnipresent, near-yet-transcendent God, Christian theologians like Justin Martyr, Irenaeus, and Origen were developing the word-concept *Logos* for a similar function. In both traditions these designations served as theological refinements of biblical anthropomorphism.

6. Jacob Neusner, trans., *Genesis Rabbah: The Judaic Commentary to the Book of Genesis—A New American Translation* (Atlanta: Scholars Press, 1985), 2:184.

7. Ibid., 202.

8. Walter Brueggemann, *Genesis* in *Interpretation: A Bible Commentary for Teaching and Preaching* (Louisville: Westminster John Knox, 1982), 168.

9. Neusner, *Genesis Rabbah*, 63.

10. Augustine, *The Trinity*, trans. Stephen McKenna (Washington, DC: Catholic University of America Press, 1963), 75.

11. For example, this icon graces the cover of Karen Armstrong's 1996 book *In the Beginning: A New Interpretation of Genesis* (New York: Alfred A. Knopf, 1996). Armstrong notes in her book that "Christians would see the apparition of Mamre as an early manifestation of God as Trinity, a revelation which had come about as a result of Abraham's eager yearning toward three fellow human beings" (63). Of course, in Genesis none of the three is actually a "fellow human being." One of the figures *is* Adonai; the other two are described as angels.

12. James Kugel, *Traditions of the Bible: A Guide to the Bible As It Was at the Start of the Common Era* (Cambridge, MA: Harvard University Press, 1998), 343.

13. Elizabeth Johnson, "Trinity: To Let the Symbol Sing Again," *Theology Today* 54, no. 3 (October 1997): 299.

Chapter 2 People of the Torah, People of the Gospel

1. The greatest point of divergence occurs among those Christian bodies that include the books known collectively as the Apocrypha, which were part of the Greek translation of the Hebrew Bible (the Septuagint) but were not endorsed as canonical by rabbinic leaders in the generation after the destruction of Jerusalem in 70 CE.

2. David Hartman, *A Living Covenant: The Innovative Spirit in Traditional Judaism* (New York: Free Press, 1985; repr., Woodstock, VT: Jewish Lights, 1997), 214.

3. M. A. Salahi and A. A. Shamis, preface to Sayyid Qutb, *In the Shade of the Qur'an*, vol. 30, trans. Salahi and Shamis (New Delhi: Islamic Book Service, 1998), vii, viii.

4. I do not mean to imply that subsequent Muslim tradition has not undertaken the burden of interpretation that inevitably also implies disagreement, debate, and difference; it most assuredly has. Beyond the well-publicized differences between the Sunni and Shi'ite traditions, there are several streams of Shi'ism, at least five major schools of legal interpretation, a decidedly rationalist theological tradition, and of course the uniquely mystical path trod by Sufi Muslims. I only mean to imply that by all appearances from the Qur'anic text, Muhammad yearned for an ideal religious situation in which there would be no appreciable difference or debate over the holy texts taken to be divine revelation.

5. The most elegant and attractive interpretation I have encountered is Muhammad Asad's in his magisterial *The Message of the Qur'an* (Gilbraltar: Dar Al-Andalus, 1980). Asad actually proposes an interpretation of the Qur'an that challenges much of my reading presented in this chapter. Asad suggests that "had it not been for God's decree . . . that men should differ in their intellectual approach to the problems touched on by divine revelation," they would exist in uniform opinion on all such matters. "Since, however, such a uniformity would have precluded men's intellectual, moral and social development, God has left it to their *reason*, aided by prophetic guidance, gradually to find their way to the truth" (292n29). Though I pursue a different arc of reflection in this chapter, I would be delighted if Asad's interpretation is the more faithful one.

6. Again, this was a critique against Jews that numerous prominent Christian writers had already spent centuries perfecting. See, for example, David P. Efroymson's "The Patristic Connection," in *Anti-Semitism and the Foundations of Christianity*, ed. Alan T. Davies (New York: Paulist, 1979).

7. Hartman, *Living Covenant*, 213–16.

8. Heribert Busse, *Islam, Judaism, and Christianity: Theological and Historical Affiliations*, Princeton Series on the Middle East (Princeton, NJ: Markus Wiener, 1998), 47. Busse suggests possible rationales for this interpretation later in his book: "because of the destruction of the Temple . . . or God's response to the complaints of the people in the desert (Num. 11:23)" (183n134).

Richard Bell, in his commentary on the Qur'an, suggests that "Allah's hand is tied" was "a Jewish jibe" against the Muslim community occasioned by "the poverty of the Moslems or to the persistent call for contributions." *A Commentary on the Qur'an* (Manchester, UK: Victoria University of Manchester / *Journal of Semitic Studies*, 1991), 1:162. See also Mahmoud Ayoub, "'Uzayr in the Qur'an and Muslim Tradition," in *Studies in Islamic and Judaic Traditions*, ed. William Brinner and Stephen Ricks (Atlanta: Scholars Press, 1986), 5–6.

9. Hartman, *Living Covenant*, 216.

10. Ibid., 217.

11. Interestingly, one Islamic interpretive tradition holds that the same Jew, Finhas by name, who said "Allah's hand is tied" was also the one who claimed that Ezra was God's son (Ayoub 10). So far, then, as Muslim tradition is concerned, we are on the right track in considering these two qur'anic statements together.

12. Busse, *Islam, Judaism, and Christianity*, 57. Bell suspects the same, accusing Muhammad of "a hostile proclamation [in which] Jews and Christians are lumped together as saying much the same as the Meccan pagans used to say, i.e., worshipping sub-deities alongside Allah" (*Commentary*, 1:299–300). There is solace in the fact that Q 9:30 "created an exegetical problem for Muslim thinkers" (Ayoub, "'Uzayr in the Qur'an," 11), who acknowledged the relative oddity of this claim.

13. Lawrence H. Schiffman, *Understanding Second Temple and Rabbinic Judaism* (Jersey City, NJ: Ktav, 2003), 45.

14. Hartman, *Living Covenant*, 33–34.

15. Richard B. Hays, *Echoes of Scripture in the Letters of Paul* (New Haven: Yale University Press, 1989), 3–4.

16. There is no scholarly consensus on the identity of the "Sabeans" who are mentioned several times in the Qur'an, where they are generally associated with the "People[s] of the Book." It is certainly possible that they are the predecessors of today's Mandeans, a small group in southern Iraq and the Iranian province of Huzistan. One significant clue in this direction is that contemporary Muslims call these people "Subbas." If this identification holds, then we can say of the Qur'an's "Sabeans" that they had distinctively strong Gnostic ideas and practices, including astrology.

17. This is from Mohammed Marmaduke Pickthall's translation, *The Meaning of the Glorious Koran: An Explanatory Translation* (New York: New American Library, 12th printing, n.d.), 101.

Chapter 3 The Creative Word of God: *Be!*

1. Abdullah Yusuf Ali, trans. and notes, *The Meaning of the Holy Qur'an* (Beltsville, MD: Amana, 1999), 1224n4445.

2. Jacob Neusner, trans. *Genesis Rabbah: The Judaic Commentary to the Book of Genesis—A New American Translation* (Atlanta: Scholars Press, 1985), 1:13.

3. See Jon D. Levenson, *Creation and the Persistence of Evil* (Princeton: Princeton University Press, 1994).

4. David B. Burrell, *Freedom and Creation in Three Traditions* (Notre Dame, IN: University of Notre Dame Press, 1993), 24. We perhaps should wonder about Burrell's assumption that questioning *creatio ex nihilo* would necessitate a God-world relation characterized by competition. Why not mutuality and nurture?

5. For an insightful treatment of the issue of whether or not the Qur'an teaches *creatio ex nihilo*, answered in the negative, see Daniel Carl Peterson's entry "Creation" in the *Encyclopaedia of the Quran*, Jane Dammen McAuliffe, gen. ed. (Leiden: Brill, 2001), esp. 1:475–80.

6. Jacob Neusner, *Judaism's Story of Creation: Scripture, Halakhah, Aggadah* (Leiden: Brill, 2000), 78.

7. This theme of divine vulnerability is not unique to Christianity; it can be found in certain strands of rabbinic thought as well as in subsequent Jewish mystical speculations. In these streams of Jewish tradition, the theme tends to be associated with the Shechinah, God's presence in the world, who dwells especially in and among the Jewish people. See, for example, Gershom Scholem, *On the Kabbalah and Its Symbolism* (New York: Schocken, 1996), and Martin Buber, *Hasidism and Modern Man* (Philadelphia: University of Pennsylvania Press, 1988). For attempts by Christian theologians to appropriate the idea of the suffering, vulnerable Shechinah as a way of thinking about God's relation to the world, see Jürgen Moltmann, *The Spirit of Life: A Universal Affirmation* (Minneapolis: Augsburg Fortress, 1992), 47–51; and Michael Lodahl, *Shekhinah/Spirit: Divine Presence in Jewish and Christian Religion* (Mahwah, NJ: Paulist, 1992), 51–73.

8. See Elizabeth Johnson, *Friends of God and Prophets: A Feminist Theological Reading of the Communion of Saints* (New York: Continuum, 1998), esp. 40–45.

9. Neusner, *Genesis Rabbah*, 23–24.

10. Wilfred Cantwell Smith, *What Is Scripture? A Comparative Approach* (Minneapolis: Fortress, 1993), 52.

11. Cf. Burrell, *Freedom and Creation*, 64–65.

12. Mohammad Iqbal, *The Reconstruction of Religious Thought in Islam* (New Delhi: Kitab Bhavan, 1974), 3.

13. For a stunning philosophical exploration of our rich relations to the world around us, more fundamental than linguistically based interpretations of that world, see David Abram, *The Spell of the Sensuous: Perception and Language in a More-than-Human World* (New York: Vintage, 1997).

14. Jamaal al-Din M. Zarabozo, *How to Approach and Understand the Quran* (Boulder, CO: Al-Basheer, 1999), 78.

15. In Philip S. Alexander, ed. and trans., *Textual Sources for the Study of Judaism* (Chicago: University of Chicago Press, 1990), 68.

Chapter 4 The Revealing of the Word of God

1. Reza Aslan provides an insightful and informative description of the debate regarding the nature of the Qur'an in the early centuries of Islamic history in *No God But God: The Origins, Evolution, and Future of Islam* (New York: Random House, 2006), 140–44.

2. Michael Cook, *The Koran: A Very Short Introduction* (Oxford: Oxford University Press, 2000), 114.

3. Gregory of Nazianzus, "Letters on the Apollinarian Controversy," in *Christology of the Later Fathers*, Library of Christian Classics (Philadelphia: Westminster Press, 1954), 3:218.

4. Fazlur Rahman, *Major Themes of the Qur'an* (Minneapolis: Bibliotheca Islamica, 1989), 99.

5. Ibid., 99–100.

6. Daniel Madigan, *The Qur'an's Self-Image: Writing and Authority in Islam's Scripture* (Princeton: Princeton University Press, 2001), 68.

7. William Placher, *Narratives of a Vulnerable God: Christ, Theology, and Scripture* (Louisville: Westminster John Knox, 1994), 104.

8. Brannon M. Wheeler, *Prophets in the Quran: An Introduction to the Quran and Muslim Exegesis* (New York: Continuum, 2002), 308–9.

9. Roberto Tottoli, *Biblical Prophets in the Qur'an and Muslim Literature*, Curzon Studies in the Qur'an (Richmond, Surrey, UK: Curzon, 2002), 50n2.

10. Rahman, *Major Themes of the Qur'an*, 136. For a more critical, though not entirely unsympathetic, approach to this issue, see Alan Dundes, *Fables of the Ancients? Folklore in the Qur'an* (Lanham, MD: Rowman and Littlefield, 2003).

11. See Cook, *Koran*, 128.

12. For an insightful exploration of this qur'anic theme see Mustafa Ruzgar, "Islam and Deep Religious Pluralism," in *Deep Religious Pluralism*, ed. David Ray Griffin (Louisville: Westminster John Knox, 2005).

13. Tottoli, *Biblical Prophets in the Qur'an*, 7.

14. Dundes, *Fables of the Ancients?* 68.

15. Mohammad Iqbal, *The Reconstruction of Religious Thought in Islam* (New Delhi: Kitab Bhavan, 1974), 27.

Chapter 5 *Adam*: What Does It Mean to Be Human?

1. The classic (though far from the only) expression of this critique is Lynn White Jr., "The Historical Roots of our Ecological Crisis," *Science* 155 (March 10, 1967): 1203–7.

2. Seyyed Hossein Nasr, *Islam: Religion, History, and Civilization* (San Francisco: HarperSanFrancisco, 2003), 66.

3. John C. Reeves, "Some Explorations of the Intertwining of Bible and Qur'an," in *Bible and Qur'an: Essays in Scriptural Intertextuality*, ed. Reeves (Atlanta: Society of Biblical Literature, 2003), 54.

4. This account is found in Surah 5:27–32 and will be explored further in the following chapter.

5. Harvey Cox, *The Secular City: Secularization and Urbanization in Theological Perspective* (New York: Macmillan, 1965), 73–74.

6. My guess is that God's demand that the angels bow before Adam has more to do with the Jewish antecedents to the Qur'an's story than to any narrative element or logic within the qur'anic passage itself.

7. A. Christian van Gorder, *No God But God: A Path to Muslim-Christian Dialogue on God's Nature* (Maryknoll, NY: Orbis, 2003), 40.

8. Fazlur Rahman, *Major Themes of the Qur'an* (Minneapolis: Bibliotheca Islamica, 1989), 17–18.

9. Isma'il Ragi al Faruqi, "A Comparison of the Islamic and Christian Approaches to Hebrew Scripture," *Journal of Bible and Religion* 31, no. 4 (October 1963): 290.

10. Mohammad Iqbal, *The Reconstruction of Religious Thought in Islam* (New Delhi: Kitab Bhavan, 1974), 13. Iqbal's reading of this passage is not unlike that offered by the rationalist Mu'tazilite school of Islam, which flourished during the ninth and tenth centuries but was largely silenced by the end of the twelfth century. Mahmoud M. Ayoub typifies the Mu'tazilite interpretation: "Languages were invented by human beings; therefore what is intended is that God inspired Adam and created in him the capacity to invent languages." Ayoub, *The Qur'an and Its Interpreters* (Albany, NY: SUNY Press, 1984), 1:80.

11. Iqbal, *The Reconstruction of Religious Thought in Islam*, 86.

12. Sayyid Mawdudi, *Towards Understanding the Qur'an*, vol. 1, trans. and ed. Zafar Ishaq Ansari (Leicester, UK: Islamic Foundation, 1988), 18.

13. A. A. Mawdudi, *Towards Understanding Islam* (n.p., n.d.), 7.

14. Jacob Neusner, trans. and ed., *Genesis and Judaism: The Perspective of Genesis Rabba* (Atlanta: Scholars Press, 1985), 46.

15. Ibid.

16. Nasr, *Islam*, 66.

17. John R. Levison, *Portraits of Adam in Early Judaism: From Sirach to 2 Baruch* (Sheffield, UK: Sheffield Academic Press, 1988), 184–85.

18. Nasr, *Islam*, 66.

Chapter 6 Cain and Abel: The Commanding Word of God

1. Reza Aslan, *No God But God: The Origins, Evolution, and Future of Islam* (New York: Random House, 2006), 154.

2. See ibid., 141–59, for a helpful summary of the history and issues of the conflict between the Traditionalist and Rationalist schools during the first half-millennium of Islam's existence. A fuller treatment, with rich primary sources, is found in Richard C. Martin and Mark R. Woodward with Dwi S. Atmaja, *Defenders of Reason in Islam: Mu'Tazilism from Medieval School to Modern Symbol* (Oxford: Oneworld, 1997).

3. Aslan, *No God But God*, 152.

4. Again, see Martin, Woodward, and Atmaja, *Defenders of Reason in Islam*. See also Lenn E. Goodman, *Islamic Humanism* (Oxford: Oxford University Press, 2003).

5. Muhammad Asad, *The Message of the Qur'an* (Gilbraltar: Dar Al-Andalus, 1980), 147.

6. Jacob Neusner, *Genesis Rabbah: The Judaic Commentary to the Book of Genesis—A New American Translation* (Atlanta: Scholars Press, 1985), 1:248.

7. Norman Stillman, "The Story of Cain and Abel in the Qur'an and the Muslim Commentators: Some Observations," *Journal of Semitic Studies* 19 (1974): 235.

8. Ibid.

9. Sayyid Mawdudi, *Towards Understanding the Qur'an*, vol. 1, trans. and ed. Zafar Ishaq Ansari (Leicester, UK: Islamic Foundation, 1988), 155.

10. Eugene Borowitz, *The Talmud's Theological Language Game* (Albany, NY: SUNY Press, 2006), 55.

Chapter 7 Knowing Noah—or Not

1. Jamaal al-Din M. Zarabozo, *How to Approach and Understand the Quran* (Boulder, CO: Al-Basheer, 1999), 258.

2. While Jewish tradition could, to a considerable extent, be included along with Islam and Christianity on this point, I hesitate to do so. There is too much material in the Talmud—to say nothing of the Kabbalah, Judaism's body of mystical literature—that renders God in profoundly interactive and often anthropomorphic imagery, resisting the tendency toward abstract perfections like timelessness and perfect omniscience. I assume this is partly due to the often strikingly anthropomorphic portrayals of God in the Tanakh (especially, as I have noted, in the Yahwistic tradition). Though rabbis were sensitive to the problems of thinking of God in all-too-human terms, they continued to engage such portrayals creatively and insightfully.

3. Neal Robinson, *Discovering the Qur'an: A Contemporary Approach to a Veiled Text*, 2nd ed. (Washington, DC: Georgetown University Press, 2003), 156.

4. Jacob Neusner, trans., *Genesis Rabbah: The Judaic Commentary to the Book of Genesis—A New American Translation* (Atlanta: Scholars Press, 1985), 1:310.

5. James L. Kugel, *The Bible as It Was* (Cambridge, MA: Belknap / Harvard University Press, 1997), 115. The *Sibylline Oracles* are generally believed to have been written by a Hellenistic Jew sometime in the second century BCE. This text represents and encourages aggressive Jewish engagement with, and proclamation of Israel's God to, Greek culture. Accordingly, its portrayal of Noah becomes representative of the Jewish duty to proclaim the imminent apocalyptic end of the world.

6. Gordon D. Newby explores some of the possibilities of Jewish antecedents to the Qur'an's narrative in "The Drowned Son: Midrash and Midrash Making in the Qur'an and *Tafsir*," in *Studies in Islamic and Judaic Traditions*, ed. William M. Brinner and Stephen D. Ricks (Atlanta: Scholars Press, 1986).

7. Robinson, *Discovering the Qur'an*, 156.

8. Karen Armstrong, *Muhammad: A Biography of the Prophet* (San Francisco: HarperSanFrancisco, 1992), 105–6. See also Reza Aslan, *No God But God: The Origins, Evolution, and Future of Islam* (New York: Random House, 2006), 56–59.

9. Neusner, *Genesis Rabbah*, 2:63.

10. Ibid., 28.

11. Kugel, *Bible as It Was*, 27.

12. David Hartman, *A Living Covenant: The Innovative Spirit in Traditional Judaism* (New York: Free Press, 1985; repr., Woodstock, VT: Jewish Lights, 1997), 30.

13. Neusner, *Genesis Rabbah*, 2:29.

14. Hartman, *Living Covenant*, 27.

Chapter 8 The Sign of Sinai

1. Al-Tabari, *The Commentary on the Qur'an*, vol. 1, intro. and notes by J. Cooper (Oxford: Oxford University Press, 1987), 365.

2. For another translation, see Jacob Neusner, trans., *The Talmud of Babylonia: An American Translation*, vol. 35A, *Tractate Abodah Azrah, Chapters 1–2* (Atlanta: Scholars Press, 1991), 12.

3. This chapter's epigraph, Q 4:154, is part of a passage that functions in a similar way. The ensuing *ayat* (verses) emphasize Israel's disobedience and unbelief; in fact, Israel's recalcitrance leads directly in this passage to the Jews' "imputing to Mary a great falsehood" (4:156) of sexual impropriety in the conception of Jesus (see the following chapter of this book) and then (in 4:157) to their mistaken claims regarding having crucified Jesus (explored further in chapter 10).

4. Benjamin Blech, *Understanding Judaism: The Basics of Deed and Creed* (Northvale, NJ: Jason Aronson, 1991), 69. See also Louis Ginzberg, *The Legends of the Jews* (Philadelphia: Jewish Publication Society of America, 1911), 3:92–94.

5. The hymn is from *Sephardi Machzor*. For more historical background and a much longer quotation from the hymn, see Howard Schwartz, *Reimagining the Bible: The Storytelling of the Rabbis* (Oxford: Oxford University Press, 1998), 87. Najara (ca. 1550–1625) wrote it originally for his local synagogue in Safed, the village in the hills to the north of the Sea of Galilee that has been the center of Jewish mysticism since the mass expulsion of Jews from Spain in 1492. Today it is famous also as an artist colony.

Chapter 9 Mary, Mother of Jesus

1. Robert J. Miller, ed., *The Complete Gospels* (San Francisco: HarperSanFrancisco, 1994), 381.

2. One could, of course, raise the same question regarding the usage of *Xristos* in Luke's gospel—or throughout the New Testament, for that matter. A detailed examination of such issues is far beyond our concern here. I assume, however, that especially in the case of Luke's writing we are not far from his understanding of "messiah" if we cite the proclamation of Peter in Acts 10:36: "God anointed Jesus of Nazareth with the Holy Spirit and with power."

3. The great tenth-century Muslim interpreter Al-Tabari interpreted *Messiah* to mean "one who wipes away sickness." See Rizwi Faizer's captivating article "The Dome of the Rock and the Qur'an," in *Coming to Terms with the Qur'an*, ed. Khaleel Mohammed and Andrew Rippin (North Haledon, NJ: Islamic Publications International, 2007), 94.

4. On the other hand, one Muslim interpretive tradition argues that the "word from [God]" that is Jesus is nothing more than God's word "Be!"—a reading that certainly fits the context of Q 3:47, as we shall see momentarily. This implies that Jesus exists precisely as every other creature in the universe exists, as the direct result of divine command. See, for example, Jamaal al-Din M. Zarabozo, *How to Approach and Understand the Qur'an* (Boulder, CO: Al-Basheer, 1999), 211–12.

5. The angel's negative reply to Mary's query, "If I actually conceive by the Lord, . . . will I also give birth the way women usually do?" is actually borne out in subsequent events in the narrative. As this document tells it, as Mary nears the moment of childbirth she reclines in a cave that becomes overshadowed by a dark cloud while Joseph and a midwife stand helplessly outside—no need for a midwife in this case! As the cloud withdraws, an unbearably bright light bursts from inside the cave, gradually receding "until an infant became visible" (19:16). The midwife, doubtful of Joseph's story that the mother is a virgin "pregnant by the holy spirit" (19:9), insists on performing a gynecological examination on Mary. Upon "insert[ing] her finger into Mary," her hand begins to disappear, "being consumed by the flames!" (20:4).

Immediately repentant of having "put the living God on trial" (20:3), the midwife is healed by holding the holy child. The story supports the notion that Jesus's birth did not rupture Mary's body—presumably providing an early source for the later Roman Catholic teaching regarding her perpetual virginity.

6. See note 3 in this chapter.

7. Faizer, "Dome of the Rock and the Qur'an," 85, 93.

8. The traditional name of this document is *The Book about the Origin of the Blessed Mary and the Childhood of the Savior*. It replicates much of the material of the *Infancy Gospel of James* but merits the name *Pseudo-Matthew* for its extensive use of the prophecy-fulfillment motif so crucial in the canonical gospel of Matthew. The translation utilized here is from Willis Barnstone, ed., *The Other Bible* (San Francisco: Harper & Row, 1984), 394–97.

9. Amina Wadud, *Qur'an and Woman: Rereading the Sacred Text from a Woman's Perspective* (New York: Oxford University Press, 1999), 40.

10. Irenaeus, *Against Heresies*, in *Early Christian Fathers*, ed. Cyril C. Richardson, Library of Christian Classics 1 (Philadelphia: Westminster Press, 1953), 379.

11. It is possible, indeed likely, that the Qur'an assumes that Mary/Maryam is the Miriam of the story of the exodus—the sister of Moses and Aaron. The Qur'an identifies her father as "Imran," a variant of "Amran," the father of Moses, Aaron, and Miriam in the Bible (e.g., Exod. 6:20, Num. 26:59). This collapsing of names / characters lends support to the strong likelihood that Muhammad's knowledge of biblical stories was mediated orally. As friend and colleague Denny Clark has helped me to understand better, when stories are encountered orally it is difficult to gain a sense of historical relations, succession, or timeline.

12. See Elizabeth A. Johnson, *Consider Jesus: Waves of Renewal in Christology* (New York: Crossroad, 1996), 36–38.

Chapter 10 Jesus, Son of Mary

1. Sayyid Mawdudi, *Towards Understanding the Qur'an*, vol. 2, trans. and ed. Zafar Ishaq Ansari (Leicester, UK: Islamic Foundation, 1988), 149.

2. Gregory of Nyssa, "Address on Religious Instruction," in *Christology of the Later Fathers*, ed. Edward Rochie Hardy, Library of Christian Classics 3 (Philadelphia: Westminster Press, 1954), 301.

3. There are many other passages in the Qur'an dealing with Jesus's identity and mission, but space does not allow their examination in this book. The Qur'an's overall concern is to affirm that Jesus was a great prophet calling Israel to worship God alone, and robustly to deny the Christian claim that he was and is God's Son (e.g., Q 3:50–51; 5:72). The best extended treatment of Christology in conversation with Islam remains Kenneth Cragg's *Jesus and the Muslim: An Exploration* (London: Oneworld, 1999). See also Geoffrey Parrinder, *Jesus in the Qur'an* (New York: Barnes and Noble, 1965), and Neal Robinson, *Christ in Islam and Christianity* (Albany, NY: SUNY Press, 1991).

4. Kenneth Cragg, *The Call of the Minaret*, 2nd ed. (Maryknoll, NY: Orbis, 1985), 266. Muhammad Asad (1900–1992), however, in his impressive *The Message of the Qur'an* (Gilbraltar: Dar Al-Andalus, 1980), insisted that neither the Qur'an nor authentic *hadith* (traditional sayings) of Muhammad support the notion of a substitute, such as Judas, for the soon-to-be-crucified Jesus. Instead, Asad argued that the crucifixion of Jesus was a legend that grew up around Christians' telling of Jesus's story, "possibly under the then-powerful influence of Mithraistic beliefs" (154n171).

5. From Willis Barnstone, ed., *The Other Bible* (San Francisco: Harper & Row, 1984), 117–99. We find similar ideas about Jesus's apparent crucifixion in *The Apocalypse of Peter*, in which "the

living Jesus" is described as "laughing on the tree, glad and laughing," while the nails are driven into the hands and feet of "his fleshly part," "the one who came into being in his physical likeness."

6. Parrinder, *Jesus in the Qur'an*, 120.

7. See Robinson's careful examination of influential Muslim exegesis of Q 4:157 in *Christ in Islam and Christianity*, 127–41.

8. Mawdudi, *Towards Understanding the Qur'an*, 2:107.

9. Ibid., 1:259.

10. Brannon Wheeler, *Prophets in the Quran: An Introduction to the Quran and Muslim Exegesis* (New York: Continuum, 2002), 317.

11. Ibid., 309–10.

12. Ibid., 310.

Chapter 11 Adonai, Allah, and the Triune God

1. Though some traditionalist Muslims argue that *Allah* is God's proper and eternal name, and therefore not etymologically derived, there is little if any reason to believe this. Certainly its current usage denotes equivalency with the generic term *God*, such that Arabic-speaking Jews and Christians feel no hesitation or compunction about using the term *Allah* to refer to the One to whom they pray and render their worship and obedience.

2. Islamic scholar Sayyid Abul A'la Mawdudi comments on this passage: "[Jesus] was . . . an embodiment of truth, veracity, righteousness, and excellence. This is what the Christians had been told about Christ. But they exceeded the proper limits of veneration for Jesus. The 'spirit *from* God' became the 'spirit *of* God,' and the 'spirit of holiness' was interpreted to mean God's own Spirit which became incarnate in Jesus. Thus, along with God and Jesus, there developed the third person of God—the Holy Ghost." See *Towards Understanding the Qur'an*, trans. and ed. Zafar Ishaq Ansari (Leicester, UK: Islamic Foundation, 1988), 1:90.

3. St. John of Damascus, *On the Divine Images*, trans. David Anderson (Crestwood, NY: St. Vladimir's Seminary Press, 2002), 15–16, 23.

4. Michael Nazir-Ali, *Frontiers in Muslim-Christian Encounter* (Oxford: Regnum, 1987), 17–18.

5. See note 3 in chap. 9, above.

6. This hadith is cited in Al-Tabari, *The Commentary on the Qur'an*, intro. and notes by J. Cooper (Oxford: Oxford University Press, 1987), 1:438.

7. The Sufi tradition is the dramatic exception to this emphasis upon utter transcendence in Islam. Perennially controversial, Sufis have tended to interpret the *Shahada* not simply as "There is no god but God" but as "There is nothing but God." Thus Reza Aslan writes, "Like most mystics, Sufis strive to eliminate the dichotomy between subject and object in their worship" (*No God But God: The Origins, Evolution, and Future of Islam* [New York: Random House, 2006], 211). The most infamous instance of this tendency probably occurred in Husayn ibn Mansur al-Hallaj, a tenth-century Sufi from Baghdad who walked the streets yelling "I am the Truth!" Since "Truth" is one of the ninety-nine names of God in Islamic devotion, it is not entirely surprising that al-Hallaj was arrested, tortured, flogged, mutilated, crucified, decapitated, dismembered, and then burned to ash. See Aslan, *No God But God*, 194–219.

8. Gregory of Nyssa, "An Answer to Ablabius: That We Should Not Think of Saying There Are Three Gods," in *Christology of the Later Fathers*, ed. Edward Rochie Hardy, Library of Christian Classics 3 (Philadelphia: Westminster Press, 1954), 261–62. For a marvelous treatment of Gregory's whole argument in his essay, see Sarah Coakley, "'Persons' in the 'Social' Doctrine of the Trinity: Current Analytic Discussion and 'Cappadocian' Theology," chap. 7 of her *Powers and Submissions: Spirituality, Philosophy, and Gender* (Malden, MA: Blackwell, 2002).

9. Nazir-Ali, *Frontiers in Muslim-Christian Encounter*, 19.

10. For a more detailed treatment of this passage, see Michael Lodahl, *God of Nature and of Grace: Reading the World in a Wesleyan Way* (Nashville: Abingdon, 2003), 114–24.

11. See earlier in this chapter, note 8. This trinitarian formulation for divine activity, of course, includes God's resurrection of Jesus; indeed, it may profitably be argued that God's raising of the crucified Jesus by the power of the life-giving Holy Spirit provides the paradigm for divine activity everywhere else and at all times.

12. See Michael Lodahl, "To Whom Belong the Covenants? Wesley, Whitehead, and Wildly Diverse Religious Traditions," chap. 10 in *Deep Religious Pluralism*, ed. David Ray Griffin (Louisville: Westminster John Knox, 2005).

13. The story of Balak and Balaam is in Numbers 22–24. It has no qur'anic echoes.

14. John Wesley, "On Conscience," in *The Works of John Wesley* (London: Wesleyan Conference Office, 1872), 7:188.

15. Ibid.

16. John Wesley, "On Faith," in *Works*, 7:199. He is of course drawing upon the opening of Peter's sermon to Cornelius and his household as narrated in Acts 10:34–43.

17. John Wesley, "On Working Out Our Own Salvation," in *Works*, 6:512. His biblical source is John 1:9.

18. Fazlur Rahman, *Major Themes of the Qur'an* (Minneapolis: Bibliotheca Islamica, 1989), 95.

19. It is important to keep in mind that capitalization (or lack thereof) is strictly the decision of the translator(s) or editor(s), and cannot in itself yield theological significance.

20. Rahman, *Major Themes*, 96.

21. Amos Yong, *The Spirit Poured Out on All Flesh: Pentecostalism and the Possibility of Global Theology* (Grand Rapids: Baker Academic, 2005), 263–64. Yong astutely raises numerous important issues for any Christian attempt to think about pneumatology (the doctrine of the Holy Spirit) in conversation with the Qur'an and Islamic theology (257–66).

22. Catherine Keller, *Apocalypse Now and Then: A Feminist Guide to the End of the World* (Boston: Beacon, 1996), 282–83; emphasis hers.

23. See note 3 in chap. 9 of this book.

Chapter 12 Apocalypse When?

1. Following are some of the more dramatic qur'anic passages characterized by evocations of an impending apocalypse and ensuing descriptions of the peopling of Paradise and Hell: 52:9–28; 55:37–76; 69:13–37; 78:18–40; 80:33–42; 81:1–14; 85:1–15; 88:1–16; 89:21–30; 90:17–20; 92:13–21; 99:1–8; 101:1–11.

2. Majid Fakhry, *An Interpretation of the Qur'an: English Translation of the Meanings—A Bilingual Edition* (New York: New York University Press, 2000), 440n718.

3. See John Wesley's treatment of Micah 6:5–8 in chap. 11 of this book, 173–75.

4. The earliest known proponent of bodily resurrection was the Persian prophet Zoroaster (or Zarathushtra), who fielded similar questions possibly as much as two millennia before Muhammad. "From where shall the body be reassembled which the wind has blown away, and the water carried off? And how shall the resurrection take place?" Zoroaster's supreme deity Ahura Mazda ("Wise Lord") assures all doubters, "Consider, if I made that which is not, why cannot I make again that which was?" See Norman Cohn, *Cosmos, Chaos, and the World to Come: The Ancient Roots of Apocalyptic Faith* (New Haven: Yale University Press, 1993), 96–99. Cohn's book is a fascinating study of apocalyptic expectations from Zoroaster to Christianity but makes no mention of Muhammad, the Qur'an, or Islam.

5. Paul M. van Buren, *A Theology of the Jewish-Christian Reality*, pt. 3, *Christ in Context* (San Francisco: Harper & Row, 1988), xviii.

Reopening: Conversation Continues

1. We should acknowledge the considerable extent to which this Hebrews passage would be amenable to a qur'anic reading. Much of what follows is adapted from my essay "The (Brief) Openness Debate in Islamic Theology—And Why that Debate Should be Different among Contemporary Christians," in *Creation Made Free: Open Theology Engaging Science*, ed. Thomas Jay Oord (Eugene, OR: Pickstock, 2009).

2. Gregory of Nazianzus, "Letters on the Apollinarian Controversy," in *Christology of the Later Fathers*, Library of Christian Classics 3 (Philadelphia: Westminster Press, 1954), 218. I had occasion to cite Gregory's response to Apollinaris in chap. 4 of this volume.

3. See Lenn E. Goodman, *Islamic Humanism* (Oxford: Oxford University Press, 2003); Richard C. Martin and Mark R. Woodward with Dwi S. Atmaja, *Defenders of Reason in Islam: Mu'tazilism from Medieval School to Modern Symbol* (Oxford: Oneworld, 1997); and Reza Aslan, *No God But God: The Origins, Evolution, and Future of Islam* (New York: Random House, 2006).

Subject Index

Scripture Index